2 x (7/16) 8/16
2x (7/16) ✓ 8/17

# THE WONDER OF AGING

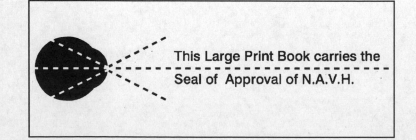

This Large Print Book carries the Seal of Approval of N.A.V.H.

# THE WONDER OF AGING

## A NEW APPROACH TO EMBRACING LIFE AFTER FIFTY

## MICHAEL GURIAN

**THORNDIKE PRESS**
*A part of Gale, Cengage Learning*

GALE
CENGAGE Learning·

Detroit • New York • San Francisco • New Haven, Conn • Waterville, Maine • London

## GALE
### CENGAGE Learning·

Thorndike Press® Large Print Health, Home & Learning.
The text of this Large Print edition is unabridged.
Other aspects of the book may vary from the original edition.
Set in 16 pt. Plantin.

**LIBRARY OF CONGRESS CATALOGING-IN-PUBLICATION DATA**

Gurian, Michael.
    The wonder of aging : a new approach to embracing life after fifty / by Michael Gurian. — Large print edition.
      pages cm
    Includes bibliographical references.
    ISBN-13: 978-1-4104-6524-5 (hardcover)
    ISBN-10: 1-4104-6524-1 (hardcover)
    1. Older people—Health and hygiene. 2. Aging. 3. Well-being—Age factors. 4. Large type books. I. Title.
    RA564.8.G88 2013
    613'.0438--dc23

                               2013037532

Published in 2014 by arrangement with Atria Books, a division of Simon & Schuster, Inc.

Printed in the United States of America
1 2 3 4 5 6 7 18 17 16 15 14

*For my parents, Julia M. and Jay P. Gurian.*
*For my wife and daughters, Gail, Gabrielle,*
*and Davita,*
*and, in memoriam, for Kathy Stevens*

It is our purpose as human beings to grow — to look within ourselves to find and build upon that source of peace and understanding and strength which is our inner selves, and to reach out to others with love, acceptance, patient guidance, and hope for what we all may become together.

— ELISABETH KÜBLER-ROSS, PSYCHIATRIST, AUTHOR, *DEATH: THE FINAL STAGE OF GROWTH*

Aging is not something that only begins on one's 65th birthday. Rather, all the choices we make regarding how we care for ourselves, how we manage our lives, and even how we think about our futures, shape who we ultimately become.

— KEN DYCHTWALD, *AGE POWER*

# CONTENTS

# Introduction:
# The Wonder of Aging

I love Mary Oliver's question, "Who will chide you if you wander away from wherever you are to look for your soul?" Don't ever stop looking for your soul, Mike, no matter how old you become.
— Julia M. Gurian, gerontologist, coauthor, *The Dependency Tendency*

In the spring of 2008, just before my fiftieth birthday, my life changed. My right hand, which had tingled somewhat for years, began to tingle far more than before. My neck, which had hurt off and on for years, began to hurt all the time. Parts of my right hand, arm, and shoulder entered a state of constant pain, and pain radiated from my neck down my back, to the middle of my spine. I could not lift things as I once had been able, nor could I hold my right arm up for more than a second or two. Because I am a writer, this was significantly destructive for me: I could

13

barely hold a pen for long, and typing was very painful.

What had happened to me? I went to various doctors in my HMO, one of whom sent me to physical therapy for three months; he assumed I was having muscle spasms. While in physical therapy, I noticed that the triceps and pectorals on my right side were shrinking. As the weeks went by, the pain continued relentlessly, as did the muscle weakness and muscle atrophy. I became angry, depressed, and, finally, assertive, returning to my HMO and obtaining a referral to a neurologist and neurosurgeon. Those visits elicited an MRI (magnetic resonance imaging), which clarified my exact situation. I suffered a herniated disk and stenosis in my neck, at C6/7. Because of the bulging disk and the narrowing of the bone, the nerve that controlled parts of my right side was being compressed at the root, causing pain, tingling, numbness, weakness, and muscle atrophy. Soon after learning the root cause of my problems, a neurosurgeon performed a cervical fusion on my spine; the offending disk was removed from my neck, and a titanium plate was placed into my spine. I spent six weeks in a neck brace so that the bones in my spine above and below the plate could fuse.

But the plot thickens, as they say. The surgery that was supposed to take care of the symptoms took care of some but not all of them. Five years later, I am still in constant pain (though the pain is much reduced from before), and my triceps and pectorals have not grown back. My right arm is still weaker than my left (which is not generally normal, since I am right-handed), I am no longer able to play most sports, I can't swim for more than a couple of minutes, I can't lift things . . . the list goes on. My nerve root had been so damaged for so long before surgery that some of my symptoms will never go away.

How should I feel, emotionally and spiritually, about this? Should I spend my days complaining? (I have done my share of that, believe me.) Should I spend a lot of time being angry, depressed, and critical of life? (I've had very dark days, full of harshness and irritability, sadness and grief.) Should I withdraw from my desires, my intensities, my dreams, and my life purpose because I am aging? My mother passed away at eighty-two, my father is still alive at eighty-four, and a number of my grandparents lived into their eighties and beyond: thus, I have a whole second half of life ahead of me. How should I spend this second lifetime, which clearly will not be as physically active or pain-free as my first?

## The Next Rite of Passage

If you are in your late forties or older (for convenience, in this book I'll often use the phrase "fifty or older"), and even if you haven't paid close attention to it, you are in your second half of life. Your story of body and soul during this time of growth might be different from mine, but you will, nonetheless, have a story. You are now, or will soon be, challenged to decide whether aging will be a positive experience for you or a journey of dread, approached like a war against the self. Ultimately, we must all face one of the most powerful choices of our lives: whether to avoid aging, or to nurture soul and spirit after fifty in ways we actually could not discover before we matured, through adversity, into the wonder of aging.

Living this choice takes a great deal more spiritual concentration than we've perhaps realized. This book is about that concentration.

## Are You in a New Stage of Life?

If you are asking some of the following questions, you may be in your second lifetime and, I believe, ready to look at absorbing that concentration into your daily life.

"My kids are in their teens or grown — now what?"

16

"I'm part of the sandwich generation — how can I manage the stress of taking care of everyone?"

"I am facing or have faced debilitating injury or illness. How do I remain vital?"

"I feel like a new sense of freedom can happen now. What is that freedom, and how do I fulfill it and myself?"

"How do I sift through all the health information available on the Internet about aging?"

"Are there stages to aging like there are stages to everything else?"

"I'm suddenly single and definitely not young anymore. What do I do now?"

"I'm retired. What is my life purpose now? Do I need one?"

"How do I talk to my aging parents about the difficult stuff?"

"Do women and men age differently or in the same ways?"

"How can I be the best grandparent possible?"

Are you asking these "second half of life" questions? For human beings in the new millennium, just the existence of a second lifetime in which to ask them is miraculous. Think back to your ancestors one hundred years ago: the average life expectancy in 1912 was forty-nine years. Our average life expectancy is now thirty-plus years past that. In a few decades, it will double that. You may remember one or two ancestors in your family before 1912 who lived to sixty or seventy or one hundred, but mainly you'll probably remember stories of just a few people per family who lived to be as old as you are now. Similarly, if you travel to many other places in the world right now, the past is present. In the spring of 2012, my twenty-two-year-old daughter, Gabrielle, traveled to a Mayan village in southern Mexico on a poverty prevention internship with the One Equal Heart Foundation. She came back to the United States saying, "Wow, Dad, there aren't many old people in those villages." She saw the reality that still exists in parts of the developing world, where older people are scarce.

The reality she saw exists in contrast to the miracle of your life and mine. The United Nations reported in 2012: "By 2030, we expect nearly two billion people in the world to be 60 years or older. This number equals the current combined populations of North America, Europe, and India." In just a few generations, one of humanity's most ambitious goals has been achieved in our developed world: to live into a second half of life that has been, for all of human history, closed to us. A certain sense of awe and wonder at that miracle is not unwarranted. As I provide you with science and spirit to help you develop a new sense of concentration as you age, I am mindful of that miracle.

## TWO WOMEN

I am mindful, also, of a calling set for me by two aging women. As I was making my gradual rite of passage into my fifties, my mother, Julia Gurian, a retired gerontologist, had begun her journey of dying and death. Her lower spine had been deteriorating for decades (in childhood she had been diagnosed with kyphoscoliosis, and she had broken her back when I was one year old, which further weakened her spine), causing her constant and extreme pain. In her late seventies, she became restricted mainly to a wheelchair. Then, in 2010, when one of her lungs shut down, she was restricted mainly to her bed.

When my mother entered her last months of life, she predicted, "There's a new wave of thought coming from you baby boomers. My generation redefined social roles, gender roles, child and human development, even death and dying, but you baby boomers are going to be the ones who redefine aging. Elisabeth and the rest of us were curious about it, but couldn't really do that work yet — you baby boomers have the science, and the need, to do it."

In referring to "Elisabeth," Mom was referring to the psychiatrist Elisabeth Kübler-Ross, who authored *Death: The Final Stage of Growth* and many other books in the fields of psychology and gerontology. My mother, who worked to help found Hospice of Honolulu in the 1970s, became friends with Dr. Kübler-Ross. A woman in her fifties back then, "Elisabeth" was a frequent visitor to our home, where dinner table conversations revolved around dying and death, spirituality and religion, family and child raising. In my mother's last stage of life, she and I remembered one particular conversation over dessert in 1976. A small, intense woman, Dr. Kübler-Ross asked a tall, pensive seventeen-year-old boy: "Mike, what do you think of all this aging stuff?" Recalling this question in her bed in 2011, Mom chuckled and said, "You used to have something to say about everything when you were a teen, but you usually just listened to Elisabeth."

I had nothing relevant to say about aging at seventeen, of course, but when my mother passed away on April 16, 2011, and as I am writing this book, I feel the presence of these two women who approached the study of aging with a sense of wonder. I owe the call to research, test, and develop a new framework for the stages of age (appearing in chapters 2 and 3) to Dr. Kübler-Ross's Stages analyses, and I owe certain aspects of the work on dying and death (in chapter 8) to my mother's dying process.

## RESEARCH AND VISION

This is my twenty-seventh book. My work as a social philosopher and mental health counselor over the last two and a half decades has integrated brain science and psychological theory with socio-anthropological data and results from my counseling practice. Over the last fifteen years, this work has been field-tested through Gurian Institute research, which includes quantitative and qualitative data, focus group results, data from online surveys, and anecdotal studies. As a social philosopher, I work to help my readers rethink and re-vision our lives in the postmodern and postindustrial world. Whether in my clinical practice or in books, I see us as a research team together — we have combined efforts to re-vision child development, gender, educational reform, workplace relationships, personal growth, and coupled relationships to fit who we are now.

The scientific research, new paradigms, and wisdom of practice you will read about in this book have been used with my clients and others in ways that I hope you will use, as needed, in your life. As we explore new ways of concentrating on and enjoying the second half of life together, I will challenge you, as I have been challenged by my own life, to fully embrace the wonder of aging. This is as much a spiritual process as a "health" process. By that I mean: we have a lot of information around us about the physical and cognitive aspects of healthy aging; we now also need to integrate that information. We are in a time of life when "taking our health to the next level" requires us to rethink and reimagine aging holistically. Both science and spirit can join together in this mission. This book provides one way of joining them together.

As you read, don't be surprised if you have to push past some hardened parts of the culture we all live in. Our culture has not yet explored aging with the developmental and spiritual focus that our culture has done for other stages of life such as childhood, adulthood, middle age, and death. We have put up a wall against aging, in some powerful ways. If you look at available conversation around you, you may notice that our culture refers to the whole second half of human life as "getting older" or "being elderly," or, at a certain point, "old age." Our culture provides us with a plethora of resources on how to handle specific physical and cognitive decline (books, WebMD, HMOs, articles, Web sites), all of which are potentially helpful, but they don't redefine aging for a new millennium. Redefining age into a new vision is something powerful, beautiful, and freeing that we can do together as we integrate medicine, psychology, anthropology, and spirituality.

The cultural redefinition of age proposed in this book stands on the shoulders of work already provided by many others, but it also includes new vision and language, and age-friendly stories from people like you and me. As we redefine aging together, I will explore seven concentrations with you. They comprise a road map for redefining age. I've had a lot of help in defining these seven concentrations. One of them involves a new paradigm for three stages of age:

*Stage 1: the age of transformation* (from approximately fifty to mid-sixties);

*Stage 2: the age of distinction* (from approximately mid-sixties to late seventies);

*Stage 3: the age of spiritual completion* (from approximately eighty to one hundred, and beyond).

As we look at each of these stages, I will connect scientific research to a holistic approach to physical, mental, relational, and spiritual health. Thus, we will work to redefine aging from not just a physical or mental standpoint, but holistically — inclusive of spiritual process. And in this book, I will not tread into territory already well covered by medicine or diet books. The wonder of aging is not about miracle cures, physical or cognitive, nor am I a doctor. My work regards integrating what you already know about healthy physical and cognitive aging (and what you will learn through many other doctors and sources through the decades) with a new paradigm for integrating that material and taking control of the growth stages of your second lifetime.

Because women and men experience aging differently, I will provide you with science-based information regarding gender differences in the second half of life, and ways to use that information to incline the male and female spirit toward greater elasticity and happiness as you age. When the genders fully understand each other's signals, we can discover a new sense of freedom in the second half of life, both separately and together.

Hidden (or obvious) in each chapter in this book are two practical goals: (a) to decrease your unhealthy psychological stress as you age and (b) to increase the quality of your relationships throughout the life span. Our human experience of longevity, wonder, and adventure depends on enjoying healthy stress while decreasing unhealthy stress, and on protecting the highest quality of our relationships. Chronic unhealthy stress and a paucity of healthy relationships are the two biggest killers of people over fifty, and the top destroyers of quality of life.

## BEING AND DOING

As you entrust me with your time, I hope you will feel a great deal, and I hope you will both do more and do less as you read. In other words, I hope you'll feel guided toward healthy action, while also being guided to (a) cut back on unhealthy action and (b) develop new rituals for living utterly in the moment. This "living in the moment" was something each of us could talk about a lot when we were younger, but now we can actually accomplish it in new, freeing ways.

Because I am a writer, I combine some of my doing and being through meditation and writing. I call this morning ritual my "daily reunion with God" because I feel reunited with my central impulse of life as I wake up, take care of bodily functions, then meditate. This half hour involves no action, just sitting — quieting the mind, letting happen whatever happens. Often, there is birdsong around me, and the sound of the small water feature in my backyard. Sometimes, there is no sound and no thought at all.

This living in the moment is all I need on some mornings, but on other mornings a theme will emerge in my mental landscape, a theme that requires "doing." A number of mornings, for instance, I have meditated on this line from the American poet Mary Oliver: "There is no end to the happiness your body is willing to bear." Especially when I wake up in pain, I seek the depth of that line in mindfulness. Then, after approximately a half hour of meditation (being), my body and mind begin their spiritual "doing." I begin writing poetry and spiritual essays longhand or on my laptop for at least a half hour, or I write longhand in my journal for an hour.

In this morning practice, I am both being and doing in a time of spiritual growth. Over the last five years especially, this practice has become a part of my own wonder of aging. Though this daily practice may take me more time than you would perhaps want to give (and perhaps you do not have time in the mornings), spiritual practice, in whatever way a person configures it to fit both being and doing, has a profound impact on attitude and growth as we age. Throughout this book, I will help you to experientially vision, in your own life, how you can bring a greater

26

spiritual practice into your days and nights.

For the purpose of inspiration and for guiding chapter themes, I will share some of my finished morning writing with you: each of the eight chapters of this book begins with a meditation on the concentration we are about to explore in the chapter. I hope these pieces help you to be newly creative in the three stages of age. Throughout the book I'll also share wise words of being and doing from saints, poets, philosophers, and ordinary people who have developed life-enhancing spiritual practices of this kind.

## BEING VISIBLE

As you read and well beyond, please consider becoming more visible as you age. Find your voice as an aging person and give that voice to the world. Become a game changer in your home, neighborhood, community, and culture. Even if you are in a highly visible profession right now, become visible about your *age*. Go inward when you must, and return outward with art and life that others can see and learn from. Be the "wise one," the "sage," the "teacher." The world needs you as a person over fifty to guide it and shape it.

After fifty, we are rarely anymore the "hero" or "heroine" of youthful quests, wielding our sword against foes and marrying the prince or princess. We've been there, done that. But we are people on a quest no less important. "Will you discover the answer to your questions before your song is spent?" the German poet Rilke asked in his second sonnet to Orpheus. In Sonnet 3, he answers, "Full living is not found only in youthful love. Truly to sing your song takes another kind of breath, a breath in the void." This "other kind of breath" is the kind of breath we are developing now in our second lifetime. It is a breathing-in-the-void; we are living and breathing in the void-time of our ancestors. Because mortality is something we feel now in ever new ways, we can come to understand that every day is a privilege. We have said goodbye to close friends, experienced a number of losses and failures, and come through. Whether single or coupled, whether we have kids or not, whatever our race or creed or sexual orientation, we need no longer feel invisible as we grow older. The planet needs our nurturance now more than ever. If our journey becomes marginalized, or the culture hardens itself against it, youth worship will destroy the civilization. The world needs us to be visible and purposeful, and we need it, too. We are breathing now with a new kind of breath. Let's fully experience that breathing and see what great journey we can make as we sing a new, mature song of wonder, love, adventure, and empowered age.

I am not done with my changes.
— Stanley Kunitz


Time is amazingly fair and forgiving. No matter how much time you've wasted in the past, you still have an entire tomorrow.
— Denis Waitely,
business consultant


Now at one's feet there are chasms that had been invisible until this moment. And one knows, and never remembers how it was learned, that there will always be chasms, and across the chasms will always be those one loves.
— Lillian Smith

# MEDITATION 1:
## TAKING YOUR CENSUS IN THE DESERT

*(This is the first of the short, written meditations that will appear at the beginning of each chapter. Over the last decade, I have written approximately one hundred of these, some in first person, some in second person, some including dialogue with God. When I write them to "you," as is this first one, the interlocutor certainly includes my Self, but also includes anyone else as well. I hope these pieces inspire your creativity, as well as thought and dialogue. The themes in each piece will thread through each chapter.)*

Have you found what you are looking for? Are you singing a song of praise? Have you fully allowed your spouse, your children, your partner, your lifework to open your heart to life's warmth? Have you arrived at the adult self you've been working toward, the one that promises the joy of "This is who I am?"

There is a time in every life when the road ahead of us becomes shorter than the road behind. At this time, we are each invited to stop walking and hear life whisper, *Have you found what you were looking for?* This is a time to take a census of our treasures and set a future course.

So I stand at the mirror in the morning, with my fingers pressed to my reflected face, squeezing back the lines of love and pain. My face mask looks like my mother's, my father's, but is now surely my own. I am the person whose life has been put more "in my own hands" than ever before.

Have I found what I am looking for?

# CHAPTER 1
# TOWARD A
# NEW SPIRIT OF AGING

In order to come fully to the encounter with whatever gives ultimate meaning, in order to really wrestle with the angel, one must be a free agent, not defined by another, or by cultural imperatives.

— Marilyn Sewell, *Cries of the Spirit*

In 2011, my research team and I developed three surveys, asking 2,752 people to provide insights about life after fifty. We were basically asking baby boomer subjects to define "a new spirit of aging" for the new millennium. More women than men responded to our survey, at about 70 percent to 30 percent. In our work in gender studies over the last two decades, we have found this result to be consistent and robust. We have also found that, in general, men write fewer words than women.

Craig, fifty-three, from Los Angeles, responded in this brief but cogent way. "I've experienced deaths in my family and some early health problems, but I understand where I am. I am finally able to handle what is on my plate — and what is on my plate is more than it's ever been. One thing I'm especially doing is listening to life (and listening to some very good and wise friends). The metaphor in my mind is that I've now entered the middle weekend of a wonderful two-week vacation. I still have a week of vacation left but I am not entirely unaware that the plane is leaving next Sunday and the vacation will end. I call this next week of my life 'Christmases Yet to Come.'"

As I followed up with Craig, he talked about the new freedom he was seeking now in his fifties. It was not the freedom of "escape" but rather of new engagement with life. Craig had married for the first time in his forties, started a new family (his daughter was six), and had decided to leave the business world to get a teaching degree. He was also volunteering in his daughter's school and had started an educational foundation with some of the money he had made in the financial services industry. Craig was stepping forward into the second half of life with vigor, vision, and wonder.

Marcy, fifty-six, wrote a longer story, also revelatory of a new spirit of aging in her life.

"My husband and I are originally from the Northeast and have been living in Georgia for 18 years. My daughter is 19 and a sophomore at college, and my son is 23, and graduated. I am working to cut apron strings with him and give us both a new kind of freedom. My daughter left for school a year ago August, and our dog passed away in May. I decided that I would get a dog, a French shepherd, so that I could participate in outdoor activities, walking, hiking, and training her for things. That has worked out very well; it has provided for me a new set of folks that I have met (lots of people within 10 years on either side of my age). I have sort of re-created myself in this role, more laid-back, no makeup, lots of enjoyment from watching dogs play together and chatting with their owners.

"Nine years ago, my mother, 88, lived in New England on her own, but I realized that as an only child I could not hop on a plane from Georgia and help her when she needed it. So I insisted that she move here. She did and is now 97. Sometimes, being with her makes me afraid of being that old; it doesn't seem like much fun at all, especially since I've realized I could live another thirty or forty years or more. But at the same time, being with Mom more has made me want to do and try new things. Caring for her makes me want to finally become the fearless and free person I've always wanted to be, and now I think I definitely have the time to do that."

"I want to become the fearless and free person I've always wanted to be. . . ." How many of us have said those words, or something like them, over the decades of our youth and middle adulthood? Many of us. Perhaps all of us. In the survey questions, neither I nor anyone on my team used the word "freedom," but that word and its meanings showed up in many of the responses. As people revealed wanting happier, growth-ful, fearless, and vital ways of living now, they discussed their sense of living in a *new time* in life when they could develop a *new sense of freedom*. They talked about a sense of now-more-than-ever and now-as-never-before. Freedom became the spiritual goal within all other goals. In reading the surveys, I understood people to be using the word "freedom" as a sign of spiritual growth at deep levels. People were hoping to redefine and spiritualize their lives so that "problems" became "challenges" and difficult parts of life became no longer "enemies to battle" but spiritually meaningful, complimentary facets of real life, an evolving part of each person's development of a philosophy of personal completion.

There is a wonderful film about some of this called *The Best Exotic Marigold Hotel.* In it, the character played by Judi Dench speaks about aging and new adventures: "This is a new and different world . . . the challenge is not just to cope, but to thrive." Dench's character and a number of others leave England and move to a retirement hotel in Jaipur, India. They enter a completely new world filled with challenges that ultimately help them find new meaning. They grow into a kind of wisdom that frees them to care for others and themselves in vital ways. Where they felt unworthy of success or love in the past, they discover worthiness and love in the present. They reassess what they do and think, becoming the role models people need in order to see where to walk and rediscover a sense of wonder. They realize they have sown many miracles in their lifetimes, and there are more to sow. They sense that pain and sorrow are beautiful evidence of a life lived for purpose. The whole film, from beginning through denouement, "breathes into the void" a sense of what freedom and fearlessness can be for people who age with vision, growth, and self-discovery.

My wife, Gail, and I went to see this film as I was developing this chapter. The goal of this chapter is to concentrate on key standards for what might constitute a new, free, and fearless spirit of aging today. Seeing the film helped me to fully understand why freedom is so important to us as we age, so crucial to positive aging and the continuation or rediscovery of wonder as we age. It is a theme at the center of the spirituality of aging, as we will explore in this chapter and this book. We may lose a lot of our childhood wonder as we move through adulthood and middle age, but as we age we have a chance to live in wonder again (and freshly, maturely) as never before.

By way of coincidence (if there is any such thing), the evening after seeing the film I spoke by phone with my father, eighty-three, who, with my mother, had taken me to India to live in the 1960s (we lived not far from Jaipur, in Hyderabad). He and I talked about the film and about his life as an octogenarian. A number of times recently he had fallen and injured himself, so he had moved into a retirement community where he could get more immediate care. Because of ongoing issues with his lungs, he also needed to move away from Santa Rosa, California, where he and my mother had lived, to a drier climate. When my mother passed away, he chose to move to a retirement community in Las

Vegas, where my sister and my aunt live.

I shared with my father the "freedom" that was emerging as a theme in this book. He responded, "It's true for me, too. People say these retirement communities shrivel them up, but that's not what I'm feeling. I'm in a whole new phase of life. I'm doing a lot, I have a lot of new friends, I teach an adult education class online, and I have the three-times-a-day hilarious entertainment of people-watching in the dining room! I'm not worrying anymore about whether I'll fall down and die alone in the house. I definitely feel a new freedom. I tell you, Mike, it never ends, the growing-up stuff."

## FORGING A NEW SPIRIT OF AGING

"Freedom" is a multifaceted word emerging not only in anecdotal research but in the scientific and psychological research on aging. One specific area of science-based research on this subject exists in and from regions of the world called "blue zones." The term "blue zones" reflects the sense of "blue sky for miles to come" in places like Sardinia, Italy; Okinawa, Japan; the Nicoya Peninsula, Costa Rica; Abkhazia, Georgia; and Loma Linda, California. In these locations, researchers have studied women and men who are living a full, chronological second half of life — to one hundred and beyond. The researchers want to know: Why do so many people in these cities and regions live so long, and with such high quality of life?

Researchers have discovered that while some answers involve genetics and healthy food intake (eating more fish, less meat; more fresh foods, nothing processed; eating small portions, and no refined sugars to speak of), many other answers involve personal choices of positivity and spiritual principles of growth. Older people in blue zones often move into the second half of their lifetimes building more freedom into their lives. They do so by focusing on four particular elements of life, elements my team and I also found in our survey, focus group, and interview results. These elements, I believe, can comprise a foundation for the wonder of aging, and what, specifically, I would like to term "the new spirit of aging." We will explore each one in this chapter.

1. Healthy aging requires concentration, over a period of years, *on de-stressing one or more of the physical, mental, and emotional aspects of our lives.* Physical and mental well-being are now crucial, whether in the face of a pivotal health event or just as a part of natural

41

aging; we need to develop discipline regarding nutrition, exercise, improving mental functioning, and working through psychological and relational issues that cause chronic stress. We need to gradually or immediately remove these chronic stressors from our lives if we are to thrive in our second lifetime. Our new discipline of lifestyle, and our working to decrease areas of significant stress, give us quality of life and longevity.

2. *Healthy aging requires us to embrace realistic optimism about aging.* This requires a lot of active life and, often, an attitude change that sees aging as filled with free potential on all fronts, from personal to professional. Embracing age and rediscovering wonder is about rebirth.

3. *Healthy aging requires us to form and join new communities.* Most specifically, we need to develop or join a small circle of friends who share similar values, ideas, interests, and visions of age. If we move to a different city, one circle of friends may dissolve but a new circle of friends can form in the new place or

new stage of age.

4. *The second lifetime is the time to grow from "adult" to elder.* This involves becoming or remaining visible, engaging in spiritual practice, practicing concentrated service to the world, and mentoring young people. The move to become an elder is a transformational experience that we need to accomplish consciously. Elder is not just given to us as we become chronologically "old" — elder is grown, created, made, and shared.

Abkhazia, Georgia, is one of the blue zones in which these four elements are prevalent. People who live to one hundred or older focus on new attitudes (they increase the time they spend joking, socializing, and working while singing, for instance); they increase their time in small circles of influence, including circles of like-minded friends; they consciously pursue mentoring of the young (the anthropologist Sula Benet, who studied them and lived among them for many years, saw a culture that lived by its proverb: "Besides God, we also need our elders"); and they specifically de-stress their lives (the physician Alexander Leaf, who studied the Abkhazians for years, noticed that elder Abkhazians try to avoid being rushed as much as possible — they really concentrate on that; they plan their day to be able to include long periods of walking from place to place, rather than rushing from place to place).

While our busy lives involve more rushing around than in a village, especially for those of us still in our prime working years, the blue zone research is helpful in begging each of us to ask questions of ourselves that can help us focus on greater health and freedom as we age.

- Do I feel an internal pull to begin de-stressing and de-cluttering my life? At certain times of the day, do I feel like slowing down a little and fully entering my senses and "the now"? Do I let myself feel this pull, or do I remain too busy to feel it or give in to it?

- Do I feel like now is the time to look at what a "good attitude" and a "bad attitude" are regarding age, health, mission, and "time left"? Where does complaining get me? Am I optimistic? Am I so optimistic that I'm not realistic about my age, or am I avoiding age by doing everything possible to pretend it isn't happening?

- Do I feel pulled toward a circle of family and friends who can become my rock as I age? Do I have close friends? If not, why not? If my spouse used to be the "friend maker" but now I am alone, how can I find a circle of friends on my own?

- Do I feel a pull to explore what "elder" might mean for *me*? All my life I have been building a personal legacy — working, caring for others, serving, accomplishing. Am I becoming an elder who shares wisdom, or am I just subsisting? Is my community allowing me to become an elder? How do I become an elder?

We have the freedom now, in a miraculous second lifetime, to soul-search and soul-find. Wherever we are in our personal journey, if we are near or have passed the fifty milestone, we are psychologically driven toward a new spirit of aging. At fifty, we're just starting to feel the call; by sixty, then seventy, then eighty, it will become even louder. I've felt it, you've felt it, people in blue zones have felt it, and everyone around us, wherever they live, have felt it as they cross the threshold into the second half of life.

### STRESS AS THE CATALYST OF SPIRIT

Contemporary science-based research on aging and stress gives us a profound window into the urge we have all felt (even if unconsciously) to be reborn and develop new focus as we age. In this way, stress is a primary driver toward early death and low quality of life, or increased freedom and a new, deep happiness.

Bruce McEwen, a neuroscientist at Rockefeller University who studies the effect of the environment and lifestyle on aging cells in both our bodies and our brains, has discovered that any significant, ongoing stressor you experience as you age attacks cells equally in the sympathetic nervous system and the hypothalamic-pituitary-adrenal axis (the system that connects your body and brain). This attack signals the frontal lobe of the brain to try to compel personal and spiritual growth at a cellular level.

So, if you are under some kind of constant negative stress in your psychophysical environment — from lack of sleep to a diet of destructive foods to depression to relationship issues to overwork — your frontal lobe and parts of your limbic system (your emotional centers) will most likely try to deal with this ongoing negative stress by pushing/pulling you toward new activations, new ways of being, new solutions that will counter the stress. You may override your own antistress decision making with an even more powerful executive choice — that is, to disregard the chronic stress your cells are under and continue doing the things that are bad for you — but your cells, body, and frontal lobe will keep pushing you toward new decisions and new rebirth. If you avoid your age — avoid what your cells are saying — for too long, parts of your body will give out, your mind will feel even more cloudy at times, your sleep will get even worse until you drive into a tree, perhaps, your heart gives out, or you have a stroke.

Your body and brain are wired for this kind of self-direction genetically. UCLA neuroscientist Steve Cole has taken the body-mind stress research into the area of genetics. He has shown that our physical cells reflect our gene growth, and our physical genes are vulnerable to any significant stressor affecting any other part of our system — mental, relational, spiritual — especially as we move into and beyond fifty. Because the bodies and brains of people over fifty are not as naturally resilient as they once were, our immune systems are not as strong in their natural life cycle as they were in our youth or middle age; thus, our brain's decision-making centers in the frontal and temporal lobes — centers tasked with guiding our thriving — must activate to protect us. This activation is manifest in our conscious (or unconscious) pull toward seeking a new spirit of aging, a new freedom, a "downsizing," a "new approach to life" as we age.

This pull is not a pull toward a completely stress-less life. That does not exist. It is impossible to have no stress or to avoid crises in life and be crisis-free. Even while working to de-stress parts of your life in your fifties and beyond, you may be, like me and most people I know, working forty-plus hours per week; volunteering in service communities; still raising or launching your children through teens, twenties, or beyond; caring for your parents and your spouse's parents; and, in all these areas, dealing with crises as they arise. To seek a new approach to stress is not to put on rose-colored glasses. Stress and crisis are a part of life.

But if you have felt the internal pull to figure out how to de-stress your life, you are feeling your cellular, physical, and neurological systems trying to guide you toward new freedom, which is freedom from the stresses you no longer need. Your physiopsychological and cellular systems are saying to you: "If I am going to flourish through the decades of my future, I must de-stress the parts of life that are destroying me." They are pressing: "If you don't choose this course, you have a greater chance of becoming mentally ill (to say nothing of physically ill) as you age." Dr. Cole notes our genetic reality here: when we were younger, many of our cells, once destroyed by stress, could regenerate, but now many of our aging cells cannot regenerate when destroyed by stress. And even more troubling is the fact that stressed-out cells now can mutate genes such as our IL6 genes; this age-related mutation leads to increased mental illness. If we continue to live highly stressed-out lives in our fifties and beyond, the stress keeps attacking us until it kills us quickly or alters our cells to the extent that we spend the second half of life in battles with mental illnesses — depression, rage, dementia — that we could, at least in part, have avoided.

So the pull you may be feeling to "change your life" is a natural one. I believe it is the reason so many people in blue zones (and many in your own neighborhood, we hope) pursue freedom so consciously. As we move through the fifty-year-old milestone, our psyches stand at a threshold between two worlds — adulthood and elder. Our cells, bodies, and brains feel the threshold as a spiritual state, a very real but also somewhat hidden state. Stress creates opportunity for rebirth into a new lifetime. If we make the transition through this new time, it is going to feel physiologically and neurally like "less stress." Spiritually, it will feel like freedom.

"My husband and I are tired of the grind we're in just to keep up," Elaine, fifty-nine, wrote in our survey. "Our kids are grown. We're going to sell our house. We're downsizing." Paul, sixty-two, wrote, "I'm letting go of some of the 'having to always be right' that drives people away from me. I'm listening better, detaching myself from some things that used to be important — now, I don't understand why I spent so much time stressing out about them." A client, fifty-five, said, "I have become more patient now. I had to. My impatience was killing me." Another client, sixty-one, said, "My job is literally killing me. I have to find a way out." Another client, fifty-one, wrote: "We have to end our marriage. The stress isn't good for me or him." These survey participants and clients felt the need to change attitudes and, in some cases, shift relationships; they felt called to develop freedom from what they feel is, literally, killing them, and freedom toward new life.

There is an ancient Chinese story of a sage who walks one day to the ocean, sits down on the shore, and uses a knife to cut boils and sores off his body. As he cuts each one off, he tosses it into the sea, and as it touches the sea, it grows gills and fins and swims away. When he is finished cleansing himself, he walks away from the sea, back to his daily life, feeling lighter, reborn. I see this sage as someone who has come to the sea because he or she feels an internal and very real pull toward freedom. Feeling that pull, he acts: he gets rid of the boils and sores (chronic stresses) of his previous self. For the Chinese sage, doing something about his stresses — freeing himself from them — altered who he was.

And so it is with us. Research in epigenetics conducted at Rutgers University confirms that our bodies and brains can regenerate some cells if we de-stress our lives as we age. It is getting more difficult for us to regenerate cells when we are under profound stress, but if we follow the "pull," the primal survival urge, appropriate to our fifties and beyond, to take control of who we are and where we want to go, and if we plan our lives in ways that allow us lowered stress and higher quality of life for the second half of life, we can

51

grow new cells; we are, literally, reborn.

## But It's Not Always Dramatic, at Least Not at First

Recently a client in her late fifties, Tammy, came to my clinical practice and asked for help to become healthier as she aged. She said, "I buy the idea that I have to make changes, especially in my stress levels, but I just can't do anything dramatic right now that involves life change: I still have a kid in college, and I'm just climbing to the place I want to get in my company. So, you'll lose me, Mike, if you don't just give me a few things to do to de-stress myself physically right now, in the middle of my busy life."

Part of my counseling practice is giving resources and best practices, so even though I am not a doctor, I felt comfortable helping her look at certain ways to deal with physical and cognitive stressors. After listening to her describe her everyday life, I homed in immediately on her sleep patterns. She slept, it seemed, too little for her aging brain's health. She was always exhausted. "I can't sleep anymore," she said emphatically, "but there's nothing to be done." She described a schedule of rising at four a.m. to commute to work and needing to spend time with her husband and child in the late evenings, and then an hour of e-mail at eleven p.m., just to catch up, and time for only a few hours of sleep. I told her point-blank that this was killing her, and she agreed, but she said, "I don't want to hear 'Don't do e-mail before bed' or 'Sleep more' right now. What else do you have?"

Unable to help her alter her stress levels in huge ways, I settled for four concrete things that might help decrease stress and increase freedom under the parameters she gave. I practice these myself, and Tammy promised to concentrate on these in the midst of her very stressful life.

If you are a person who feels the pull toward new freedom, but your life is immensely busy, these four things will at least help you start heeding the call toward a new spirit of aging. They are baseline stress relievers for anyone and everyone, though we all need to go even further than these to fully realize the goal of freedom.

- **Food.** Food grounds body and soul. A good breakfast gives Tammy's body and mind fuel for the day, which decreases unnecessary stress on her cells and primes them for growth all day. If, however, she eats a huge dinner, her cells will need to process the food during the night — carbs are more likely to turn to dangerous fat during the night, when she's not active, which increases cortisol (stress hormone) levels in the brain.

- **Water.** Tammy didn't drink enough water during the day. But she drank a lot at night, she said. This was most probably increasing her stress hormone levels. Lots of water during the day could help allow her brain to be more oxygen-filled and thus more intelligent, vital, relationally savvy, and spiritually at peace. But lots of water near nighttime was probably interrupting her sleep, which is a life-threatening stressor.

- **Alcohol.** A little bit of alcohol can be healthy, especially a glass of wine a day. Too much alcohol, however, especially as we age, can have a negative holistic effect on us. It can become such a stressor as to lead to ongoing mental and physical disease and destruction of spirit. Tammy confessed to me that her husband was saying she drank too much. If someone we trust is telling us we drink too much, we probably drink too much, especially in a high-stress life like Tammy had.

- **Chocolate!** Chocolate is, potentially, a physically, mentally, relationally, and spiritually useful food. Really? Really. Unless your doctor tells you otherwise, you might think about having a bit of chocolate every day. I asked Tammy to consider it. Chocolate can de-stress our brains and thus lift our spirits. It tastes good and can help our mood, especially in the winter when life can seem gray and somber. Some people have even reported a sense of spiritual euphoria from eating chocolate in the middle of a particularly dreary day.

Whatever large and small things we can do, we should do. Whether stress catches up to us quietly or dramatically, it catches up to us. Whether regarding food, sleep, relationships, work . . . or all of the above . . . stress is a factor. The earlier we let dialogue about our stress levels enter our personal, familial, and conscious conversation, the sooner we engage the primal, protective drive within us toward developing our own new spirit of aging.

Positive attitudes are somewhat correlated with genetics (some people are naturally more optimistic than others), but everyone can alter their attitude toward increased optimism in given situations. This alteration has an internal logic to it, and it is not just an "attitude" task but also a spiritual task. To set a foundation for positive attitude as we age, we have to each, personally, decide what we mean by "positive attitude" and "optimism" for *us*. "Optimism" and even "positive attitude" are clichés and are easily scoffed at. Let's look a little deeper into them.

Someone you know — or you yourself — has stopped dyeing his or her hair, letting it go gray. This is a symbolic gesture for this person that says, "I'm here, I'm ready, let's see what's next." The person is being both realistic and optimistic about age in his or her own way. "Okay, I see reality," he or she is saying, "and it's not going to be easy, but I'm going to enjoy it, live it, be with it as it is, and see what happens. I'm going to be free of the fear of aging." This is all a part of the pull toward freedom for this person, an inherently positive pull, a part of optimistic thinking. As with all of life so far, things certainly won't go as planned all the time for this person or you or me, but whatever happens, it's going to be interesting.

This combination of realism (things won't necessarily go as well as I wish) and optimism (things are going to be fine indeed) is of great value. It is an attitude that embraces age on both fronts — the reality and the dream. Nancy Snyderman, sixty, a physician and throat surgeon, who provides medical reporting for NBC's *Today* show and NBC News, has traveled to all continents in her work. In interviewing hundreds of scientists and researchers, she understands the term "realistic optimism" to stand for "significantly important attitude adjustment as we age."

She recently told me, "I've seen the power of this attitude in blue zones, and just recently I attended a forum on aging and interviewed former president Bill Clinton, who is just hitting a new stride in his late sixties. He said, 'I'm just getting started!' There is no scientist or doctor I've interviewed who doesn't agree: if we look at issues such as stress, loneliness, what we eat, how we interact, how we transform our identity, we become the greater for it, and it comes hand in hand with changing our *attitude* toward aging."

I asked Nancy to define this attitude shift. She said, "It's about being both happy and real, in equal parts. For instance, if you have tried to hang on to your youth, there is nothing wrong with you. You are doing something natural — you love the success you had in your youth, the feeling of running hard, playing every sport, attracting other people's healthy looks and glances. But to be healthy now, you may need to bust the myth of the fountain of youth. While it can be very useful to use hormones, dye your hair, take a food supplement . . . your *intention* in doing these things is important."

About "intention," Nancy said, "Your doctor should be able to help you decide your intention as you discuss with him or her the 'why' of what you are doing. If your intention is health, you're probably fine with using the product, cream, or dye; if your intention is to avoid your age, you might need to rethink. Embracing our age does not mean letting ourselves go completely. It doesn't mean thinking, 'I'm over the hill.' Just the opposite: research shows that we can negatively impact our emotional and, in turn, our physical health if we think we're done, finished, over. But it does mean taking control of what is real and what really makes us happy."

I hear Nancy saying that it is freeing of the soul to embrace age in a way that is both real and projective of best results. While we may think initially that "freeing" would correlate with staying young, and while, at times —

especially when we are ill or in pain — we might think it is quite enslaving to grow old, still, in the long term, it is actually enslaving to *avoid* who we are. Avoidance of identity is always slavery to another person or ideal.

New research regarding the biochemistry and neurology of happiness confirms this idea. Happiness is a feeling of immense emotional and spiritual freedom — freedom to be who we are with the people we are with. Happiness is directly linked to aligning ourselves with positive attitudes and realistic goals. Happiness as we age feels like an embrace rather than an avoidance, a source of power rather than a sense of irretrievably sad loss. As science-based research in "happiness development" has confirmed over the last decade, we can especially feel it manifest in our lives through basic elements of happiness: a prevailing sense of gratitude, engagement in the world, discovery of meaning, and a sense of faith. The more these are active in our everyday lives, the more we should be able to feel realistic optimism.

- **Gratitude.** At some point in our new growth, we realize we have come to feel greater appreciation for what we have and focus less on what has not come to be or what has been lost — such as a youthful body.

- **Engagement.** At some point in our new growth, we feel constant engagement of our personal energy in purposeful life, that is, less of a shotgun approach to doing "everything" and more of a directed approach toward the most important things and people in life.

- **Discovery of meaning.** In both small and large ways, as we take time to experience life as it is lived, including "smelling the flowers" and connecting with people who build meaning in our lives, we feel more greatly like we are living lives of meaning, not futility or "I'm on a treadmill and can't get off."

- **Faith.** Over a period of years, even decades, we may find ourselves exploring involvement in new spiritual thinking, mindfulness, and rituals as we move some of our life focus to mysteries of spirit and soul, God and faith, with a new energy to fully engage in the gifts of mortality.

Even if you are living a very busy life, and

even if you feel you can make no changes right now, you can focus just a little more of your daily time and energy on gratitude, engagement, meaning, and faith. You really can. You can do it during your meditation time, during a walk or run, while you are reading or talking with a friend, or while in a state of prayer. Each of these concentrations will enhance your sense of being freer now than ever before, happier, more fearless. Life is coming at us hard as we age, and realistic optimism helps us move more freely toward a new, protective spirit of aging as we live this life.

---

Lori, 54, wrote to me:

"Two days before my 53rd birthday, I received the greatest lesson in life. My 22-year-old son was diagnosed with a life-threatening brain tumor, and every day since then has been a lesson in faith, perseverance, love, and progress. I quit my job to be with him 24/7 and in the process learned that I was a lot stronger than I had ever imagined. I started my own new business in the process. As my friend *Wall Street Journal* columnist Jeff Zaslow wrote to me in an e-mail, 'Life is fragile. We don't always see that — until we have reason to.' Five months after that note, Jeff tragically lost his life in an automobile accident."

Kathy Stevens, 62, a mother, grandmother, and executive director of our Gurian Institute, had been battling cancer for two years when she said, "I'm going through a lot, but when I read this blog (below), I look at my attitude and remember how good I have it. Since I am off to chemo this morning, it again made me stop and count my blessings . . . for having the past two years of treatment to keep me alive, getting to spend time with kids and grandkids, having time to collect my thoughts on life past and present, continuing to fulfill my legacy."

The blog post Kathy referred to was this:

*I lost both my only child, my daughter, Beth, and her newborn baby, my only grandchild, a few weeks ago. December 1st, 2011, was parent-teacher conference day. Beth, a teacher, was talking with a parent of one of her students when she suddenly felt light-headed, collapsed, and stopped breathing. The 911 call was made.*

*An emergency vehicle soon arrived. At the hospital, we learned that Beth had a cyst, fed by large blood vessels, that was positioned in an area that hid it from ultrasound scans. The cyst ruptured, causing massive internal bleeding. All attempts at resuscitation failed. The loss of blood to her brain deprived it of oxygen, so that by the time she reached the hospital, there was no trace of brain activity. The emergency room crew performed a C-section in an attempt to save the baby. However, the baby had been without oxygen for too long as well. Her little organs began to fail, one at a time. Within a few hours baby Natalie Danielle joined her mother, Beth, in heaven.*

Kathy finished with, "What do I have to complain about compared to this? Tragedies like this really make me want to change the way I treat other people. The world needs a lot more of my love and less of my negative thoughts, no matter the amount of pain I am in, and no matter how scared I get of cancer."

Kathy passed away from cancer a few months later, on April 1, 2012. She worked part-time right up until her death, serving schools and children through a company she had cofounded twelve years before. At her memorial service, every eulogist noted in their speeches that Kathy was a person constantly focused on positive attitude and meaningful purpose.

## Keeping a Record

If you have read the *You* books by Drs. Mehmet Oz and Michael Roizen, you will probably know the term "real age." If you feel fifty but you are really sixty, your "real age" is actually fifty. Similarly, if you live the lifestyle that protects your "real age," your real age will always be as young as it can be. By taking care of your real age, you are gaining happiness, clarity, quality of life, and longevity.

I see journaling (keeping a record of your life) as a way of caring for your "real age" and your soul. I help my clients use this tool as a way of embracing age and furthering the cause of spirit, meaning, purpose, and happiness. Research on the power of self-expression through writing and the arts corroborates the potential of this action of body-mind as care of spirit. Sian Beilock, psychology professor at the University of Chicago, is the author of *Choke: What the*

*Secrets of the Brain Reveal About Getting It Right When You Have To.* Beilock has gathered data from studies regarding attitude shifts and happiness. A consistent finding in the research, she reports, is this one: "Self-expression (as for instance through writing) decreases stress and focuses attention on positive success-outcomes." Writing things down has been proven in clinical trials to relieve anxiety, focus the mind, and improve attitude.

If you haven't already, I hope you'll purchase a notebook of some kind or open a new document on your computer or tablet. Let this "journal" become a significant part of your journey as you embrace age with personalized, realistic optimism. This notebook can become a sharing of who you are now and who you have been — a sharing of your life legacy. If you haven't begun a "memoir" yet in your life, this book might evolve into that kind of life record. And this record and sharing has probably already happened in your life through photo albums, oral stories to friends and family, videos or video clips, drawings or art, sculpture, recipes you've given to your kids, and any other form of expression. By starting a journal, you are now organizing the disparate elements of your record. Take time to look at photographs, video clips, and diaries you've kept. Take a week or a month or many years to do this, all the while devoting a new notebook to the efforts of aging with wonder. As you proceed forward, fill your notebook and memoir with new words, new doodles, drawings, insights, questions, answers, action plans, and many surprises.

The spiritual writing with which I begin each chapter of this book (my own morning reunions with God) are part of my notebook and memoir. I am a person who embraces age (and experiences a great deal of self-therapy) by writing about that embrace, exploring it in the action of revising my words constantly until they fully capture the spirit of aging I am living. I will pass on parts of this notebook to my family over the next decades. It is a way to be visible as I age, and thus work toward helping the next generations ponder this new second half of life.

While you don't have to revise (over and over again!) as I, a writer, compulsively do, your notebook can still become your own expression and guidebook for your children and grandchildren (now or in the far future) as they understand you and see the world through your eyes. Your "doing" (writing and creating in your own way) can lead to greater visibility for the attitudes and spirit that aging needs. Your work can become part of your family's "family bible." Your ideas and thoughts will be sacred objects and ideas that rise above the over-information and detritus of your family's busy lives, even after you are gone.

If in keeping this journal you write very private things that you want no one to see, tear those pages out and store them in a different place (or move them to a different file in your computer). And while I'm coaching you now toward keeping a journal and using words in a journal or notebook or memoir, please don't feel that I believe words are the only way to communicate. If in the rest of this book I say, "Pull out your journal . . ." and if you don't like using words, please read my suggestion as a way of motivating you to turn to whatever media work for you. Make a video, take photographs, or develop some other way of creating and recording this life that is *your* beautiful and fleeting life, which is immensely valuable to record right now.

## A CIRCLE OF FRIENDS

Leo Tolstoy said, "True life is lived when little changes occur. The big changes take care of themselves if we make the little changes." Looking at our stress levels, embracing new attitudes, asking, "What does freedom mean now?," focusing on developing a new spirit of aging . . . each of these little and big changes can be made on our own, but, just as powerfully, each can be enhanced depending on whom we hang out with. As we age and our children grow up, our friends, to some extent, need to become our family. Science tells us why.

The Harvard neuropsychiatrist John Ratey, sixty-three, has studied the "social brain": how the brain looks when we study "human beings as social animals." When I met Dr. Ratey at our institute in Colorado, I met an optimistic, free-flowing scientist who provided his keynote speech in shorts and an aloha shirt. John is very comfortable in his own skin! We discussed together the social brain, about which John has written, "Our highest human virtue is our connection with other humans, and social activity is basic to our health and happiness. Our brains are preprogrammed to look for other humans from the moment of birth, and continuing social interaction is essential for normal development throughout our life." To bring the point home, John said, "As much as individuals must be able to fight or flee in order to survive, we also need sociability if we are to survive . . . we have a central dependence on others. We are designed for group living."

John's research joins with that of numerous other scientists who study the effects of social relationships on the brain. This research distills to two main points: (a) people who become significantly lonely as they age die younger than people who spend more time in healthy social groups, and (b) healthy social groups can alleviate symptoms of depression, among other mental illnesses. We are wired to be together, even though, at times, we just want to be alone.

Developing and maintaining one or two small circles of good friends is essential to a new spirit of aging. It is healthy living at any age, but it is something specific to aging, too; as we age, we often need more help than we did before. We need a kind of support that a circle of similarly aged friends can give us — support, love, freedom appropriate to who we are *now*. We need the rush of dopamine, oxytocin, serotonin, and other brain chemicals that constitute the generous internal pathways of love and happiness. As John told me, "Friends make us stronger and happier — usually!"

Gail, my wife, and I belong to two circles of friends. One for each of us is made up of "good women friends" and "good male friends," respectively. These are gender-specific "kinship systems," supportive and loving women and men who have become like our "kin" as we age. Each of us meets with these women and men spontaneously or in scheduled ways for lunch or dinner, book group or game night, and to support one another through both joyful milestones and difficult times.

As a couple, Gail and I also belong to a circle of friends that has grown together organically through our children's lives. There are five couples in this circle; our children grew up together through our religious activities and through school and sports; we as couples gravitated toward one another. All five couples in our friendship circle are aging together; we are all between forty-eight and sixty-two (all in or around the first stage of age, the age of transformation, which we'll look at in the next chapter). We all have grown children between the ages of nineteen and twenty-eight. We have similar interests — family, movies, books, conversation, sports, food, games, personal growth, health concerns. While we each also have our own personal interests and activities, we get together a few times a month, even if some of us will be missing from the social time.

No subject is off-limits in our dialogues, but we've agreed to spend little time in angry gossiping. We also joke, "Okay, enough about

70

our health. Let's talk about something else!" We try to keep our eye on being of use to one another. To that end, I've relied on Gail and our circle for help as I write this book, bouncing ideas off of them, sharing research results, and applying practical strategies.

I asked our circle of ten friends what they found most valuable in having a circle of friends. I heard:

"We (Mark and I) like to make dinner for all of you and get together that way because we feel really good being with you."

"It's fun to be together, the conversation is therapeutic, very healing. I understand everything better because I get so many different opinions from you all."

"No matter what else is going on in my life, I always know that being with you will make me feel better."

"The surprise party you threw for my sixtieth made me realize that all of you have become like my family."

"Facing health challenges is less stressful because we have each other. I don't know what I'd do without you guys."

"You guys ground me."

"We know each other so well, things make sense when we're together."

"Work is busy, life is busy, but I always know there will be some peace and companionship when we're together. I trust you guys."

A circle of friends is a spiritual ground, a place of health, a time of freedom, a concentration of life force, a source of passionate life-energy. It is good for our bodies; through a circle of friends, we can help one another through surgeries and illnesses, and we can keep one another honest about bad habits, such as overeating. It is good for our emotional life, as we support one another in working through life's issues and challenges. A circle of friends helps us de-stress. It is also a source of hope; as concerns and cares arise regarding age, death, and dying, we are there for one another to find and give meaning to life. The love and friendship in the group unifies being and doing into a single experience; as we talk, cook, eat, play games, and "do" many things together, we also feel that we are just "being" together at a deep level. We often find that after spending time in this circle of friends, we feel immensely free and fulfilled.

My Circle of Women: I have always had a group of close friends, but it is my circle of friends who are constants in my life. They are my support and my trusted confidantes. This is a reading that I use in the women's retreats I lead for our circle of friends:

*A circle of women can provide a container for emergence in a way that a woman alone, or even a one-to-one relationship, cannot. Intimate relationships and even friendships can break or at least be greatly strained by life changes. But from the combined wisdom and energy of a small group of women who are committed to "hearing each other into speech," a continuity and trust can develop that can be relied on over the long term. And, witnessing each person's direct knowing of her truth, we can be empowered to love our own.*

Seeing the many threads of my life come together to weave a tapestry of purpose . . . recognizing that all the events of my life, no matter how diverse, were strands on the same tapestry and what has emerged is quite acceptable to me now.

— Beth, 62

If you already have a positive, life-affirming circle of friends, celebrate and nurture it! If you are laboring under some age avoidance, pessimism, or loneliness, hopefully you can start looking around for one or two or more people or couples with whom you can form a circle of friends, have dinner together, go to movies together, do some fun activities together, watch sports together, take trips together, take walks together, and otherwise talk and be present with one another in the ways that can make aging feel adventurous, even when it is happening in your own living room or backyard.

## BECOMING AN ELDER

A family asked for my help. We met together a number of times to talk about the constant tension between the mother and daughter. Among the family's particular issues was this one: the mother, seventy-five, was angry at her daughter, Pauline, forty-eight, and son-in-law, Hank, forty-nine, for not respecting her and not treating her "as a mother should be treated."

As we delved into the situation, this conversation occurred (this is a condensation of a much longer set of dialogues).

Me to the mother: Do you act respectably toward Hank and Pauline?

Her: What do you mean? Of course.

Me: I mean, do you respect your daughter and son-in-law, keep good boundaries, not tell them what to do, that kind of thing? Do you treat them with respect?

Her: Of course. But anyway, it shouldn't matter. I'm the mother. I should get respect from them.

Me: I'm not so sure. You will get *love* for being the mother, but *respect* might be another thing.

Her: "Honor thy father and mother" doesn't make a distinction between the two. Kids should respect me for giving them life and raising them. Period.

My disagreement with her on this point became like a verbal 360-degree circle for a number of sessions. We kept returning to it, but she didn't budge from her opinion that no matter what, she should be made to feel totally comfortable, always, in her children's home.

Then, one day, I agreed to come to the daughter's home. It made sense to meet with the whole large family there rather than in my small office. The day before, I had been phoned by three people in the family and told that the level of conflict in this family became severe enough that the granddaughter, seven, had run from the room weeping at her own birthday party because of a verbal conflict between her grandmother and her mother.

When I arrived at the house, I said hello to everyone, then we settled quickly into conversation. Gradually, everyone admitted fault for the tensions, everyone, that is, except the seventy-five-year-old mother/grandmother. So I asked her about her actions. She told me to "hold the bullshit" about "love and respect." I confronted her again, suggesting that respect has to be earned. Our discussion echoed our argument in my office.

Me: What do you gain by saying people should just respect you because you're the mom? It's not working. People around you are just respecting you less, getting angry at you more.

Her: You're blaming me. Talk to them. They don't give me a chance.

Me: But what do you gain?

Her: What the hell are you talking about?

Me: You must be gaining something by causing all the tension you cause? What is it?

Her: This is bullshit.

Me: Let's switch gears then. What are you afraid of?

Her: This is psychobabble. I'm not afraid of anything.

Me: You're afraid of something. You see all the tension you're causing, but you won't give an inch. What are you afraid of?

Her: Nothing. I'm not afraid. I just want to be treated with respect.

This back-and-forth continued for a few minutes until finally I took the risk of saying, "Look, maybe you're afraid you've failed as a parent, so you have to bully everyone to make sure you never have to feel that failure. Could that be it?" With clients who will not give an inch, one guesses at times to stimulate a dialogue.

Her: That's bullshit. You're taking their [the family's] side and coming up with some psychological crap to justify it.

Me: I'm actually more on your side than you realize. If you don't fix this problem, your kids are going to shut you out. They won't want to see you anymore.

She turned away, looking toward the window. She knew this last sentence was true. Also, she was getting overwhelmed by the dialogue. "Please just think about what you're afraid of," I suggested. "That fear must be creating a lot of the tension and stress for you. Let's talk more when you want to talk." She walked out of the room. I spoke with the family a bit more and then left the house.

A week later, both the mother and daughter called. The daughter said, "Mom wants to see you. Some good things have happened." The mother asked to see me a couple of weeks later. In my office, she confessed, "Until you convinced me about the difference between love and respect, I hadn't thought along those lines. I just assumed I should get love and respect because of my age. It pisses me off that you were right about this, but I'm glad you were direct. Life is a lot better now." She did not bring up our dialogue around fear at that moment, and so I did not. (In chapter 2 I will further explore the role of the fear of failure and inadequacy during our aging process.)

This anecdote is ostensibly about a mother becoming less domineering, and thus safer for, and more enjoyable with, her family members. I believe it is also useful in helping us define an "elder" in today's complex society. As I compared the Gurian Institute survey and focus group research with broader research from anthropological studies, I could not help but note that "elder" comes up constantly, yet its meaning is often unclear. "Elder" is an essential component of aging in any generation, and it constitutes a crucial element of the new spirit of aging we are defining in this book. But what do we really mean by "elder"?

In the case of this mother and her family, while the climax of the confrontation took place over a few weeks, the journey of the growth of this mother and this family took a few years. As this mother matured toward a lower-stress, healthier way of being in her family, the word "elder" didn't come up, yet it represents her intention. She felt an internal drive to become a respected elder in the family and exert healthy elder influence. She needed help in discovering how to do it because her assumption about how it happens was an assumption that might have worked a few hundred years ago but was not working now. However, she absolutely knew she wanted to have a positive influence on this family.

As she better understood what an elder was and could be, she moved into a more positive relationship with her family and the family with her, and she herself felt much freer as a person. Something almost indefinably subtle occurred, something natural to human development and something immensely valuable. During the next three years of her life (she passed away at seventy-eight), she and her children and grandchildren became closer, and she passed on a number of recipes, ideas, hugs, wisdom, books, and family stories that she would not have passed on had she not become an elder. She became the role model and identity model she was trying to be.

## An Elder's Way

In this second half of life that so many of us now experience, we have the opportunity to shift from being an "adult" to becoming an "elder." All previous civilizations have asked adults to become elders, so this concept is by no means new, but for us now it is a part of a living miracle: literally, billions of us will actually get the chance to become elders, if we will take that chance. Think of what the world will be like if that miracle — and all the wonder, awe, and good work it implies — actually takes place.

What does the word "elder" conjure up in *your* mind? Are you an elder or just "getting older"? Becoming an elder requires consciousness and concentration, especially in our present century when an elder's way is not clear. For a starting definition, we can look up "elder" in a dictionary or on Wikipedia. We see that "elders are repositories of cultural knowledge and transmitters of that cultural information" or "elders are thought of as reservoirs of certain skills that need to be passed on to younger people." In Sardinia, one of the blue zones researchers have studied in depth, elders spend a part of their days passing knowledge of their trade or craft to younger villagers. In Okinawa, elders seek out opportunities to support and help their family and community members "when asked." In both these places, elders spend less time in sedentary lifestyles (sitting and staring at screens) than do older people in many parts of the United States. In Nicoya, Costa Rica, and in Loma Linda, California, elders report "having reasons to get up in the morning," and they are known as "older people who are comfortable exploring and passing on their faith." They feel that mentoring is a part of their "sense of higher purpose." In Japanese, the principle of the elder has a name: *ikigai.* In all these places, many elders hold positions of wisdom and authority; they run families, tribes, marketplaces, governments; they are judges, teachers, leaders. They are not perfect — they are elders.

Summarizing all the research, I think we can say with some safety that an elder in our society is someone of fifty or older who:

- passes on specific work and wisdom (occupies a niche, a "lifework," a legacy, and teaches it to others, while also providing wise counsel when needed);
- models life purpose and maturity (fewer power struggles with others, more insightful respect and admiration of others, more "drawing out" of others' gifts);

- remains as physically and mentally active as possible (takes control of damaging body-mind practices and transforms them so that the body and mind remain healthy as he or she ages, so that the elder can be "of use" and "enjoy life" for as long as possible);
- connects young people and society to mysteries of success, compassion, freedom, and faith (takes the risks of modeling both humility and self-confidence in the face of real life, while protecting others' rights to live their own way, in their own mysteries).

In some cases, in some blue zones (as it was for our own ancestors, if they lived long enough), some elders just ease into becoming elders. They are just bestowed the title and grace of the elder because they get older. But in our culture this happens more rarely. Part of embracing the wonder of aging is really taking hold of where we are as elders. We cannot turn back the social clock; we live in an age when "elderhood" is rarely bestowed on us just because we're older. Our culture focuses more on young people and middle-age journeys, and we are challenged as elders to be visible. We can complain about this, or we can take our own responsibility for it and correct this course. We can *take* the elder role rather than waiting to receive the distinction. We can (and we must) concentrate so fully on what an elder is now, today, that we support one another in thinking, acting, creating, serving others, enjoying life visibly, and take our place. This "taking" is part of the redefinition of age that we can make happen. By embracing the wonder of aging, we can embrace a new role in the family, neighborhood, group, marketplace, and world, a life position we must not passively wait for people in today's society to give to us. Each time we volunteer at a child's school, teach a child a craft or skill, provide insight to others, or lead, guide, and help younger people sustain life and vision, we can be an elder.

As we continue together in this book, we'll explore all this a great deal more. Each chapter of this book constitutes an aspect of becoming an elder. As we explore this together, we may need to support one another in realizing that in our day and age a person can live to seventy or eighty but still not be an "elder." This is what the mother/grandmother ended up realizing. Becoming an elder means realizing that a person can still act like a child, not an elder, and our society and our families are relatively unforgiving of that kind of behavior, especially in America.

A person can complain constantly, which an elder probably ought not do if he or she is going to be respected as an elder. A person can spend his or her last decades of life in power struggles with others, which an elder does not. An older person can withdraw from family and community, which an elder does not do. By now, an elder has generally looked death and mortality in the eye — through his or her own difficult illness, by losing a job or dream that cannot be regained, by burying a spouse or many friends, or simply by living long enough to see the inevitable. Thus, for the elder, free will is even more powerful than it might have been before we went through trying times. Having come through, an elder no longer avoids his or her deepest fears through manipulation and dominance of others. It is partially because we are going to die (and we know it) that we will, hopefully, seek to concentrate on serving others, connecting with the world intensely, taking care of everyone who needs us, making peace with who we actually are, and seeking a new spirit of growth. Ultimately the "glory" of an elder is the choosing to take hold of freedom. The kind of freedom we hint at here (and we will keep getting deeper into it throughout this book) is not about escape; rather, it is the next stage of growth, the next mature kind of love.

To become an elder in our society is not as cut-and-dried as it may be elsewhere or might have been in the past, but it is a maturity on which family, community, and even the soul and spirit of our race depend. As we move forward in this book and keep exploring what a true elder is in the context of our lives in postindustrial culture, please keep this phrase in mind: "on which the spirit of our race depends." By the end of this book, I hope it will resonate even more fully than it does now: part of this concept of embracing the wonder of aging is the concept of our role as elders in a world that desperately needs our active, meaningful, and well-delivered wisdom.

### CHOOSING FREEDOM

There's a certain new spirit of aging, a sense of freedom, that aging promises. It is different in many ways from the freedom we felt when we were young, left our childhood homes, and went out on our own. That earlier freedom was laced with the attitude that we would have few limitations ("You can do anything you want! You can reach any dream!"). The freedom we are talking about now exists with the understanding that we do each have limitations. We've been around the block a few times. We know what's what. And we know that it is time to feel the freedom that exists commensurate with our present wisdom. It is now, in fact, when we are fifty and over, that we can grow into the next stages of life, in which we can finally feel the freedom to be ourselves and the freedom to really take care of the people we love the way they should be taken care of.

Feeling this sense of freedom, we can potentially live in the emotions and activities of a freer life for many decades of new growth — at least three stages of new growth, as we will detail in the next chapters. This sense of growing freedom is a sense that we are, as a generation, creators of a new spirit of aging that will become increasingly essential for billions of people going forward, billions who will be here long after we are gone — the future generations of empowered age.

What, if not transformation,
is our deepest purpose?
— Rainer Maria Rilke


Friends, remember, to be born a human
being is a rare event. That is why we ask: If
I fail to achieve liberation in this life, where
do I expect to achieve it?
— Zen Master Szu-hsin Wu-hsin


You must open your eyes after fifty years of
living
if you want to cross over from confusion.
— Jalal ad-Din ar-Rumi

## MEDITATION 2: FORESHADOWING

Tennis racket in one hand and pen in the other, I am a man who no longer moves with the same vigor he felt in his youth. I see the direction I will go to reach the finality of life — it will be a summer day, I imagine, when I will lift my glasses off (or a daughter will do it for me), and lie down on dewy grass,

my skin covered with scars that no medicine can rub off, tattoos of transition from servitudes and arrogances to a laconic knowledge that I'm going somewhere else than I imagined in my college years,

so that when children and grandchildren look at my head, they see white hair floating on the air like foam left behind by the tide, and with the shovel of their own thoughts they will fill dirt into the spaces my new silences have left them,

while I remember a man who hoped to become a tribute to God (and accomplished it, in his way), his children whispering how the old guy took a whole life to become himself,

and I on the summer day sitting down in a chair on the back porch, my mind a mist of thoughts, will let it happily occur to me that my constant itching eczematic skin and my dented, wrinkling thighs and these droopy shadowed eyes and aching neck and scarred knees and endless canker sores and sleeplessness incurable and paunched belly and skinny arms — what else? what more? — these boiled-baked-bumped feet, this gray weed-covered peanut, these sagging pecs (where once I wore armor), these bent shoulders —

each is a reason for applause, each a slowing stubborn challenge to the loss of the single breath that delivered me into the world, each a centaur battling in my bones against death,

while my eldest daughter walks up to me, "Dad, come on, let's go play tennis. There's a court open," and my youngest one, "Daddy, you're squinting!" lifts my thick glasses back onto my eyes, both women bending to read over my shoulders this poem I've been writing,

"Dad, come on, you're only fifty-four, don't think like this,"

Ah I see it so well,

how both of you will chide me for looking beyond you to death, when I should be living, with you right now, the many stages of my miraculous age.

# CHAPTER 2
# THE AGE OF TRANSFORMATION

The labor you have performed up to now has transformed your environment, and that environment, now, is transforming you.
— Brett McKay

Four women and three men talked together in a living room. Our ages ranged from fifty to eighty-three. We had just finished dinner and now drank decaf coffee and ate dessert. Outside, snow fell; inside, the gas fireplace emanated heat, and our conversation felt soulful and gentle. Gail and I had brought this focus group together to hear and record what people fifty and over were thinking. Everyone in the group knew I was writing this book and knew my theory of "age stages" (which I will share in this chapter and the next). Some of the people had used my research in their lives and work. I asked them, now, to recall moments when they knew they had left "midlife" behind and entered new stages of age.

Judy, fifty-seven, an attorney, recalled, "I was fifty-three when Liam and I became empty nesters. We had been a part of the sandwich generation, caring for my folks and raising kids, but then it just sort of happened that our kids became seventeen and eighteen, basically on their own, and we realized we were becoming empty nesters. I missed the little kids and actually got pretty depressed by their loss, and then Liam's father died. We got into therapy and explored where we were for quite a long time. I learned that my husband and kids couldn't be my major source of joy and identity anymore, and that I couldn't 'save' my parents — they had a right to their own lives, even when they did things I wished they didn't do. And I learned that food couldn't be my source of stability either. Whenever I got stressed, I ate. I had to get free of, essentially, a food addiction. My work fulfills me, yes, but it had become rote, too. At fifty-three, I basically paused to breathe and look at a lot of aspects of who I was; I was now a woman who was aging, a woman in a whole new stage of life."

Mark, sixty-three, a small-business owner, spoke after Judy. "That's what's great about it: the opportunity to do something new, enter a new stage of life. I cried for a few days when my last kid left home, and I miss my kids, but my attitude is: I did my job; it's their turn to make a life now. What Judy is talking about . . . I get that. I had to look at who I was and decide what to keep and what to throw out. That's been big for me as a divorced man, a single man, going forward."

Hank, a tall, lanky seventy-one-year-old who wore bow ties, set his coffee cup down and added, "It happened for me somewhere around my sixtieth birthday. Kate and I realized we wanted to sell the big house, downsize. We wanted to do more volunteer work. I want to play more golf. I've got my fly-fishing, we've got the grandkids. I remember ten, twenty years ago, I had no time for anything. Now I have time. It's that 'freedom' you talk about. I get what you mean."

These comments moved us into a discussion of the influence of money on our age groups and the fact that "retirement" had become something of a lost dream for so many people. Then, Tricia, sixty-nine, a social worker, mentioned the idea of freedom again, saying, "But aren't we capable of some kind of freedom that goes beyond our parents' 'retirement' dream? I mean, that is important, and I do plan on retiring, but aren't we talking about something else? I remember, in my thirties, I saw my parents and their friends 'getting older' and it was like a huge wave of white hair to me. I was brought up in a middle-class black household. We didn't have a lot of interaction with 'old people' when I was growing up. We also didn't have a lot of old people left. Now that I'm getting older, I realize I don't have a lot of models for the stages of aging or getting older, but even with the financial changes, I feel like there is a kind of freedom I can have that none of my elders back then could have. I feel like this really is a time like no other."

Peggy, eighty-three, a retired administrative assistant whose husband had died the year before, chimed in. "If I didn't have my daughter to help me, I wouldn't really know what to do with the health care system. It's a maze. And there's not much out there written for me at my age. So I guess I'm 'old,' and I know I am, but then, other times, I think I've got a whole other stage of life left in me. I'm still living independently, so I'm free to do as I please. I miss my husband, but I have long-term health insurance, my health is okay, and I have money to live on. I could live another ten or twenty years. I might just be getting started with a new stage of my life, for all I know."

The people in our focus group sensed the inner and outer drama of distinct life stages after fifty. They sensed that biological, emotional, social, and spiritual growth, including growth of the spirit of freedom as we age, occurs in distinct eras or epochs after fifty. Debra Gore, a physician in the Group Health Cooperative, recently told me, "One of the primary areas of medical growth in HMO study is research on life after fifty, and we all agree that post-fifty living is not just one huge stage of life. It is a number of stages, lived sequentially, one after the other, and also lived simultaneously. There is a chance to reach certain goals and accomplish certain milestones in each stage that each aging person can tap into."

Neuropsychiatrist Daniel Amen agrees with Dr. Gore. Founder of the Amen Clinics (which utilize SPECT [single-photon emission computed tomography] scans to help diagnose mental conditions), Dr. Amen is also the author of several books, including *Change Your Brain, Change Your Life* and *Use Your Brain to Change Your Age.* One of his many assets is his ability to synthesize information gleaned from more than sixty thousand brain scans.

Daniel and I discussed aging together one

afternoon in Colorado Springs after our conference sessions. We were fifty-four and fifty-one, respectively. We walked along a number of trails overlooking the Rocky Mountains, huffing and puffing a bit from the high altitude (feeling our age!). Daniel was writing *Use Your Brain to Change Your Age* at that time, so I asked him what was new in his research, and he revealed a bit of his own journey.

"Fifty was a milestone," he said, "even though I started feeling my age before that, and there have been some issues with aging. But you know, I've also never felt better. That has been a real pleasure. I am at the beginning of a new stage of life." I asked what he meant, and he said, "I'm breaking new ground in ways I couldn't have before. I'm clearer about some things. I'm not as scared to go in certain directions as before — a little more fearless. I feel like I'm changing, morphing, shedding old skin and becoming a new person. It's pretty neat!" (I have always loved Daniel's very scientific use of the word "neat"!)

We huffed and puffed a bit more, and I asked Daniel if he thought there might be actual, discernible stages of age that were unexpressed and unsynthesized in the present literature. "Absolutely," he nodded. "We are living out various stages of age without fully realizing it." Would those stages be hinted at in brain and biochemical research, I asked. Again, he nodded. "The stages of age will fit the stages of the brain's and body's arcs of aging."

I then asked what, for me, is the million-dollar question — a question of spirit and soul: "Do you think that beyond the science, there will also be a spiritual basis for the stages of age, with evidence in the world's spiritual and poetic literature, for instance?" He asked what I meant. "In other words," I said, "as we identify brain stages of the second half of our lives, will we also find that those stages track along the lines of what spirituality has been teaching us about age over the centuries?"

Daniel pondered this silently for a moment, then responded. "A scientist who doesn't also look at spirituality is too narrow in his thinking. Science and spirituality should correspond to one another if we look deep enough, especially as we look at life stages. Science and religion, science and spirituality . . . these are probably two sides of the same coin."

## THE STAGES OF AGE
The *age-stage paradigm* I will present in this

chapter and the next is the result of research in both science and spirituality. Conscious staging of your life after fifty is the second concentration I will ask you to pursue as you age. It has taken me more than a decade to develop and utilize this paradigm. I have gradually increased my integration of science and spirituality, following Dr. Elisabeth Kübler-Ross's process of detailing the "stages of growth" she associated with the final stage of life. Dr. Kübler-Ross, like Debra Gore and Daniel Amen, and like so many of the most progressive medical thinkers of our day (Andrew Weil and Deepak Chopra come to mind), was committed to finding evidence, if available, for developmental epochs in both scientific and spiritual literature. In presenting the age stages in these chapters, I will, thus, present both scientific and spiritual proof for the research on what I call the age-stage paradigm.

The stages are:

*Stage 1: The Age of Transformation* (from approximately fifty to approximately sixty-five);

*Stage 2: The Age of Distinction* (from approximately sixty-five to the late seventies); and

*Stage 3: The Age of Completion* (from approximately eighty to one hundred, and beyond).

If it turns out, over the next decades, that an increasing number of people begin to live far beyond one hundred worldwide, this paradigm will, I believe, be added to with another stage that is perhaps unrecognized now.

Each of the three stages includes elements of one another, but each one is developmentally distinct. The year thresholds for the stages cannot be measured exactly, giving each stage a two- to three-year cushion either way. Throughout the three stages, women and men approach aging differently. Thus, as I present the stages here, I will point out useful male-female differences to add into your exploration and conversations. I will not divide available physiological and health literature into the stages — that is, I will not give diet or nutrition advice for each stage. Rather, I will look more closely with you at the psychological and spiritual aspects of the stage in which you are living so that you should be able, by the end of this book, to tailor available physiological and cognitive self-care advice in the media and in other resources to the developmental growth-stage in which you are living.

Mary, 51, shared these thoughts in our July 2012 survey:

I realized that I was aging:

- When my muscles were not as toned as they used to be.
- When my daughter wants to stay up late and I need to go to sleep because now I am tired by 8:30 p.m. (She is 11 years old.)
- When I look in the mirror and see more wrinkles on my face.
- When I see more varicose veins on my legs.
- When it takes forever to lose a couple of extra pounds.
- When I am told: "Thank you for bringing your granddaughter to the birthday party," and she is my daughter!
- When a cashier tells me that I can get a senior discount.
- When I forget things that I am supposed to do.
- When I get offers for the scooter store, AARP, burial insurances, grandparents' life insurances . . . etc.

Being 51 years old, I feel the effects of menopause: irregular cycles. I am tired very often. A woman seems to be the one who is more responsible for the children, and she has no problem putting herself after the kids and her family. It is tiring!

The wisdom I've been learning in all this is that I have to enjoy life as much as I can. I feel closer to women as girlfriends more than ever. I think we understand each other much more than men understand us. We are great support for each other. I want to enjoy every little moment of life. A glass of wine, music, and relaxing. Appreciating a sunset . . . things that you don't always take the time to do.

## STAGE 1: THE AGE OF TRANSFORMATION

Julie Taymor, fifty-nine, the Tony Award–winning director of *The Lion King,* recently said this about aging: "It's all the circle of life and death. The sun rises at the beginning and sets at the end, after an incredible tempest of events and even some dark times. If you don't have those experiences, your life is probably not as rich. I am realizing this for myself now." Inspired by the Lion King story she has helped to tell for decades, Ms. Taymor was reflecting on the first stage of age, the age of transformation. She talked about "aging" and "health issues," "facing mortality" and "seeing a lot of life in the rearview mirror." She saw the "tempest," the "circle," "the dark times," and the light. She also reported feeling more joyful than ever.

The age of transformation includes all these things. As we will explore in detail in this chapter, it is a psychological journey of internal and external change that transpires from around fifty to around sixty-five. As our bodies and brains go through significant transformations into the second half of life via menopause, andropause, and physical aging, our souls are transforming as well, living through more than a decade of life in which our psyches transform from who we were to the elders we will become.

Archana Singh-Manoux, research director at the French National Institute of Health and Medical Research in Paris, asks us to concentrate on this new time in our lives as an essential step for quality of life going forward. "Healthy lifestyles and good cardiovascular health now are important for cognitive outcomes later . . . the fact that cognition declines implies that [understanding] these factors — health behaviors and cardiovascular risk factors and disease — become important for cognitive outcomes later in life." She advises us to look carefully at what our bodies and brains are doing in this stage of life in integrated and holistic ways. If we do not — if we avoid our age and the necessity of age transformation — we will suffer much more later. And if we only transform one element of life without holistically looking at the whole transformation, we will probably try a diet or other "new life technique" that won't stick, won't ultimately serve us, and may even become a setup for low quality of life later. It is as if our aging bodies and brains are saying to our souls:

"Okay, friend, will you become fearless and free through this transformation, or will you languish unactualized, lost, destructive, constantly dissatisfied?"

"So — will you take control of the inevitable changes, and make health and meaning from them?"

"As your body changes during these ten to fifteen years, how will you use this time to become a new person?"

"What will your new worth and identity in society be, since you are not going to be young anymore or even middle-aged?"

## Pre-Aging and Middle Age

If you are not yet fifty years old, but some of

the body-soul dialogue fits where you are, don't be surprised. The *British Medical Journal* recently featured a ten-year study on memory and cognitive function in seven thousand women and men forty-five and older. In the youngest cohort, forty-five to forty-nine year olds, the brains of both women and men had already shown decrease in memory and cognitive function associated with aging. Among men, there was even greater loss of memory than among women.

Similarly, a recent study at the University of South Carolina looked at the physiological side of turning forty-five — muscle mitochondria and physical exercise. The researchers found that when people are younger than forty-five, muscle mitochondria (the DNA of muscle growth) resuscitate more quickly, with less muscular exercise. As the subjects moved through their late forties, their muscle mitochondria resuscitated less quickly, and they needed more conscious exercise time in order to resuscitate muscles. In this study, forty-five years old was a possible marker for "aging." While we generally call our forties "midlife," and that is a good name for it, our forties are also a transition into the first stage of age, the beginning of our second lifetime.

That said, by fifty we fully enter Stage 1.

If you are over fifty, you may remember that your fiftieth birthday felt very different from your fortieth. Your fortieth felt, perhaps, like you had entered midlife, but your fiftieth felt like a rite of passage into a whole new journey. You felt that it was a "major milestone," and it was.

## MENOPAUSE AND ANDROPAUSE AS SPIRITUAL QUEST

Ultimately, I believe, our being conscious of the first stage of age, the age of transformation, is about seeing menopause and andropause as vital spiritual quests rather than burdensome processes. That "other kind of breath" we mentioned earlier, that breath in the void, can be our breathing now, as we sense certain inevitabilities and meet those with transformative, quest-like spiritual passion. This attitude turns menopause and andropause into tools of a transformative journey. It makes new meaning of them in the context of the wonder of aging.

In both menopause and andropause, which can begin while we are in our "middle age" or "pre-age" (in our forties), we experience some or all of these eight elements of physiocognitive change. These are elements of biology that I believe we must convert into spiritual concentration in order to mine the age of transformation for all that we can. After listing these elements for your review, I will provide some analysis, then reframe the elements to become catalysts for a new stage of freedom.

But first, here is what is known as the "symptoms of menopause and andropause." I see these "symptoms" not as parts of a disease but as possible, worthy, and important signals of spiritual transformation.

1. Sometimes, even often, in menopause and andropause, you may experience mood swings, irritability, grumpiness, increased rudeness or harshness, even (and often, especially) to people you love. Your hormonal and brain changes, especially the drop in former hormonal levels, can create "dark times," even create suicidal ideation, which can be especially shocking.

2. You may develop a sense of your former identity as inadequate or feel you have lost your identity, and you may feel you have failed at life, not fulfilled yourself, and need to start over. As your hormonal systems and brain change, your psyche experiences a sudden sense of lost or confused self. Much more of

this is neurally and hormonally caused than we often realize.

3. A "crash" of body and soul can occur, for example, "hitting bottom" in an addiction or experiencing a climax in former mildly self-destructive patterns, losing or quitting a job, destroying a marriage (whether overtly by having an affair or covertly by not working through decades of stored-up disappointment in a lover). The need for transformation you are feeling biologically and internally will often manifest in outward relational transformations, such as marital separation or divorce.

4. Reduced libido or sex drive, or reduced potency or ability to obtain and maintain an erection for men; reduced vaginal functioning and lubrication for women, and in some cases, increased physiological pain during sex. The creative, sexual, loving force you once took for granted in body, mind, and soul is now going through physiohormonal changes that send ripples, often painful ones, into intimacy, creativity, and physical/sexual functioning.

5. Intermittent or constant feelings of fatigue, loss of "verve," lack of sleep as compared to previous sleep patterns; depression, boredom, restlessness. Nearly everything about your body and brain can change in some way over these ten to fifteen years, which can affect various parts of your life. Especially if your lifestyle remains set for a thirty-year-old's energy level, you can become overstressed and dangerously depressed now.

6. Constant aching, stiffness, pain, and new or worsened physiological problems related to muscle or bone decay; increased obesity (acquiring a potbelly for men, finding weight loss "almost impossible" for women). Metabolism is not what it was; bones and muscles are transforming; your body is hoping to challenge you to accommodate and reboot toward a new era, new ways of living that decrease stress and increase health. Your body will keep hitting you with this charge until you heed the charge and take it to new levels of life energy.

7. Hot flashes, night sweats, skin condi-

tions (irritations), decreased will to get exercise or move around, increased sedentary life — all can feel like repeated shocks to your whole system. Especially for those women and men who have "harsher" menopause or andropause "symptoms," some personal motivation can dissipate and motivation itself may need your attention; you may sit in front of the TV a lot. Your experiences may also collide with a major illness, which surprises your system and can take your life over for a while.

8. You will sense that you are getting older and the environment around you knows it, as if your workplace, community, and family are judging you differently, in a negative way. At first, this can be quite depressing. Perhaps at work, you are replaced by someone younger, or, in your family, you are replaced by a new spouse. This is a social/cultural element of the transformation experience. Inevitably, some of your social relationships will change or need to change.

If you are in your mid-forties, you may feel a few of these signals of transformation in a nascent way; if you are in your mid-fifties, you should be involved in even more of these experiences, and even more intensely, than before. By fifty-five or sixty, your father or mother or other family members may have passed away, or you have lost at least one aging friend or mentor to various diseases. Your hair is probably graying in all sorts of places, even if you dye the hair on your head. Your body's aches and pains feel more like age than "midlife." If you have had a life-changing health problem already, you know this is not midlife anymore. You are involved in something far more intimate with mortality than middle age.

It can be a worthwhile and soulful exercise to sit with a journal open and with the list of eight elements before you. To study the list, think about your life: breathe, process, reflect, feel. If you are in counseling, or if you can go to lunch with a peer friend, and if you have a circle of friends, look at all of this together. Bring your silent thoughts into the open, discuss them, review who you've been, where you are. Share your stories in a group over dessert. Find people who understand where you are and what you are going through. Go through some of it alone. Find solitude. Take your time. Fully engaging in Stage 1 takes a lot of patience.

When you lose everything, and I mean everything, you sit there in this empty room in the dark, and the only person who can get you out is you. The hardest thing in life to do is to change. I worked really hard to make changes. I went to therapy; I realized the person I molded myself into was strong in one part, but he was weak in others. I thought I could fix it in a year. It was a humbling experience that took 12 years.

— Mickey Rourke, actor, 59

As you review your journey and process, think, and feel over weeks, months, and years, you might see how your natural, biological growth constitutes *an age of transformation* in which the eight elements might come to look like this:

1. Now we have a ten- to fifteen-year period in which to heal inward terrors by learning, finally, to take very little personally; to detach when needed; to be angry only in healthy ways.

2. Now we have the time and a mission to build a new identity, finally fight through our fear of inadequacy (more

on how to do this in a moment), and free ourselves from chronic stress so that we can fulfill ourselves, finally, in ways we could not when we were young.

3. Now we have a chance to finally get free of an addictive behavior, change self-destructive patterns, and get help to make the right choices for our family. In some cases, the quest will take us to divorce, but in many cases the divorce we thought inevitable in our transformation shock may, over a period of years of transformation, become a new kind of marriage, more whole and freer in new ways.

4. Sex can become liberating and freeing now in new ways, as well. Now we can follow our changing bodies in preparing for a new way of seeing intimacy as we age, a new, freer kind of intimate separateness that is not based as much on quantity of intense contact as on deep quality of intimacy (more on this in chapter 5).

5. Now we have time to work through natural patterns of fatigue and re-

charge certain aspects of our lives, while letting go of other attacks we used to make on the world, attacks that will debilitate and kill us now because of our age. We can develop new sleep habits, new rituals of rest (a nap in the afternoon, if we're lucky!), new energy (meditation every morning), and some actual peace of mind, things we tried to develop before, perhaps, but over a decade now, can fully actualize and enjoy.

6. Now we can transform our bodies into even more of a spiritual temple than they were — spending a decade altering our eating and physical habits, matching who we are with how we act. "My body is my temple" is, perhaps, something we said when we were young, but back then we could put nearly anything into that temple and still thrive; now, we must fully value what it means to say, "My body is my temple."

7. We can work very hard, accomplish a lot, build a legacy, but in an integrated, graceful, energy-saving way now, a way that shows the world we are embracing life because we know what life is, finally; we have, over a decade or more,

the freedom to finally clarify our new, wisest priorities.

8. We can now experience this transformative rite of passage and, thus, rebirth into a second lifetime. The inevitable losses we will experience in our ten to fifteen years of transformation can grow our psyches deeply if we see them as losses that are required for growth, grief that is necessary, new triumph that is waiting for us as we awaken to the elder's way of thinking and doing in a second lifetime.

Transforming ourselves consciously, gradually, completely, we can feel what Mary Oliver meant when she wrote that it was specifically when she was no longer young that she realized what a kiss was worth. This "what a kiss is worth" can be a metaphor for enjoying the world. While mowing the lawn, or having a meal, or shopping for clothes, we might now feel the sensual world as never before. As our biology transforms us, even our senses are changing; the olfactory parts of our brains, for instance, transform just a little bit during menopause and andropause, as do a number of other sensorial and emotive centers of the brain.

113

To reframe menopause and andropause toward spiritual quest is to concentrate, through the lens of the changing body-brain, on the engaged soul. It is to know that youth is only one life. There are several more lives we can find now, including becoming wild in ways we never had the confidence or freedom to be before. We have ten to fifteen years of transformation in which to internally, environmentally, and relationally change from busy living to busy living with full meaning. We know what we know and we're wise enough now (or can be, if we will concentrate on it) to know what we don't know. "Sometimes," Mark Twain quipped, "what gets us into trouble is not what we don't know; it's what we know for sure that just ain't true." For each of us, there are things we "knew for sure" that are no longer true. We have time now and internal propulsion to figure these things out.

## DEVELOPING FEARLESSNESS IN OUR FIFTIES

One of the things that I believe, after physical health, is the most psychologically freeing during the age of transformation is confronting, finally, one's root fears — the fears that constitute the bases of our overreactions, anxieties, excessive needs to control others, and relational errors. These root fears, in psychological terms, all taper backward and downward into a single root fear: the fear of being inadequate. This anxiety is more pervasive in us than we realize, especially when we are under constant stress. Stage 1 is our time to fully understand it and transform the psyche toward new concentrations and new life.

Here are two case examples to illustrate this.

**Tom and Alice.** Seventeen-year-old Brandon came into my office accusing his father, Tom, fifty-four, of being a "hypercritical, irritable, judgmental" man. Brandon was a smart, underperforming "geek," a lover of video games, a boy ready to drop out of school; he was on depression medication; he was smoking marijuana every few days. "I'm in trouble," Brandon confessed as we walked together and talked during a counseling session. "I need help. But it's not all just me. My father is so critical of me, I can't breathe. I want to leave home and never come back. I think I hate him sometimes."

When Tom and Brandon's mother, Alice, fifty-one, came into the next session, I met, in Tom, an imposing man, six feet two inches tall, stocky, much larger than Brandon or his quieter mother. Brandon, I could see, had more of his mother's body and features than Tom's, but his eyes were Tom's: strong, piercing.

As our conversation evolved, we relatively quickly came to discuss Brandon's feelings about his father's dominance. Tom defended himself. "I want him to grow up. I don't want him to fail. That's why I'm hard on him." Toward the end of a session, Brandon yelled, "Just let me go, let me be! Stop trying to control me!" Tom yelled back, Alice tried to run interference, and I saw a father and son at war.

I also realized this was a father of fifty-four, beginning or perhaps halfway through andropause, who projected his own lifelong anxiety of inadequacy on his son. Andro-pause — its moodiness, irritability, and naked emotions — exacerbated the father-son dynamic. While Tom was definitely trying to be a good father to his wayward son, he was clearly haunted by the fear of failure — both in himself and in his son. The mother was not sure what to do as she sat in the middle of this. The son just wanted to be free of it all, carrying in his defiant attitude the weight of freedom that all three people actually wanted but were unable to realize.

For some weeks, little change occurred in this counseling or in this family; then, in a particularly difficult session, I stopped the flow of argument and asked all three partici- pants to spend the next week looking at how afraid of failure, rejection, and inadequacy they were. Over the next few weeks, all of this made sense to them, and we worked together on this dynamic in the family. Each person in the system looked at where they each were psychologically, at their present stages of life, in relation to how they felt worthless, like failures, rejected as human beings, and un- able to succeed.

Before giving more detail on this, let me give a second case.

**Amy and Allen.** Amy, fifty-four, and Allen, fifty-three, came to see me for marital diffi- culties. Amy, a successful lawyer, said, "Allen interrupts me all the time and he gets angry and irritable with me over little things I do to try to improve our lives. I feel like twenty-two years of marriage are a failure. Truthfully, I think there are times when we hate each other."

As soon as I heard the word "hate" directed toward a family member, my antennae for the fear of inadequacy went up. Allen said, "Amy is the most controlling person I know. She insists I always tell her where I am, what I'm doing, like I'm her kid or something. I love to hike and she doesn't, but if I go hiking, somehow I'm 'robbing our relationship' or 'not valuing her.' I can't satisfy her." The words "controlling" and "can't satisfy" also raised my antennae for this issue.

As we continued talking, I learned that this couple was in an entrenched pattern of controlling each other. This had gone on for most of the relationship. The couple had been in therapy before, and separated, ten years ago, for three months. A month into our work together, they separated again — Allen moved out and roomed with a friend who had just divorced; Amy and Allen planned their divorce even as they kept coming to counseling.

During this time, I helped them with a number of issues they faced, but finally a time came when I was able to challenge them as I had Tom, Alice, and Brandon. I asked them to look at how their individual fears of inadequacy forced them to control and dominate the person they loved. By then, these two people, who deeply loved each other, were living separately and missed each other a great deal (even despite their anger at the other). We were able to look at their individual and collective fear of inadequacy in a way that each of them felt to be transformative. This work does not always bring a separated couple back together (it is only one aspect of psyche and relationship), but in their case, it did bring them back together.

## Transcending the Fear of Inadequacy

With many of my Stage 1 clients, I look carefully at the anxiety of inadequacy because I have found that this baseline human fear can finally, now, be dealt with in the psyche as never before. Our Stage 1 lives are changing or have already changed in a number of ways — internal and external, hormonal and social, emotional and relational. In Stage 1, it becomes possible to advance our identities and psyches to a richer sense of success and confidence than we were able to develop before. This advancement of self, this concentration on root fears, is the next psychological growth stage in human development. As we confront an anxiety that has plagued us for decades, we become freer than before.

At fifty-five years old, I am honest when I tell clients and audiences that as a person in Stage 1, I am working on this very issue. I have my own fears of inadequacy that manifest in various worries, anxieties, overreactions, and stresses. Understanding and healing these is part of my own transformation into an elder. Because I am smack-dab in the middle of this journey, I am highly sensitive to the fear in others and am especially interested in the roots of the fear. For Tom and Alice, as for Amy and Allen, the anxiety of inadequacy was the emotional ground of many of their present difficulties; Tom's sense of inadequacy made him constantly feel vigilant, even desperate regarding his son; Amy and Allen felt unrealized as individuals and as a couple, yet they wanted to have a relationship with each other. By dealing with their fears of inadequacy, they transformed their relationships and themselves.

In studying all available research on psychological fear, I see no one who is immune to feeling inadequate in certain situations: the fear itself is not a disease or something wrong with us. It is a fear housed in each of our psyches naturally, no matter our age; thus it is actually a useful one, a psychological fear that helps us survive and thrive. It responds to what twentieth-century psychologist R. D. Laing called "the ontological insecurity built into the human condition," an ontological (baseline) insecurity that drives us to work hard and succeed. The universe and nature are huge, we can easily see, while we are small; we live in natural fear of that large universe (and our own puniness within it); we constantly wrestle with feeling insecure and inadequate, and from that wrestling, we advance up hierarchies, are vigilant to protect families, never rest on our laurels, constantly seek pro-social behavior, empathy, and compassion, moral and character success; we accomplish, grow, learn, and love.

Abraham Maslow was responding to his understanding of the baseline fear of inadequacy when he provided a model of the hierarchy of needs. In *Toward a Psychology of Being*, Maslow uses the word "capacities" to help us understand the internal impetus for psychological transformation and growth of self beyond anxiety, toward greater freedom from fear. "Capacities in us clamor to be used, and cease their clamor only when they are well used. [Using] our capacities is necessary for growth and transformation. [If unused], the unused skill or capacity can become a disease center or else atrophy or disappear, thus diminishing the person. But once used, it can liberate the self." Maslow acknowledges that incapacity to accomplish the lowest level of the pyramid — survival — retards our ability to establish higher levels of self-actualization, but once we have developed enough material comfort to ensure survival, we have to deal with the fear of inadequacy in order to become more advanced, more civilized, more whole as we mature and age. For Maslow, as for all of us who have accomplished "survival," the base-line fear of inadequacy can now become a catalyst for transformation.

But for many of us, like Tom, Alice, and Brandon and like Amy and Allen, getting stuck in the fear of inadequacy feels so natural, we don't move forward. We don't fully mature into a complete elder, a liberated being, as we age; in Maslow's terms, we don't fully self-actualize. We have felt inadequate for so many decades, we no longer build new capacities; we do not transform ourselves, no matter how old we become. Brain research in the last decade has given us a number of clues as to why our psyches get stuck in our fear of inadequacy. Two parts of the brain — the anterior cingulate cortex and the caudate nucleus — handle a great deal of our psychological stress responses. They also partially control the extent to which we will psychologically mature during the one to two decades of menopause and andropause.

The cingulate cortex is an attention center of the brain; the caudate is a reward center. These centers receive and transmit Pe (error positivity) signals and ERN (error-related negativity) signals. ERN signals are associated with defensiveness and fear reactions. Pe neurotransmission is associated with increased fearlessness and freedom from the

ERN stress signals; they provide more neural cognition in areas of the brain that we would call "spiritual" and "liberating." Studies led by psychologist Jason Moser at Michigan State University, as well as studies by psychologist David Nussbaum, at the University of Chicago, show that people who feel more psychologically adequate are increasing Pe signals in activated brain centers like the cingulate cortex and caudate. By moving more signaling in this direction, the brain increases blood flow to centers associated with inspired capacities in the self for psychological growth and transformation. The more Pe signals your brain is activating — that is, the more adequate you feel — the more successful and transformative your lifework and life energy are. Body, thus, follows soul: you will do more healthy activity because your psyche feels healthier, less stressed-out, more whole and free. Awareness of the fear of inadequacy, and tracking how it is chronically stressing a person's psyche, begins the "brain work" of increasing Pe signals and decreasing ERN signals in the brain.

Counseling regarding root fears and feelings of adequacy and inadequacy for Tom, Alice, and Brandon was counseling toward a neural increase of what we call, in our common language, "psychological growth" and "spiritual transformation" (more Pe signals). For Tom and Alice, for instance, their initial, presenting issue (Brandon's failures and Tom's attacks on his failures) actually had a great deal to do with the psychology of adequacy and inadequacy. Both Tom, who was dominant, and Alice, who was passive, felt inadequate and felt like failures as they entered Stage 1. While Alice fought her fear of this inadequacy by giving up power and withdrawing from conflict, Tom did his battle more overtly and obviously, by projecting failure onto Brandon (and Brandon, of course, was also "failing" in ways that did need some response). From Tom and Alice, the fear of inadequacy — a fear constantly mirrored and exacerbated by their son's seeming inadequacies — stimulated rumination over failure and rejection in their own brain centers, such as their cingulate cortices.

Now in their fifties, these two parents got a second chance to delve deeply into the baseline fear they experienced unconsciously. They were going through andropause and menopause. Their internal biopsychological clock gave them the impetus to change by making Tom more irritable and Alice more passive. Their growing son, who sought more freedom anyway as a youth, was challenging them, even shocking them into new action —

counseling, self-reflection, personal growth, and change. These people had a chance now to create a new sense of freedom (for both the parents and the son), as well as increased quality of life and lowered stress (by changing the negative relational patterns they were in). My role as counselor and mentor to this family and these fiftysomething transformers was to guide the internal change as much as the clients would let me. I had to play this role provocatively, and by challenging the clients at times; I had to try to "shock" the clients into looking at themselves and transformation clearly.

Here is a verbatim conversation with Tom that illustrates this.

Tom: I've been thinking about last week. You seemed angry with me in that session. Were you?

Me: Why do you say that?

Tom: You said something like, "Listen, you just can't keep controlling other people because of your own fear of inadequacy. You have to transform, change, get moving. You're fifty-four years old. It's time."

Me: Why did that seem angry to you?

Tom: Your tone, maybe.

(Tom was right: I had said, somewhat confrontationally, "You know, Tom, there's not much more that I can do with you now until

125

you admit how inadequate you feel as a man these days. You need to stop projecting your own sense of failure onto Brandon.")

Me: I'm sorry about that, but was it useful?

Tom: Yeah. I'm glad you got impatient with me.

Me: Why?

Tom: Because you stood up to me. I wish Brandon would do that more. I have to get over how pissed I am at him for being such a failure. I get that now. But I'm pissed at myself. Yeah. I get that, too.

Me: You're pissed at yourself for what?

Tom: You know. The same thing.

Me: Failure?

Tom: I've failed at a lot of things. You got pissed at me, and it made me think about it. Brandon and I went golfing on Saturday and talked. I apologized to him. Can you believe it?

Me: That was huge.

Tom: Huge. I told him I got how hard I was on him because I was always feeling like a failure myself. I told him I had to let go, let him be who he was, no matter what. I told him this didn't mean he could bring pot into the house and that stuff, but it did mean I knew I had to change.

Me: What did he do when you told him all that?

Tom: Shit, man, he was blown away. We talked for a long time. Things feel different in the house.

Like so many men, Tom has difficulty expressing in words all the nuances of what he is feeling. But he was able to connect the dots. He saw, in his few words, what was going on. He revealed to himself, for the first time in his life, how much he had battled feeling like a failure all his life; his son's situation (and his own domineering attitude toward his son's failures) gave him a Stage 1 catalyst to de-stress his own psychological life, increase Pe signals, and transform into an elder.

The next weeks and months were not easy for this family or for Brandon, but a large piece of the puzzle fell into place for them. As I worked with Tom and Alice in couple counseling, I helped them explore the stages of age and the extent to which menopause and andropause were trying to catalyze transformation in them. I asked them to keep journals and to focus on watching and recording how their fears of inadequacy not only surfaced, but also could now be changed toward new identity. Tom continued his journey of transformation by looking back on the raising of his children as a series of episodes in which he wasn't around — he felt guilty and inadequate about this and now needed to

127

fully reconnect with his children. Alice had felt constantly inadequate as a person — in her words, "not smart enough to follow my own dreams." For this couple, there were layers and layers of these feelings.

Many clients do not reach a breakthrough, but most of us in our fifties are facing, without realizing it, our own version of accumulated psychological life stress that Tom and Alice faced: leftover or locked-in inadequacy we now have a chance to transform into new identity. As I mentioned, at age fifty-five as this book is published, I have my own impatience, irritability, overreactions, projections, anxieties, worries, and fears. Much of my own time in therapy, conversation, group time, friendship time, and personal reflection is spent helping myself while helping others to move through the age of transformation with the goal of quieting the chronic stress of feeling inadequate.

Most of us make enough money to survive now and can finally look at this internally stressful and stress-causing part of ourselves with personal transformation in mind. We have the freedom, capacity, and wisdom to reach out to others who can help us realize how much of the carnage around us is caused by the fear of our own inadequacy, a fear that is natural to the human brain but one that got revved up in our busy, stressful lives to whatever extent that fear was needed by our personality and life circumstance. Now we must realize the extent to which that fear is a greater source of negative stress than we may have had the chance to realize before, and we must decrease that stress through years of self-reflection and change.

Allen and Amy did just that. As we talked together and contextualized their present stage of life as an age of transformation, we worked on seeing the opportunity to explore the baseline fears that kept them from maturing and growing. I helped them reframe their interruptions and controlling behaviors from the viewpoint of adequacy and inadequacy. It took time, but gradually Allen and Amy both understood this in a revelatory way, each in his or her own consciousness. Amy said, "Okay, I get it: I control him because I'm afraid he'll leave me. It's almost like I've got a disease. I just keep replaying this stupid way of living. I've always felt like I wasn't worth very much, and that drives me to be a success in work, but it's not good at home."

Allen said, "I interrupt her because I'm afraid. I can't even let her speak or have a voice because my ego is so afraid of her brains. I've always felt like Amy is smarter than me, and that hurts my pride. I've got the fragile ego thing that men have, I guess, I don't know, but when I cut her off and interrupt her and talk about myself and my way of thinking and all of that, I'm just like a weakling kid and she just ends up hating me."

By working on self-understanding, then changing their behavior patterns, these two people were, like Tom, Alice, and Brandon, increasing Pe signals and decreasing ERN signals; they developed personal and couple language for transforming themselves out of enslavement and ascending the hierarchy of needs; they used their present life situations as a foundation for stepping into new ways of trusting themselves and others; they faced the crises inherent in the age of transformation — which can be a decade of crises with kids or parents, financial and work crises, crises with life-changing disease, crises with relationships, including possibly divorce — and reframed negative behavior and relational patterns to become positive catalysts toward transformation from adult to elder.

Letting go of my kids was so tough. They grew up, my marriage ended. I went through really difficult times. But what a joy it all was, too. I mean, it's not like we were all trapped together before — I loved raising my kids — but now there's a feeling of freedom that is amazing, too. I have a new partner, I am in therapy, I have my work and my good friends. A lot has changed. I think I trust myself finally. That's the biggest thing. I don't think I ever really trusted myself before.

— Sandra, 59

I wanted to share some news with you — I will be leaving B_____ Center after 25 years. As you probably know, I have a long history with B_____, first in the Human Resources department, then as the Conference Director, and most recently running the Education program. B_____ has been a wonderful place to call "home" for the past 25 years, but as I have had many life changes in the last few years, and now have sent my youngest child off to college, I decided that 2012 would be my year to look within myself, trust myself, and find new passion in new work. I am looking forward to stepping out of where I have been and now having new opportunities and experiences in new environments.

— Sally, 56

## THE ROPE AND THE SNAKE

The Buddha told a story of a monk who, when bathing in a river, stepped on a rope and thought it was a snake. Because he could not see to the bottom to view what the rope really was, he anticipated agonies, pains, venomous bites, worrying, panicking, crashing his way out of the river, looking for a stone with which to crush the snake. When the rope rose up and he saw that it was not a lethal snake but, instead, a rope, he was immensely relieved. The Buddha said, "The cause of his fear lay in his error, his ignorance, his illusion. When the true nature of the rope was recognized, he found tranquillity of mind, and he was happy. This is the state of mind of one who has recognized the fears inside the ego that cause his troubles."

You, I, and all of us exist in states of fear that can be revealed, worked on, and integrated into the psyche as nondominant during the age of transformation. The fears will always be with us, but they will not dominate us from Stage 1 going forward. This is perhaps one of the greatest promises of menopause and andropause, and Stage 1 of age. We have ten to fifteen years now in which to come to grips with fear and our lack of self-trust. We can (and most of us will) change jobs over a decade. Some of us will change our relationships. Becoming an elder will become increasingly important. At a deep level, we will come to sense that to fully become a respected, essential part of a community and family now, as we age, we need to look carefully at our own sense of adequacy. There is a great deal about ourselves we need to make peace with as elders. The psychological fears we have grappled with throughout our lives can continue to create chronic stress for us, or we can finally, now, deal with them positively, so that we move forward psychologically, spiritually, holistically toward the next era of service — being a grandparent in our family and being an elder mentor to the world around us.

Ultimately, this transformative process is about becoming stronger, wiser people for ourselves, and it is about becoming wiser people for others, to whom we will be (and already are) essential role models and elders. The first stage of age is our first major chance to embrace the wonder of aging as if our lives depended on it, which they do.

I have never felt radiant like this before
I have never felt free like this.
— Nazim Hikmet


When I'm weary . . . I ask my dead friends
for their opinion
And the answer is . . . "Whatever leads
to joy."
— Marie Howe


It ought to be lovely to be old,
to be full of the peace that comes of
experience.
— D. H. Lawrence

## Meditation 3: Take Yourself, and Go Forth

Freedom is confusing, isn't it? Even though we know the world is an amazing masterpiece, just when we gather the courage to hold it happily in our small hands — when we clutch a bouquet of flowers to us, "Yes, this life is beautiful! I am ready to carry it forth" — life betrays us. A loved one dies, a relationship falters, we lose our job, our body begins to give out; we have everything we need, but we greedily hunger for more.

Have you felt how confusing freedom is? It easily becomes suffering and pain. And yet, whenever life is most confusing, haven't you also felt you must go on, as if, somehow, even in the darkness, a voice whispers: *You have assets. You can succeed. Just take yourself and go forth! I'll always be with you.*

Somehow, isn't it true — no matter our conflicts with loved ones, even when we discover we cannot be the person we thought we would be in our youth, still we sense beauty, truth, and love right near us? It is as if God says to us every day, *No matter your suffering, have faith in your life, courageously choose to go forth, trust yourself, carry your legacy in your small hands.*

Every day a new hint . . . this is what we get; every week, a new glimpse. In our lives we are asking, "Lord, do I deserve to be completely loved?" One day we arrive at a new stage of life, one where we can be sure we hear back: *Yes, you do. It is time now to become the people you hoped for many decades to become, the ones who carry the universe like a masterpiece in your small hands.*

# CHAPTER 3
# THE AGES OF DISTINCTION AND COMPLETION

Something has reached out and taken in the beams of my eyes.

— Mirabai

Rabbi Jack Isakson, sixty-eight, is a big, powerful man with a broad smile. For nineteen years he was the rabbi of Temple Beth Shalom in Spokane, Washington. He is an inspirational speaker and teacher, and he and I have had many a debate about meanings of parts of the Bible. One of our most powerful dialogues occurred regarding the story of Aaron, the brother of Moses. Much of Jewish lore is based on the journey Moses made, and the Jews with him. But wasn't Aaron's distinct identity and role, Rabbi Jack wondered, just as important — different, but equally important? While Moses wore the face of the Hebrew nation, Aaron was the high priest (in Hebrew, the *kohein*) who led sacrifices and services, and a people's connection with God through ceremony and ritual. Rabbi Jack said that the distinct value of Aaron is demonstrated in an incident in Numbers 16:1–18:12, which echoes Moses's use of the staff to scare Pharaoh back in Exodus. In Numbers, God orders all of the chieftains of Israel to inscribe his name on a staff. Aaron is one of those chieftains, and he inscribes his name. The staffs are left overnight before the Ark of the Covenant. Of all the staffs left before God, only Aaron's blossoms on that night — it blossoms like the tree of life, growing flowers and almonds. Everyone in the nation sees this distinction, and God proceeds now to instruct Aaron on his duties and the duties of all his descendants forever forward, which Aaron performs until his death.

In interpreting this incident, Rabbi Jack said, "There is a midrash [story, interpretation from ancient rabbis] that talks about how each of the staffs was cut from the same beam of wood. Thus, no staff was holier than any other; all were made of God's material. But only Aaron's flowered and bore sustenance, so we can see that Aaron's distinction, his importance, got clarified in this incident. He had an identity, a lifework, a legacy that he would work on until he became very old. That role, that distinction, as with everything

139

else in God's world, would always in some way be associated with service, or end up being most important for the service it provided others."

I asked Rabbi Jack what he thought of the fact that only Aaron's staff flowered. Did this mean that he had the only sacred role or distinction and everyone else was inferior? "No," he said, "this single flowering of Aaron's staff relates to Korach and the rebellion against God that Korach made. It is incident-specific to this section of Numbers. The ultimate meaning of the story in the whole Torah [Five Books of Moses] is that all roles that serve God and others are distinct and equally valuable. Thinking that one person's distinction as a human being is more valuable than another's often gets us in trouble. Legacy and service may look different, but they are our equalizer. All of us have equal value in the body of God.

"Remember Jacob and Esau. When Isaac was blind, he tried to bestow his legacy on one son, Esau, and ended up bestowing it on Jacob; this nearly tore the Hebrew nation apart with assumptions that one brother's legacy was 'better' than the others. It took generations to show that everyone has a purpose, a legacy, a distinct self of great value to life and God."

140

As I have developed and taught the age-stage model, I have thought a lot about what Rabbi Jack said. My work helping clients navigate life after fifty often takes my thinking toward the wisdom of many of the books and stories that founded our civilization. Dr. Daniel Amen's comment that science and spirituality are not worlds apart echoes through this work. With all the contradictions built into the Bible, there are also resonances with life stages we can now understand as a part of the wonder of aging. The resonance of distinction, lifework, legacy, and service is one of these. As we leave Stage 1 somewhere in our early to mid-sixties, and as we navigate Stage 2 from approximately sixty-five to our late seventies, we take stock of who we are, who and what we have created, what our identity and roles have been, what our lifework is, and what legacy we are passing on. The age of distinction is a time of celebration of soul, if we will let it be.

Author Roger Housden, an anthologist of inspirational poetry, introduces an anthology called *Risking Everything* with these words: "Have you ever longed for a life in which every part of you is entirely used up? Have you . . . dared to take a step forward and down into the known and humdrum details of your daily existence and suddenly found there a fullness of love and meaning as rich in its own way as others may know only through wild adventures?"

Answering these questions for himself, he continues: "There is, I believe, a longing in many of us, often unrequited, to give ourselves utterly to our lives . . . [to feel that] . . . our failures, our losses, our sufferings of all kinds, are inextricably woven into everything else — into the flowers, the sunrise, the great achievements of mankind, and into our own successes, too. It is all one great, swirling, unending creation, and every last drop of our life, its darkness as well as its light, has its part to play."

Housden's words reflect the kind of self-mastery that we can develop in Stage 2. It is a self-mastery we can mine with a sense of wonder if we become conscious of it. In this new self-mastery, we are not now mistake-less, not perfect, but also we are less mistake-prone than we were in previous eras of life. Stepping through the age of transformation into a more mature self, we are distinct, called now to fully teach and share what we know. We consider words like "grace" worth studying for years, rather than moments. Our sense of self is based more in a sense of having arrived somewhere than in constant, effortful striving to get somewhere. We have longed desperately, and now found what we longed for. We are in our mid-sixties now, and beyond. We have become, legally and socially, "senior citizens." We experience love, peace, sorrow, hope, and courage with greater sense of their worth in our lives than before. We are not as easily deceived as we once were by our own inadequacy, or by the machinations of others, nor are we as abjectly moody as we were just a few years ago, in the age of transformation. We live more carefully than before, ready to risk everything, but not willing anymore to risk the loss of what and whom we love. Adventure and service occupy our time, but ambition is no longer dominant, nor must we "define and distinguish ourselves even more." We have distinguished ourselves.

## STAGE 2: THE AGE OF DISTINCTION

Sarah, sixty-five, wrote from Atlanta. "I am an art teacher, close to retirement. I'm glad to say that people mistake me for being at least 10 years younger. I attribute that to working with young people and keeping up with the latest technology in my field. I laugh and smile a lot every day and enjoy my work. My greatest sources of joy have been my work and my children, who are still very different from one another. I love talking about these jewels.

143

"My daughter talked, walked, and did everything early. She loved social interaction and did not like to be by herself. She loved nursery school and was always a leader, involved in every aspect of social life and very organized. Now she works for a large country club community organizing all of their events . . . perfect for her personality.

"My son loved to be at home. He has always been a deep thinker. As a child he could entertain himself for hours. He was and is fairly quiet. He takes in all that's around him before he acts or speaks. People have come to respect his thoughtful opinion, his compassion for others, his truth telling and dependability. I always thought of him as an old soul in a young body. He works as an IT problem solver . . . again perfect for his personality.

"It has been a challenge over the last few years to lose family members and friends. The only immediate family I have left is my sister, and we live far apart. I have been blessed with good health, but I am coming to understand that good health is everything and it can change overnight. On top of this, my husband and I went through a lot of difficulty . . . losing our house, business, and almost one another.

"But I have enjoyed learning how to take care of business. As we patched things up a few years ago, I realized I missed the male thought processes of daily life. It's good to be back with him, but I also know I have built myself into a strong, solid, happy person. This has taken me a long time, but now I'm braver than I've ever been. I'm ready for whatever comes. I'm going to keep working on living life for everything I can, and giving back everything I can."

Sarah has entered the age of distinction. This age stage begins, generally, as the age of transformation ends; biologically, the transition to Stage 2 occurs as menopause and andropause come to an end. Personally, our age of distinction might clarify itself within us as we feel, for long stretches of time, that we are now "strong," "solid," "happy," or other words to that effect — our self feels transformed to one no longer plagued by inadequacy, regret, self-destruction, or severe stress, though we still have hard times and we know hard times wait ahead. In this stage of life, we generally feel proud of what we have created, nurtured, and been through in life. For Sarah, coming through meant reunion with her husband. For others, Stage 2 may be a time of aloneness, we may be widowed, divorced, or remarried. Whatever our circumstances, we will sense that we are distinct, not dependent completely on another. We may be saying the word "retirement" a lot, and saying it now with clarity as to when we will retire (or at least cut back to part-time work). We may well find ourselves, as Sarah did, looking back on work, family, and social life with a concentration on what has and will give us joy.

**Have You Entered the Age of Distinction?**
You will know you have entered Stage 2 by certain physical and cognitive changes in your body and brain. Medical science predicts at least some of the following for us by the time we move from sixty-five to eighty:

- We may ache a lot, especially if we exert ourselves physically. Those aches are not all bad — they are proof of life and proof that an exercise regimen is generally good for us.

- Our skin is becoming wizened. It is wrinkling, thinning, becoming more like root than flower, more like rough loam than primed and toned for constant stimulation.

- Our bones are becoming more brittle, more easily broken; our skeleton emerges to greet us more, perhaps,

146

than it did before. As we have surgeries for various osteopathic maladies, we come in closer touch than before with the frame that has held us up in this world.

- Our brains are condensing their areas of use. Quite literally, our brains are pruning away certain cells, such as memory cells. Our lifetime of filling our brains with things we have to remember is now catching up to us: our brain can't store everything anymore, and so we will forget more than we would like to forget. Lists become essential memory tools.

- Our ability to learn whole new worlds is diminishing. As our brains become more stingy in cell creation and cell use, we feel ourselves concentrating on what we know, and modifications of that, rather than on taking on a whole new part of life. Who we are — our distinction as a human being — is more about culminating who we've been up until now rather than making a whole new self, though this does not mean we won't try new things: we will. But we will have different expectations of what we can accomplish than before.

- Our brain chemistry has by now significantly changed from one that was actively transforming itself from a fertile, childbearing adult into a generally nonreproducing elder; now — with the exception of a minority of men and a tiny minority of women who do still reproduce at this age — nature has instructed our hormonal system to move energy away from the generosity of reproduction toward the mysteries of grandparenting, mentoring, being an elder, and exploring the life of the soul.

And so, within all the changes we are going through, we may well have a sense that a lot of meanings are clearer than they were in Stage 1 or in earlier adulthood. When we are speaking with others, reading the paper, or listening to the news, we may notice that words like "fairness," "justice," "honesty," "corruption," "values," "resilience," "duty," "honor," "compassion," "hope," and "love" make some real sense. To a great extent, we may finally know what these words mean because we now know a great deal of what they mean for us as individuals. We still have a sense of adventure and new learning, but we have less time to waste on other people's corruptions and silliness. We can still be surprised, hurt, and confused in Stage 2, but we are not kids anymore, nor are we still trying to figure out what an adult or elder really is. Where we used to be filled with desires and fears, now there is a beautiful exhaustion to our knowing, a kind of inward quietude that allows for certainties. Because we have lived around seven decades or more, the percentage of what we know is larger now, and we are comfortable with what we know; we do not need "experts" as much as we did because we have, to a great extent, become our own experts. About our physical and mental health we may need experts, but about our soul's journey we have a great deal of clarity of our own.

## The Grandeur of the Beloved

In Matthew 5:15–16, Jesus says to his disciples, "No one, after lighting a lamp, should put it under a bushel basket; they should put it on the lampstand so it gives light to all in the house. In the same way, let your light shine before others, so that they may see your good works." For people in Stage 2, this wisdom is powerful. All through our lives, we hoped to accomplish things; now, hopefully, we can let our accomplishments shine with maturity and distinction in ways beyond desire and battle. "This is who I am," we say to the mirror, "this is what I represent, these are my accomplishments." If we say this at thirty, we're still not sure we're right. At seventy, we know we are. If we were people who hid our light previously, there is no reason to do so now.

And we have, hopefully by now, become elders who understand what it means to say, as did the thirteenth-century Muslim poet Rumi, "The only way to measure myself is by the grandeur of what I love." We, our family, our community, and our legacy are the beloved. We are measured by them, do they know it? Now we can make sure everyone knows how important family is — family is one of the ways that God makes the masterpiece of a life visible. Once we see this divinity clearly, we may feel a love for this beloved that drives us to give back, serve, and mentor family and friends (and the larger world) usefully and powerfully. Sarah's yearning to give back was not a yearning borne of "I *should* do this" but of the deepest heart calling her to fill the world with what she was and what she could give.

Though we may often look in the mirror during Stage 2, noticing more and more wrinkles, our mirror search is generally not narcissism but rather humility at the grandeur of the world, the beloved. While in many of our daily activities we still long to have our ego stroked, we long to be admired, and we still feel inadequate (that survival fear never leaves the human psyche completely), we also can now feel humility and gratitude in deeper ways than before. Like Sarah, we can connect our greatest joys, including a sense of still being young, with a life lived fully for every moment of grace it can contain. "Break your pitcher against a rock," Rumi writes. "You don't need to hoard pieces of the ocean anymore." Seeing what is what, what life really is, how grateful we are, we can contract certain parts of life so that we can shine the parts that involve purpose and legacy. In our honorable work, our "tending of the temple," whatever that temple is for us — our scrapbooks we make for the family, the small gifts to grandchildren of furniture we want them to remember us by — will be accepted now not merely as markers of our ego accomplishments but as gifts we have created for the sake of community, family, and friends. We may start a scholarship fund, slip our children extra money, look for younger people to mentor. While some of us, like a Bill Gates or George Lucas, may have the means to start giving back whole, massive legacies before the age of distinction, and while each of us may, hopefully, always feel pulled to give back to others throughout our lives, it is in the age of distinction when most of us now have enough things, money, and time to advance our legacies fully.

If you think of diplomats and inspiring speakers traveling the world in their sixties and seventies, hoping to heal the world (Kofi Annan, Desmond Tutu, Maya Angelou), you are seeing people of distinction committed to their legacies. They are tending the temple. Most of us will not be world-traveling diplomats or speakers, but we can still be local ambassadors. We may never actually retire — for economic or other reasons — yet we are "retiring" in our sixties and "retired" by seventy even if we are still working because we are now working for soul. As we give things away and contract our lives, we may get increasingly interested in spirituality, an inwardness that is generally not an escape from the visible world but a sense of personal passion integrated with the visible world. As we "slow down," we will, hopefully, self-reflect, remember, feel contentment, converse with nature and our God. We may become the person who sees the garden we have planted and finally enjoys touching the grass and flowers. "To elder" is now a verb for us, an accumulation of character, actions of being, and spiritual quest that distinguishes us from younger people, especially if we actively connect with those younger people. These youth will see that Maslow's self-actualization can fully and with a certain quiet purity happen for elders because they will watch us; these younger people will set their compass by us. We have built a legacy, and now it is time for that legacy to humbly, usefully, fully, and lovingly shine.

## Identifying Your Distinction and Legacy

The word "legacy" is an essential marker of Stage 2, a word with many meanings. For our purposes, a "legacy" is the inheritance you have and are creating for personal accomplishment and the good of others who will survive you. It is the way you have tended the temple. It is the body of work you will pass on "to your descendants" (which means your communty, not just blood relatives) and are beginning to pass on right now, in a conscious way, as you "give back." This legacy is your birthright, as it was when Isaac tried to pass it on to his children, a birthright that you have mastered and developed far beyond where your ancestors took it, and are ready now to help make a clear part of the next generation's birthright.

Your legacy is also, in practical terms, evidence of your personal worth. To "have a legacy" means to possess something of value that positively affects family, community, and society. If we think about the iconic "gold watch" of former corporate life, there is a metaphor for what we mean. When a person "retired" and was ceremonially and publicly given a gold watch (an object that could stop and start time), the watch was symbolic of the person's value and body of work. While most of us don't get gold watches today (and it seems to many of us that we will never retire!), somewhere in your life, if you are in Stage 2, you have developed a lifework of enough value that it deserves that gold watch. Even if you spent very little time in a large workplace in your life — if you spent most of your time raising your children — your legacy is still sacrosanct now. Your job is to be conscious of it, find it, reflect on it, help it to become of the kind of use that will extend through generations. This legacy is what matters most in your life — for Sarah, it was her work at school and her children and family; for Aaron it was his role as priest: if you concentrate on it, you will see it clearly, and it will combine both work and family. Stage 2 is a time in life when concentration on our legacy brings a sense of the miraculous.

The writer and ethicist Michael Josephson speaks of legacy by speaking of "what will matter." He writes: "Ready or not, some day it will all come to an end. . . . All the things you collected, whether treasured or forgotten, will pass to someone else . . . your grudges, resentments, frustrations and jealousies will finally disappear . . . so, what will matter? What will matter is not what you bought but what you built, not what you got but what you gave. What will matter is not your success but your significance. What will matter is not what you learned but what you taught. What will matter is every act of integrity, compassion, courage or sacrifice that enriched, empowered or encouraged others to emulate your example. What will matter is not your competence but your character. . . . Living a life that matters doesn't happen by accident. It's not a matter of circumstance but of choice. Choose to live a life that matters."

This "life that matters" is your legacy. The older you get, the freer you get to be who you really are. That amorphous "who I really am" is your legacy. Your legacy, in all its forms, is connected to your sense of freedom by its connection to the choices you make. If you have not chosen to focus on legacy before now, the age of distinction is the time when you can actively and freely choose that focus, that life, that service. If you take at least a decade to identify, protect, define, refine, and begin to give away your legacy, people will sense your legacy in you and of you; they will see it around you, know it as yours, and feel it in their lives as you share it with them.

I want to give the world and my grandchildren the idea that I know I deserve to be respected, and now I don't hesitate to say so if necessary. I believe all of us need to respect ourselves as children so that we can respect others throughout life. I know we do not have to agree with others, but our opinion needs to be respected, as does theirs.

I want to give also the idea that I know the rewards of acknowledging mistakes and asking forgiveness. This affords peace, which is all I want in life. If I can show other people that I am always trying to forgive, I will have given a great gift, I think.

My husband is more stubborn than I and tends to try to make everything work as he wants it. However, age seems to have softened him so that now he steps back and gives the issue time before gently addressing it. I know some of the legacy he wants to give. He still believes he can play tennis and golf (at age 77) in 100-degree heat. He will do that even when I've asked him not to. Recently, I've realized how important this is to him, how much he is trying to pass on to others through this bravery, so I've decided not to fight these battles. I let him take chances just as long as he kisses me good-bye before venturing out in the extreme heat.

— Pat, 72

We never stop creating a legacy. There is no end to this spiritual work. Researchers at Stanford University decided to study the time period I am identifying as Stage 2 by tracking the legacies of four hundred of the world's most famous people. The researchers discovered:

- A third of the accomplishments of the four hundred most famous people came when they were between sixty and seventy years old.

157

- A quarter came when they were seventy to eighty.

- More than half of what researchers called "the world's greatest work" was achieved by leaders, thinkers, creative people, businesspeople, and others who were sixty or older. More than half! Some examples:

  - Hillary Clinton was sixty-two when she became America's secretary of state.

  - Golda Meir was seventy-one when she became prime minister of Israel.

  - Michelangelo was thirty-three when he began work on the Sistine Chapel.

Julia Child was forty-nine when her first cookbook was published. Louise Nevelson was a prolific sculptor well into her eighties. Tony Bennett is a regular Grammy Award winner, and he is an octogenarian.

Many people write memoirs of their legacy when they are in the age of distinction. Your journaling process can be your memoir. By the time you have written down thoughts, memories, experiences, and ideas from your life, you will have the foundation for a memoir. Fill pages of your journal or other notebooks with stories you were born to tell and wisdom you have gained. Here is a brief questionnaire that you can use to focus your thoughts as you journal, write, and process. These questions do not have to be answered all at once; in fact, returning to them over a period of weeks or months or years can be a fruitful practice.

1. What is my life story? Where am I from? Who are my "people"? What is my lineage? What have my life-defining events been so far?

2. In what ways do I most matter in my family? What are my most important roles in my community? Are there roles I need to take on more passionately now? Are there roles I need to let go of?

3. What are my most important accomplishments in life? In what ways have my jobs been useful to my own growth and to others' growth? What plaques, commemorations, photographs, and other emblems of my work exist? Look-

ing at them now, how do I feel?

4. What are my regrets in life — in my family, work, community, and friendships? Are there conversations I can have with others, new alliances I can forge, that can help me adjust my legacy toward more positive relationships? Are there people around me who can help me make peace with any regrets I have, so that those regrets don't tarnish my legacy?

5. What three to five areas of life do I want to devote my identity and life to now, as I grow older? Who needs me now more than ever? What do I need now more than ever? Have I done all that I can in this world, or is there more for me to do?

Don't be surprised if, when concentrating on elements of your life story, identity, role, and even any regrets, you make the same decision as a man in one of my focus groups: "To get off my duff and do something again." Joseph, seventy-two, began writing his memoir and ended up stopping that for a while to go to work at Albertson's food store. He said, "I know I'm living the stereotype, but you

160

know what, I wanted people to see smiles when they came in the door. People are just too damn unhappy." He had been a machinist and then a union executive, retiring after forty years, as the unions began to disassemble. He had done many other things in his life, and "smiles" might seem small, but to him it was a part of the legacy he wanted to live now.

Simone, sixty-seven, told me: "For the longest time I felt guilty for being such a caretaker of other people. But all my life, I have felt that my purpose in life was to respond to people, help them feel better, care for them. I have always been one of the people that my husband, children, parents, friends, and others come to when they need something (I am a registered nurse). But the truth is, for at least two decades I've been conflicted, thinking I should achieve more, make more money, move higher up in my HMO.

"Luckily, a lot has changed for me over the last few years. I accepted myself. I let go of those other goals that were really other people's goals. And an amazing result has been my mental clarity. I feel like I just *think* better, *accomplish* more, *do* better at my job because I am at peace with myself. I believe making peace with who I, Simone, am has made me a smarter person, in many senses of the word."

Simone's sense about personal comfort increasing cognitive clarity is backed up by good science. Research shows that mindfulness and contentment with identity can both decrease stress hormone (cortisol) levels in the body and increase the chance of nurturing new cell growth in the brain. This is an aspect of "change your brain, change your life." The mental clarity Simone feels in Stage 2 is enhancing her quality of life and most probably increasing her longevity.

We can all do this. We each have about fifteen years of distinction to fully reach the next stage of elderhood. We may "retire" away from a particular job during these years, but we will also, hopefully, retire into a life of distinction, gracefulness, and decreased stress. And if we retired into what is now called a "retirement community," one day, hopefully, all these communities will be called "elder communities," for we are actually quite vital in the age of distinction, and our "retirement" is only economic, not spiritual. We are becoming or have become elders who are very much of use to the world, people in our sixties, seventies, and beyond who choose to live with one another in order to feed one another's communal needs and support one another in getting their second, third, and fourth winds.

## A Second Wind
A friend, Dakota Hoyt, sixty-seven, spoke about getting a surprising "second wind" in her age of distinction. "I had a good friend who was running a company that trained teachers on how to become more effective with kids. She was doing great work, work that was really changing lives and helping children. I started working with her part-time eight years ago, at fifty-nine, after I retired from school administration. Over these years, my friend and I got closer, and I got deeper into the work, but still, I was pretty much retired, enjoying my grandkids, developing hobbies, taking care of my garden.

"Then my friend got cancer and needed more help. Then she needed more help and more help. I did more training engagements for her, ones that the chemo and radiation stopped her from making. I started helping her and her other staff members to run events locally. Honestly, I only started this as a post-retirement sideline to help my friend; but then I started earning more income, too, which helped a lot. I thought, 'Well, I'll just do this a little while for some more money.'

"But about a year into this, I found myself getting a second wind. As my friend got closer and closer to losing the battle with cancer, I started feeling something more than 'earning money' or 'just assisting a friend.' I felt my*self* in the work. I said to my friend, 'This is what I've been doing all my life, in a way, professionally, and it's my calling.' She was nearly bedridden by then; she saw my passion and said, 'I want you to be my successor as executive director. This work needs you. It is a calling, it is my legacy, and I think it is yours, too.'

"It was and is. I think that's why I have such a second wind now. What I thought would be exhausting isn't exhausting as much as regenerating. I'm doing, again, what I am called in this life to do, and it fulfills me. I love it and I will do it until I just can't do it anymore."

This is the drive, the calling that emerges in a "second wind." We work mainly for love now, for calling and legacy. Our second wind energizes us. However we spend our days, we sense the presence in us of delightful pulls toward giving and receiving, helping others and thus helping ourselves grow. We are growing now as elders, who give their legacy to others as much as develop it for their own gain.

# THE ELDER'S LOVE

There are people who get "second winds" in their sixties and seventies but who do not act as elders. They do not wrap legacy around love or devotion. They still see legacy as only about accomplishment and ambition. This can happen. It is possible for any of us to put only one toe in the age of distinction, even though we are chronologically and neurologically old enough to be in Stage 2. With only one toe in, we can be dominating, cloying, immature, enraged, selfish, hoarding, and essentially frightened of life. We can be a person reflected in the line from the Turkish poet Nazim Hikmet, who said, "You are only 'old' when you love no one but yourself." With only one toe in the age of distinction, we may hoard our legacy; we are stuck, psychologically and spiritually, in the age of transformation, or still stuck, in many ways, back in one of the stages of adolescence or adulthood. We have not dealt with our compulsive fear of inadequacy.

Anything can happen in a growing, evolving psyche, and so we must concentrate on the age of distinction consciously, study it, understand it, feel it, live it. One powerful book we must read in this time is the book of grief — as we lose friends, family members, and more and more personal powers in Stage 2. This grief may trip us up, confuse us; we may want to avoid it, but soon, it must become our inspiration toward sharing our legacy. Nobel Prize–winning poet Pablo Neruda wrote, in "There Is No Clear Light," "My griefs confirm my existence." This is a comment made by a man of distinction who understood that the deaths of others around us and all the griefs we feel and move through confirm that we are here, worthy, real, alive. They are wells from which an elder drinks, each in our own way. We are now the sum of all our parts; the sum of both griefs and joys confirm our existence, so that we both long and do not long for the crushing weights of life. We have come to the time in our journey when we say with equal energy, "Ah, I want to be filled with longing again," and "Ah, I'm so glad my longings no longer rule me."

Something has changed for me. I don't have to have my obsession with people's flaws anymore. I've gotten to a less critical and judgmental age. I thought I saw things clearly before, when I was so watchful of others. Now, actually, by decreasing how critical and judgmental I am, I see things much more clearly. It is great. The thing I think I always wanted

> — to change people to fit some idea I had of what would make me safe — is kind of gone from me. My hard work has paid off. I really like this freedom.
>
> — Carl, 69

### DEVOTION AND A LIFE OF JOY

Part of the wonder we are able to protect now, in the age of distinction, is the wonder of living long enough to carve out a life of joy. This age of distinction is a time of freedom, when we can choose to experience joy by choosing to spend our time on activities that give us joy, with friends who enjoy life, and in attitudes that promote joy. Joy is a dopamine producer; it feels good and brings all the new cell growth along with it that "feeling good" can bring. Murray, seventy-one, works into his business trips and board meetings two vacation days so he can take the train from L.A. to D.C. "It just makes me happy to take the train," he says. "It's just a great feeling for me." Vernice, sixty-three, wrote: "I hadn't had a vacation in eight years and realized that was not where I wanted to be now, so I took three weeks to travel around India. It was an amazing trip. I came home with a much clearer sense of who I am and what I want to do with the rest of my life. One thing

I will definitely do is go somewhere different than my hometown every year, for as long as I am able."

Cindy, sixty-seven, told me, "Every year I do a one-week silent retreat in the mountains near Shasta. We have a community of elders that supports each other in our growth. All year I look forward to that week of community. With these people, I feel comfortable with who I am. I come back home completely reenergized to give back to my community. It's like a formula, almost mathematical."

Tim, sixty-four, said, "Claire and I were in bad shape and trying to fix our marriage. We decided to take a break. I went for a month to New Zealand and worked from there (software support). It was one of the happiest times in my life. It proved to me I could be happy, and I realized that Claire is not the problem. I think that month of being so happy showed me how to be happy again anywhere."

Barry, sixty-nine, loves music. He said, "I'm actually a better musician than lawyer!" He still works as a lawyer, but spends more and more time practicing with a jazz band, doing shows, mentoring younger musicians. He recalled to me how his second family didn't like that he invested so much time in music, but they ended up seeing that his time playing music with his band at bars did not take away from them but instead fed them, because it helped him to be whole and distinct. Now, his wife, Sherrie, and his son, eleven years old, travel to some music festivals with him, all together in an RV.

## WOMEN, MEN, AND DISTINCTION

Is Stage 2 lived differently by women and men? In many ways, no, but in some ways, yes. One potential difference that involves wealth can surprise us.

According to the 2010 census, women control nearly 60 percent of the wealth in the United States. And interestingly, the number of wealthy women in the United States is growing twice as fast as the number of wealthy men. Women now represent more than 40 percent of all Americans with gross investable assets above $600,000. Forty-five percent of American millionaires are women. Forty-eight percent of estates worth more than $5 million are controlled by women, compared with 35 percent controlled by men. Sixty percent of high-net-worth women have earned their own fortunes. Some experts estimate that by 2030, women will control as much as two-thirds of the nation's wealth.

An obvious reason for women ascending

in wealth is that more women than men are living longer; thus, more women than men are living long enough to enjoy the freedom that money can bring to us as we age. According to the Women's Philanthropy Institute, "Because women live longer than men, they will end up in charge of much of the $41 trillion expected to pass from generation to generation over the next 50 years." This is something of a miraculous legacy for women. Just a few decades ago, wealth was so much controlled by men, this kind of women's empowerment did not seem possible, ever.

## Self-Image Differences

But, as with everything in nature and life that involves the genders, if we look deep enough, we will find a basic cost-benefit balance to the age stages. While more women are living longer, women are also more prone than men to battle the kind of self-image issue made iconic by the words "the beauty trap." This trap still hits more women than men during the age of distinction. Generally, women feel more depression related to lost beauty, while men feel more depression related to lost power. Neuroscientists David Buss and Helen Fisher believe the hormonal and brain biology we inherited from tens of thousands of years of women needing to be attractive in order to continue their genetic line has led to women now feeling a propensity toward the beauty trap. Many aging women may feel that they must be youthfully beautiful to be whole. Similarly, for tens of thousands of years, males needed to be powerful and successful in order to attract women and continue their genetic line. In large part, they still do. Men, thus, fall more into the success trap. Both men and women may have to look closely at how hypervigilant and constantly agitated they are about whether they will be rejected by others for their lack of beauty, success, or other marker of distinction.

Recently, my twenty-two-year-old daughter asked me what message I would give my own twenty-two-year-old self if I could travel back in time. . . . It's nothing short of astonishing, all that we learn between the time we are born and the time we die. . . . We can look back and identify moments — the friend's betrayal, the work advancement or failure, the wrong turn or the romantic misstep, the careless comment. But it's all a continuum that is clear only in hindsight . . . we understand ourselves, our lives, retrospectively. . . .

I would tell my twenty-two-year-old self that what lasts are things so ordinary she may not even see them: family dinners, fair fights, phone calls, friends. But of course the young woman I once was cannot hear me, not just because of time and space but because of the language, and the lessons, she has yet to learn. It's a miracle: somehow over time she learned them all just the same, by trial and error.
— Anna Quindlen

In the age of distinction, we will hopefully hear the inward music we have been dancing to all along. We will hopefully slow down enough to hear and sustain the inward music that has always been inside us. Other people, when they look at us, may admire our faces and our dance, see who we are, see what we have accomplished — as lovers, parents, grandparents, workers, inventors, caregivers. These family members, friends, and acquaintances are seeing our spirits existing in a miraculous time of distinct, trusted, clear self. As they admire us, we are further able to hear our inward music and help them move more deeply into finding theirs.

The Buddha said, "Happy is one who has overcome ego; happy is one who has attained peace; happy is one who has found the truth." Stage 2, our age of distinction, can be a beautiful decade to decade and a half of relative ego-lessness and happiness . . . these can glow beautifully in us at dinner tables, in time with grandchildren, or on vacations, on tennis courts, through letters and e-mails we write, in board meetings and pleasant human interactions. An elder in the age of distinction is ego-less, happy, and truthful because he or she embodies a life legacy that is now incontrovertible. As elders, we are or are becoming so aware of life's real internal workings that we may be finally getting to a place where we do not have to force "truth" on people anymore (we become better listeners now); we may now be in a stage of confidence without ego attachment (we lead without a selfish agenda) and may now become happy in that way that invites people to join us, but does not say, "My way is better than your way." In some way, perhaps, we are more Moses and Aaron than Jacob and Esau; we are no longer in competition with the universe but instead, distinct each in our own way, we are ready to arrive at a place of inner peace.

## STAGE 3: THE AGE OF COMPLETION

Reverend William Houff, PhD, a retired Unitarian-Universalist minister and author of a number of books, including *Infinity in Your Hand*, has, like Rabbi Jack, played a significant role in my own development as an elder. Bill, eighty-six, and I have been friends for almost thirty years. He officiated at Gail's and my wedding in 1986, led the baby-naming ceremonies for our daughters, and performed Gail's and my first renewal of vows at ten years of marriage (Rabbi Jack performed our second one at twenty years of marriage). Bill and I were activists together on various causes, including battling for environmental safety at a regional nuclear facility.

For ten years, Bill and I have met for lunch, spending our time in companionship and dialogue. Bill calls it "getting together." For me, it is both pleasant time and spiritual and practical mentoring. Bill had been a pastoral counselor for almost thirty years, and I often bring cases to him, especially those that involve counseling elders. Bill is thirty years older than I am, and though his health has been failing for some time (Parkinson's disease is one of his main companions now), his mind is sharp. There is also deep calmness and humility in his personality that he has carried into his final years of life; "detachment" is a key word for him, a vision of life that pierces through illusions to "what is." This detachment, he says, is both an ability to know and tell one's own story and hear the stories of others, and a way of renouncing a life story, detaching from everything that previously gave a life meaning. Bill is in Stage 3 of the age stages. This stage, quite distinguishable from Stage 2, is generally no longer a time when legacy is still being defined. For Bill, legacy has long been defined and is now something to detach from.

In one of our lunches, I asked Bill to help me understand the stage of life he is in by sharing with me the spiritual questions he had been answering in his lifetime. Bill took a couple of months to ponder my request, and at a next lunch he told me, "Okay, the four questions of my lifetime . . . you wanted them, you got them. (1) Why do we suffer? (2) Do I really have faith? (3) Am I finally free? (4) Have I learned how to love? They are just small questions," he chuckled, "but will they suffice?"

Grinning and nodding, I wrote the questions down and asked him to explain more, since I would put this in my new book on aging. He chewed a bite of burrito (we always went out for his favorite, Mexican food), he crinkled his face (his head is bald, so wrinkles show on his forehead), and he said, "Well, sure, I can help you lead people astray." From there, he explained why these four questions seemed, for him, to be the questions he hoped he was answering with greater completeness in his last years of life.

I have condensed his words into the four answers:

1. Until I understood the cause of suffering, I didn't understand that happiness is about detachment. In every stage of life I thought I did, but it's in my mid-eighties I'm really growing, really getting it. When you're old, and you've got significant disease guiding you toward death, you can finally get it. Until you get really old, you can't.

2. We all know what faith is, right? It is a serene state of trust. I have that now. I thought I had it before, but I didn't. Now, my life comes down to a little bit of exercise, taking care of Patty, taking my meds, and hoping for a bit of human contact every day. My mind has definitely turned inward to God. This is faith.

3. I used to struggle with a lot of demons. It was always in my eyes. It's in your eyes, you young pup. You're still breaking free of psychological chains. But for

me, those chains are broken. I'm not perfect or anything, but I'm free like never before. And listen, I wish that freedom had come fifty years ago, or more years ago, but what did I know? There's a special form of it that comes when you are very old.

4. I have learned how to love. I'm very proud of that. I can't tell you exactly when it happened, but now I get it. 'I'm a lover, a real lover.' Closeness is a miracle, actually, a miracle. You really realize it, Mike, when you see your wife leaving you, detaching from you, going to the lost world [Patty, his wife, had early to mid-stage Alzheimer's disease; she passed away a year after this conversation]. You never stop learning how to love — disease of a loved one, and disease in oneself, is a great teacher about the next stage of love. Love is about caring for your loved one, and it is completely about letting go.

Soon after this lunch, Gail and I saw Bill and Patty for dinner, catching up on the exploits of our children and theirs, their grandchildren, and various topics of life. At our next lunch, Bill and I talked more about his and Patty's situation, and he asked if he had been helping me at all with the book. Absolutely, I assured him. "I call the psychological stage of life you are in 'the age of completion.' Does that title make sense to you?" This question stimulated him to say, "Absolutely. Completion is about detachment, Mike. Study detachment, and you'll understand the age of completion. Patty and I sold our farm, sold our house, moved into assisted living. Now she's in the Alzheimer's unit. In the end, we have to detach more and more, in the deepest spiritual sense of that word, or we will die one day having lived someone else's life, not our own lives, and on the day we die, our souls will not have detached, freely, at all from these bodies and brains.

"I still live my life with as much vigor as I can, but I have no illusions anymore — my ship has left the port — I am floating away. I am definitely all about completing my life journey in the way that will most beautifully set me free."

## Are You in the Age of Completion?
Whatever our circumstance, the brain and biological changes that occur as we move through our eighties, nineties, and beyond create a new stage of age. It is not without

its challenges, but it is a miraculous time of life, a time, as Bill was implying, when physical limitation, disease, and death can be balanced, should we choose to balance them, by concentration on the next stage of a soul's journey, a stage as invested in detachment as we were in attachment when we were born. In this way, the arc of a life moves toward completion. We came into the world needing to attach completely to our mothers, fathers, community, and world; in Stage 3, we are still attached to life and love, but now we move with the most spiritual depth and grace if we seek to integrate into our lives the kind of *detachment* that will complete our journey.

This said, I found in surveys and focus groups that a profound difficulty affects the defining process for Stage 3. The difficulty lies in the need to avoid seeing "completion" as a word representing only "the end" or death. While our bodies and brains are moving more greatly after eighty toward diminishment of vigorous function, we are not done with this life and its joys of attachment. Especially in our new time and new millennium, some people have the science- and medicine-driven ability to spend one, two, even three decades being close to others and life, helping others complete themselves, and learning the lessons of wonder, detachment,

179

and completion ourselves.

In surveys and focus groups, as I asked people to define life after eighty, I learned one thing that I hadn't expected (in retrospect, I don't know why I didn't expect this): Stage 3 women and men, like Bill, often have a great sense of humor, and one that tingles with sardonic, honest wit. My mother-in-law, Peggy, eighty-six, gave me a book in this tradition, smiling. "I think you'll like this novel for your aging book. This book is funny, and so true. I don't know if you have to be in your eighties to get the humor in it, but see what you think."

The book is a detective novel by Daniel Friedman called *Don't Ever Get Old.* It features Buck, an eighty-seven-year-old retired police detective, irascible to the core, who solves crimes with his grandson in tow, and cracks jokes along the way. As he prepares to take on a case, he describes his body and life in these two ways. First, he discusses his changed body:

"My skin had become dry and thin, almost papery in texture. If I jostled my arm too hard against a doorknob or bumped a knee into the bedside table, I could tear open and leak thin, watery blood all over the carpet. A couple of times, I hadn't been able to stop bleeding, and Rose had to take me to the emergency room. And it was easy to bump into stuff, because my eyes were failing. I needed a pair of glasses to see distance and a different pair to read. That fuzzy vision was, I guess, a minor blessing; it spared me from having to take a clear look at the mess of bruises and liver spots on my arms and cushioned the blow of seeing my collapsed and sunken features in the bathroom mirror."

Second, he notes the pain of having to detach from previous ways of being useful.

"Back when I could push a mower, I used to take care of the grass. It was something that Rose and I could do outside, together; she maintained the flower beds. Our yard was the best on the block, and we took a lot of pride in it. But since I had heart bypass surgery in '98, we'd been paying some kind of Guatemalan refugee to handle that stuff. He was a hardworking, fastidious man, and his crew did a good job. I hated his goddamn guts, and I carried a deep resentment against the lawn. The Guatemalans had replaced me, and the indifferent grass had gone right on turning green in the springtime."

If you are in your second half of life, I recommend this fun, touching novel. The latter paragraph captures a sentiment I heard in surveys and focus groups regarding the pain of detachment. In the age of completion, a new reality is the feeling of being replaced, unneeded, much too fragile, and almost obsessed with one's own and others' health. By eighty, we may be more sedentary than we wish we were. We may feel like we are constantly having to be repaired. Because we spend so much time trying to hold on to physical and cognitive health, others may see "old people" who are "used up," "defeated," "finished." We ourselves can feel that way. This stage of life, for Buck, becomes revitalized by solving crimes. Similarly, we will not be "used up" if we find our own way of being a "useful elder." We will not be "defeated" or "finished" if we concentrate on completion with our own form of the questions Bill asked, searching our memories and our present lives for answers to the mysteries of detachment. Completion is a part of spirit, and it comes into our spiritual concentration in two ways: (a) keeping active in order to extend our lives and quality of life, and (b) moving our soul's forces toward consciousness of the mysteries and meanings of the endgame.

After retiring from many different careers, Shirley Aresvik, now 87, began writing poetry in her early eighties. This journal entry is a poem she wrote for her friend Bee on her ninetieth birthday.

*You Wear It Well*

*Bee, you wear it well,*
*That special mantle*
*That salves and freshens*
*Those around you*

*You wear it well*
*The aura that time*
*And heart have*
*Invested you with*

*You wear it well,*
*The natural grace,*
*Good will and gentleness*
*That infuse your being*

*You wear it well*
*This emanation of innocence*
*Beauty and love*
*That breathes you*

*You wear it well.*

With a focus and urgency like no other time in life, during Stage 3 the aches of the body are doorways to the soul. Completers are completing the life of the body, including the life of the brain, by working toward keeping body and mind as healthy as possible until the very end of life. Until the internal switch turns off and we decide, unconsciously or consciously, that it is time to die, we seek to do what it takes to be healthy. It is part of our survival instinct. While we physically move around the world much less now, still we know that we need to move around as much as possible to remain as alive and brain healthy as we can. Clinical studies from around the world show that completers who take a walk most days for just thirty minutes will tend to have less cognitive impairment, and just this one thing, exercise, buys us time and enhances life energy. Neuropsychiatrist Dr. Daniel Amen points out that, especially for the elderly, "Exercise elevates the heart rate, which forces oxygen and glucose to the brain, which improves cognitive function. When we exercise, increased blood flow brings more oxygen to the brain and sends out more protein, which nourishes brain cells and promotes the growth of new neurons (brain cells) and synapses. Studies have shown that people who walked 7 to 9 miles per week had larger brains and better memory than those who did not walk as much."

At our highest state of being, this is about body and brain staying as active as possible to enjoy the life of the soul. Galway Kinnell wrote in his poem "The Road Between Here and There" about what he thought of as still possible: "inspired work, faithfulness to a few, and a last love, which, being last, will be like looking up and seeing the parachute opening up in a shower of gold." Completers who are flourishing tend to seek not only reliable exercise routines, but also brain-enhancing activities that involve higher standards than others might believe a completer is possible of and, as much as possible, there is the need to be with others, connect with others, experience the joy of others. In both solitude and in our attachments, we experience what Mary Oliver called "the brittle beauty of understanding," a sense of knowing how fragile life really is, yet how beautiful. If you have seen the movie *Young at Heart*, you have seen people in the ages of completion touring prisons and other venues to perform solo and choral arrangements of popular songs. In one prison, the hardened criminals were moved to tears by the sight and sounds of octogenarians moving, swaying, dancing, and singing. In my own home-town, Spokane, a group of elders has formed a group, Riversong, in order to stay active, keep moving, and share social time. They give free concerts for the public, learning ten to twelve new songs for each fall and spring season. Even the elders with Parkinson's in this group choose to physically stand up as much as possible to deliver their songs. Bob Moylan, seventy-eight, comanager of this group, says, "They have fun, they don't just work. If they came in timid, they won't leave that way." Patricia Moylan, seventy-five, the other comanager, says, "You can just sit back and let death come slowly, or you can live life fully and use your brain, lungs, and spirit."

## Self-Mastery in the Age of Completion

Completion, thus, is about remaining as healthy as possible for as long as possible, and it is about concentrating on a soulful life as it is and may be without body. In "Meditations of an Old Woman," the poet Theodore Roethke gives the word "crone" to the part of completion that involves sedentary life, silence, and detachment. He talks about feeling like "a strange piece of flesh." What is left, he tells us, feels light as a seed. He realizes, "I need an old crone's knowing." He describes the quiet, sensual part of this "knowing" and time of memory as crystallized in the times "I have learned to sit quietly, watching the wind riffle the backs of small birds." In this silent time, the Polish poet Czeslaw Milosz realizes that wherever he has wandered in life, "my face was always turned to the river." Completion comes in discovering the deep place of silence in our room, garden, bathtub, and memories when we realize we have actually been pointed toward the river (the great unknown, the source of life, the center of meaning) all along. Completers come to a time of self-mastery and may not even realize it.

---

I have no regrets and no misgivings. Actors take chances, but there's always something good about them and something we learn from them.
— James Earl Jones, 82, actor

In Switzerland, I was educated in line with the basic premise: work, work, work. You are only a valuable human being if you work. [Now I know] this is utterly wrong. Half-working, half-dancing — that is the right mixture. I myself have danced too little. [Now I know] you will

> find peace, that deep place of silence, right in your room, your garden or even your bathtub.
>
> — Elisabeth Kübler-Ross,
> psychiatrist

For some completers, consciously expanding traditional or progressive faith in God is a part of the self-mastery. Shimon, eighty-seven, wrote in our survey these words from a Jewish mystic, Ibn Gabirol, that he now repeats among his own Sabbath prayers every week: "The infinite heights are too small to contain Thee, yet, if Thou wilt, Thou make thy abode in my heart. Shall my heart not treasure this hope of harboring thee, or shall I not entreat Thee till my tongue can call no more? Nay, I will surely worship Thy name, till my nostrils no longer breathe." Shimon added, "I know myself as a religious Jew now. I did not used to be religious, but now I am."

A completer may feel depth of life in making the short steps to the bathroom and in prayer to infinity. Both are a part of self-mastery. Both are ways to enter a state of consciousness that elders throughout time and history have sought the time and courage to enter, a time in life when an elder can become fully united with the source of life and death. This "becoming" is a miracle we have one to three decades to wonder over and realize, as some of us live well beyond one hundred. This state of consciousness involves the sacred task of "renunciation."

## THE FINAL JOURNEY OF RENUNCIATION

India is a beautiful, overwhelming place made up of thousands of smaller beautiful, overwhelming places. I lived there as a boy and came to love the homes, markets, businesses, buses, trains, cars, bicycles, cows, snakes, babies, the living, and the dead all basically sharing the same spaces, with few boundaries between. There is little room to hide in India from the stages of life and of age: all stages coalesce in busy, multigenerational homes, markets, and doorways, where the smallest baby and the oldest adult live and die together.

Among the most interesting people I met in India were the elder *sanyasi*, the old people who, with begging bowl and walking stick, maneuvered through streets and cities and villages until they became too tired to walk. These people practiced the portion of self-mastery that relinquishes ownership of life's "things" for the sake of searching for ultimate detachment. In Hindu or Buddhist terms, these *sanyasi* hoped to "fully realize the self" before they die. Shankara, an Indian writer of the seventh century, helped refine the art of *sanyasi*-renunciation. He insisted that to fully complete our search for soul in a lifetime, we must, at some point, consciously renounce the distractions of the world of "things" and realize:

"You are actually pure Consciousness, the source and witness of all experiences. Your real nature is joy. Because you identify yourself with the ego, you are tied to birth and death, but when you renounce your bondage to the ego, when you complete the renunciation of distraction and outward experience, you will become free to discern Reality, and realize, 'I am Self.' You will experience the greatness of true knowledge."

This language is old, one might say, or at least it is the language of another place and time. What does it have to do with us? And really: few or no people we know are going to take up a begging bowl and walking stick and wander the streets in search of the self! In fact, in America or Europe, if someone saw you do this at any age, he or she would assume you had wandered off from your safe Alzheimer's facility and need to be returned. Yet there is something important for us here. It involves deep reflection on the power and opportunity of spiritual renunciation during the age of completion. If renunciation, which is a deep self-mastery of soul life, has not happened for us before Stage 3, it can happen now. What do we mean by renunciation?

It is somewhat defined in the Tao Te Ching: "The wise person shuts his senses, closes all doors, dulls his edges, unties all knots, softens his light, renounces the sources of agitation — this is called the attainment of unity with the One . . . by renouncing desires, one sees the Secret of all life; without renouncing of desires, one does not see all the way into the Way."

Do you remember reading the Tao when you were younger? I read it many times. When I read the Tao (and the Bible and any parts of any religious texts that brought up renunciation), I tried to take into my soul the dynamism it had for me — the sense that I should be "desireless" in order to succeed. Perhaps you did this, too. Perhaps you looked around at your life as a young person and saw your compulsions and desires and said, "Wow, what if I could renounce everything now at twenty (or thirty)? What would happen in my spiritual life?" But perhaps, like me, you had a lover, spouse, children, or work path by then. Renunciation was, actually, not an option. Perhaps most of us ended up saying something like, "I'll try to live with a hint of renunciation now, but let's face it, it's not realistic to renounce my life. I'm not a monk and can't afford to be." Renunciation went to the back burner, as it needed to do.

Now, however, as we come into our eighties and beyond, we are in a stage of life Reverend Houff was talking about, when renunciation, whether we like it or not, is actually an intrinsic part of life. The beginnings of full spiritual renunciation, and thus of completion, are already in us, even if we have not taken up a begging bowl and staff. If we look at our life in our eighties and beyond (or, if we are in earlier stages and are taking care of parents or others in Stage 3), we will see that these elders by now have renounced much of the daily, hourly contact they had with a life mate, either because a spouse has died or because the interior world of love is a calmer one now; life and love exist now in more quietude than before, more sleeping in separate beds perhaps, more sitting quietly in each other's presence at the breakfast table, less constant talk; less planning, less distraction, more reflection; less desire and longing, more oneness with the inner flight of thought; less immersion in the fifty challenges of fifty errands; a greater sense of the body's decline, which can, if we let it, compel our mind toward soul. Renunciation is a part of life now in ways it could not be when these elders were younger and merely experimented with humility and the deep reward of inner peace.

If you are one of these elders or working with one, perhaps, like Bill and Patty Houff, you owned a second home for much of your later life; now, you've sold that home, unable to keep it up. Perhaps, too, you've sold your primary residence and live in a community of other elders, enjoying conversation there and the quiet of your own room. Elders who sell and give away things, homes, the pieces of a life that once seemed all of life, are renouncing the material world to a great extent. That renunciation can turn mind toward soul, if we concentrate on that spiritual completion, or it can just make us feel unneeded and dead while still breathing. Renunciation, especially in our very material Western world, needs cultural and personal focus in order to enliven us.

Bill Houff and I spent a great deal of time looking at renunciation in the context of world religions. I am grateful to him for this year of lunches, research, and dialogue. He led me to see that all religions connect renunciation with completeness of spiritual awareness. We've mentioned Hinduism, Buddhism, and Islam already in this context.

Jesus on the Mount of Olives preached: "The kingdom of God belongs to those who give up all things and become again as little children." Jesus goes on to say, "When you surrender everything, you surrender your heart to God, and God will give you peace." Jesus learned some of his passion for renunciation from his predecessor, Moses, who, more than a thousand years before, was forced to complete himself through renunciation — in his case, by renouncing his desire, late in life, to enter the Promised Land. He, like all of us in our last decades of life, had to give up something he thought he wanted more than anything in the world.

It was difficult for him as it is difficult for us to give up going on the trip to China we had on our bucket list (our legs just won't carry us anymore), give up the spouse whom we wanted to outlive (he or she dies, leaving us alone), give up our independence (we can't live alone anymore), or give up driving our car (because we are now a danger to the world). Will we see these forced renunciations as part and parcel of the spirit of completion? Moses began his renunciation by complaining to God, "Why won't you let me into the Promised Land before I die?" but ended up realizing that the renunciation itself *was* the Promised Land — it was his destiny, one in which he as leader did not arrive there so that his people would be inspired to fight harder to arrive there later.

## Renunciation as Spiritual Task

Some completers never heed Moses, Jesus, or anyone else on this. They experience the natural renunciation of body and mind as they get old but see no soul in it. A friend in her fifties talked to me about her parents. Her father, eighty-one, was domineering and angry. His health had taken a turn for the worse, and he was afraid. He raged at his wife and lived without spirit, unhappy, and — this was a significant clue to his spiritual poverty — unable to be humble. His wife or one of his daughters would say, "Dad, let's play a game, let's play cards, let's go on an outing," or "Dad, can you teach Jeremy [his six-year-old grandson] chess, like you taught me?" or "Dad, will you talk to someone about how scared and mad you are?" but he shut down or lashed out. Because he was scared — because his natural renunciations caused anxiety in him without a compensating sense of spiritual search — he was not able to join his natural renunciations with the soulful re-nunciations Jesus or Moses or the Tao or the *sanyasi* called for — purification of the heart and renunciation of thoughts and deeds that

195

ran counter to love.

Gradually, his family members withdrew from this angry, anxious patriarch. They had little choice — they had to keep themselves and their children safe from his dark world. They cared for him as best they could, but he did not die in the kind of loving embrace the family hoped to give this man who had done so much for them in his lifetime. During the man's later months, I met with him and his family to try to help, and found myself powerless. The language of "completion," "renunciation," "humility," and "peace" were not helpful. Though the man had been raised a Christian, religion did not speak to him. His family brought a minister to meet him, and it did no good.

But, still, from his family experience came a gift. The patriarch gave a gift of *sanyasi* even though no one knew it at the time of his dark living and his lonely dying. His children, born-again Christians, talked with me after his death about seeing in the dark grandfather a spiritual poverty they did not want to live when they became his age, in his circumstances. Into the lore and life of the family now came spiritual themes that would not have emerged had this angry grandfather not so resisted spiritual life in the end. The family promised to live their own future renunciation, dying, and death with less attention to the lost body and more attention to the gained soul.

My own father, at eighty-three, experienced a very painful form of renunciation, one so devastating that he could only make meaning and peace with it by understanding it as part of his spiritual path in the age of completion. The renunciation occurred a year after my mother died. Because it involves a criminal case still pending, I cannot give a great deal of detail here; suffice to say, these details are the tip of the iceberg. In essence, when my father lived in Las Vegas, he was defrauded of all of his money by a career criminal who practiced on him a combination of identity theft and predatory grooming. By the time my father (and we, his family) found out that the criminal behavior had gone on, my father's IRA and bank accounts were all cleaned out. His credit cards were maxed out. He awoke one day in July 2012 with nothing material to his name except the sparse furniture in his room, a 1983 Nissan station wagon with 250,000 miles on it, and my mother's ashes.

The first month of work in the face of this renunciation did not include concentration on the principle of renunciation. It involved dealing with the material issues — working with the police to get the predator off the streets (it turned out that this predator had already been in prison for five years about a decade before he cleaned my father out), working with banks to understand the fraud, moving my father to Spokane so that he could be close to me. The first months were, on the surface, so busy with details of the material world that the spiritual act of renunciation was less clear, and too submerged to discuss proudly or with detachment. And in the first month or so of dealing with the crisis, my father's emotional state was as fragile as I've ever seen it. Life, in that month, was mainly about survival.

But my father was the person who first introduced me to *sanyasi* culture when we lived in India during his early academic career (he was a professor of American studies until his first retirement at fifty-three, then joined the foreign service, retiring again at sixty-five). In both his time as a professor and as a cultural officer for the U.S. government, he had lived for many years in India. It was about a month into the new, difficult, frightening time in his life that we began to discuss detachment, *sanyasi* culture, and completion. These spiritual rigors first came up in conversation among Gail, him, and me when he came up to Spokane for a few days (previous to moving here). He remembered Janis Joplin's famous "Me and Bobby McGee." "Freedom's just another word for nothing left to lose," my father said as he smiled (for the first time in a long time). "I guess I have nothing left to lose now, so I must be free." The sad, wry quip turned his thinking and words toward what had happened to him, and he mourned the loss of what he had thought of as his material identity; but then we talked about his children, his grandchildren, and the legacy of sixty years of marriage; we talked about his world travels and explorations, his published books, the thousands of students he touched all over the world, and all the things he had been and accomplished.

My father seemed to become somewhat happier, his eyes beginning to light up. He resolved, "I'm going to move to Spokane and I'm going to get rid of just about everything I own. Wouldn't that be an amazing feeling! My life is so filled with clutter anyway. What do I need with all the stuff?" The instinct of renunciation rose in him, and we began to plan how he could do this — give the couch and bed in Las Vegas to his sister (my aunt), Denia; give his old car to his grandson, Justin; give some of his memorabilia from his foreign service years in India and Pakistan to his daughter (my sister, Maria, whom my parents adopted in India when I was five); give other items to his son, my brother, Phil; and give furniture and jewelry to his grand-daughters (my children). This "giving," this relinquishing began to feel very good to my father. Planning out gifting what he had to his family members gave him joy. "I'm going to just come up to Spokane with our family papers and my picture of Gandhi and not much else," he said. He resolved, "I'm going to see this as the next stage of my life. I really can be free now in some new way I am meant to explore." He sat with that thought a moment and then said, "I mean, son, how else can I see this whole thing? If I don't see it this way, what has my whole life of explor-ing the world been about? If I let this crisis destroy me, I will have been one of those old people who becomes so ashamed of losing his money that he thinks he has no life at all without the money. That's not who I want to be. I want to be like the *sanyasi* in India who have a purpose even after they've given everything up. That's what I want to be."

I had never known my father completely until I knew him in this moment. His cour-age was profound. He saw life and loss as completion rather than new emptiness, re-nunciation rather than destitution or utter destruction, meaning-in-victimization rather than constant shame or withdrawal from the world. As he inspired me and my two siblings, Phil and Maria, he began to develop a new adult learning course that he wanted to teach through the Osher Lifelong Learning Institute regarding how Stage 3 individuals could protect themselves from predators and how family members, like my siblings and me, could help our parents to protect themselves.

The shame my father felt for being so unprotected, and the guilt my siblings and I felt for not better protecting him, will probably never fully leave our family's development or history, but it does not dominate our family, in large part because of my father's spiritual leadership. Dominant now in my family is the sense that some kind of profound renunciation happened for my father, one that his life development could support through spiritual understanding and activity. The self-realization of detachment in my father's psyche brought a light to his eyes and renewed vigor to his life. That light and final vigor were worth as much as anything else could be. It was a light that I, as a son, had never quite seen in that way before.

We never know how the *sanyasi* will be a *sanyasi* — we never know how he or she will complete the spiritual task of renunciation and teach us about life. In America, certainly, very few of us will be like those old women and men in India I met as a boy, and, hopefully, we will come to a time when no elder will ever be a victim of a predator as my father was, but the ideas of *sanyasi* and renunciation can add a layer of meaning to the third stage of age, even in tragedy. These ideas provide a concentration for our energies and influences in Stage 3. The Hindus, Taoists, Muslims, Jews, Christians . . . all religious voices of renunciation, are very wise in positioning many of the acts of renunciation into the final stage of life, the stage we are calling "completion." May each of us have the courage in our late stage of elder living to fully embrace the part of being an elder that might ultimately be the most difficult: the letting go.

## MOSES LOOKS BACK ON HIS LIFE

When I meet with Stage 3 women and men, I ask that they journal, write memoirs, write poetry, and write statements of their lives. This writing process, especially around lists, details, and things to let go of, was important to my father during his time of renunciation. Watching elders connect with the creative possibilities of recording renunciation, detachment, and completion inspires me to try to project forward to what my own age of completion might be like one day. I find that by projecting myself into my father, Bill Houff, Shirley Aresvik, and other Stage 3 individuals, I can increase my attunement to their needs by walking in their shoes in the one way I, as a writer, have available to me: writing.

In this projection, I have over the years created a long piece called "Moses' Farewell Song to His People" (which follows, in content, the last chapters of Deuteronomy). This is a part of the "family bible" I am going to pass on to my children at some point. In the short prose poem with which I am ending this chapter, I speak as Moses in his last years of life. I hope this short piece helps you "write" a bit of the detachment and completion our Stage 3 elders gift us with.

From "Moses' Song of Farewell to His People":

"Lovers of life, do you remember your youth? How we moved through the universe like seeds! Even the abyss seemed to adore us, for we learned its secrets. And the many stormy days — do you remember? Exhausted, we left behind any storm that would have us for long; yet, still so young, we returned to every scene of carnage. We sang, 'I will give all my energy to gain a journey beyond the

203

stars!' To settle down, we believed, was to be a slave! Young, we walked by a small painted house — old people planting seeds in their gardens — and we sighed, 'What quaint loyalty they have to a task sadly measurable!'

"Now here we are, quite old. We have very little anymore to call our own. We've returned from the wilderness and found our homes. We are now the ones young wanderers see as they wander past our quaint rooms with their lovely, driven faces. If one of them should stop at my small fence and ask, 'Are you happy, old one?' I will sing, 'Life is worth every drop of blood and every tear. Young friend, you must wander from star to abyss and back home again.'

"I will cry, 'O young souls, look at my flowers!'

"And I know, I know, they will walk busily on."

[As women and men] we need each other's qualities if we are ever to understand each other in love and life. The beautiful difference of our biological selves will not diminish through this mutual fusion. It should indeed flower, expand; blow the mind as well as the flesh. When women can cherish the vulnerability of men as much as men can exult in the strength of women, a new breed could lift a ruinous yoke from both. We could both breathe free.
— Marya Mannes


Let us return to imperfection's school, no longer wandering after Plato's ghost.
— Adrienne Rich


Wisdom is learning what to overlook.
—William James

## Meditation 4: The Dance of Eggs and Stones

Every day we must risk something. Life is a dance of eggs and stones. Things must break if we are to say, "I've lived!" Arrogant or just dreaming, ignorant or testing the world, our risks break shells before little birds can be born. We are that powerful.

You know this, don't you? You've felt the guilt and shame of your errors. We who carry light in our heads are so smart, we often remember people's fragility *after* we've broken their hearts with our dancing.

What will it take to be a better person — to dance with more grace, to know when my harsh steps are the right ones or the wrong ones? With people different from me, what will it take to be more empathic, more understanding, lighter of foot? If I lie down at night recalling a day for which I should be judged, mustn't I change? The next morning, mustn't I rise up and say, "Teach me, I want to learn"?

I must learn the next piece of choreography the other sex has written for me.

I must work to meet brothers and sisters who will advise me. I must listen to what they say, see what they see, wander toward their wisdom as does the stone from the original mountain, falling toward the nest of eggs below.

God made us from both eggs and stones so we can fulfill the eternal commandments of intimacy: repair.

Friends, isn't it wonderful this life is so fragile?

How else would we teach one another how to love?

# CHAPTER 4
# HOW MEN AND WOMEN
# AGE DIFFERENTLY

The term "soul mate" suggests two people who have everything in common. But our gender, with all the differences it implies, divides us. . . . And that's fine with me.
— Anna Quindlen

My wife, Gail, and I have been married twenty-seven years. With both of us in the therapy and counseling fields, we like to joke that we had better stay together; how would we have any credibility if we did not? We also like to joke that our marriage is strong for two other reasons: (a) we argued, bickered, even fought like cats and dogs during our first few months of marriage ("getting a lot of it out of the way," Gail quips), and (b) I try to live by the advice I give to male clients, "If you want a marriage to work, marry a reasonable woman, and then do everything she says." Gail joins in the teasing, "But are you sure she has to be reasonable?"

And so goes the decades of tête-à-tête on which we have based a marriage, one in which Gail and I know ourselves as very different people — our personalities are different by nature, I an extrovert, she an introvert; I a judger, she a perceiver; and so on, and while our moral values are mainly similar, many of our interests differ and we are very different in the way we approach life as female and male. Gail can spend a great deal of time talking with her friends about how a room looks, colors that match or don't match, what fits where and how, why something should or should not be set up a certain way. I notice little of it. As long as no one gives away the couch on which I watch TV in the evenings, I am happy!

And for Gail, an emotional moment with a friend, a child, or with me is a beautiful moment to be savored. If the emotional situation includes negative emotions, the savoring will become agitation, worry, rumination, but rarely will the emotions of the moment be seen as lacking in importance.

For me, emotions are important, no doubt, but I don't see all of their colors, I don't hear all of their music. I miss whole hours and days of emotion. I don't hold on to arguments with friends or suspicions I can't immediately prove. I take very little personally

— Gail takes a great deal personally. And even as counselors, she and I differ along gender lines. If a client comes to me with an emotional issue, I listen, ask questions, listen some more, but ultimately the client knows I will see their issues as design problems to solve. For Gail, the listening is the thing. In the listening is the life story, and that life story has its own music, color, and taste, all of which need to be touched with empathy for as long as the empathy can last.

Our children are grown now, but in parenting we were very different as well — I was much more paternal than she, she more maternal. At root, what I mean by that is that we both loved our children unconditionally, but in a typical "paternal" way, I required them to *earn* my respect and I expected independent action and risk taking from them. Gail gave them everything she had, including respect, in every moment of their lives, and unless they trashed her in some huge way, she tried to help them with anything they needed help with, including trying to protect them from the very things I tried to push them into. For me, parenting was more about saying, "Go do it yourself if you can. I'm around if you can't do it or if you fail. I'll pick you up, I'll support you, but respect has to be earned, so go give it a shot before you call me."

Neither way of parenting is better or worse; both were equally important for the core self-development of our children. But they were generally different along a number of gender lines that have, over the last forty years, been corroborated and defined in neurobiological research.

### BEAUTIFUL AND LIFE-SUSTAINING DIFFERENCES

A focus group participant, Tammy, sixty, told me, "From the popular press, I got the idea that as we age, especially during or after menopause, differences between women and men went away. That's not the experience I'm having. Sure, some differences aren't as big as they used to be, but Alan (sixty-two) is still a man, and I'm still a woman, and some of those differences we saw clearly when we were younger are still around. We've gotten so accustomed to most of them that we just forgive them. A few, though, still rankle us — especially me. I admit it: I am still hoping one day he will change!"

While Tammy said this last part with a smile, she was quite serious about the fact that gender differences really matter. Some of the scientists working in the field of gender neuroscience are Tracey Shors at Rutgers University, Ruben Gur at the

University of Pennsylvania, Simon Baron-Cohen at the University of Cambridge, Jay Giedd at the National Institute of Mental Health, Sandra Witelson at McMaster University, Daniel Amen at the Amen Clinics, Louann Brizendine at the University of California–San Francisco, and Richard Haier at the University of California–Irvine. Using PET (positron-emission tomography), fMRI (functional magnetic resonance imaging), and SPECT (single-photon emission computed tomography) scans on human brains, as well as laboratory research on animals, and combining brain research with biochemical analysis of both animals and humans, these and other scientists refer to "the male brain" and "the female brain" to help define the neurobiological differences in our gender. The scientists are not looking for stereotypes. As Richard Haier has put it, "Human evolution has created two different types of brains, male and female, designed for equally intelligent behavior." These scientists have shown that all of us fit on a "gender-brain spectrum." "Male brain" and "female brain" are code words for a spectrum of seven billion–plus brains in the world, approximately half of which are male and half of which are female, and among which some brains and bodies are transgender.

If you are curious to take a "test" to see where your own male or female brain fits in the "maleness and femaleness" spectrum, try going to the Web site www.bbc .co.uk/science/humanbody/sex/add_user .shtml, where you can take a "Brain Sex ID Survey." Take this test with someone of the other gender, and you will take a step toward decreasing stress that gender differences can cause. This chapter is here to help with the third concentration of the wonder of aging: focusing on gender differences in order to decrease the stress of aging. In the Gurian Institute's focus groups and surveys, we found both a lively humor about gender differences and also a sense of urgency to the questions women and men asked about one another after fifty. As we age, the genders are living proof that women and men together are one of the strongest forces on earth; women and men who don't understand one another, however, become a war zone. By the time we reach fifty, most of us have probably realized that our partnership with our loved one can be a foundation for our other successes. You may have felt over the years that gender partnership is a healing mechanism for what ails you; you may have felt how your own flaws need the other gender's wisdom. Where a man feels consumed with things that may feed ambition but starve him of soul, he may need a woman to guide him back to freedom. When a woman feels lost, a man may be there to help her discover a way home. We may also sense that if we do not understand and forgive one another for our maleness and femaleness, we can destroy the societies that civilizations try to build. The destruction happens not in masses of soldiers destroying cities, but in one couple at a time destroying each other, homes, families, neighborhoods, communities, and, ultimately, our ability to live in wonder as we age.

## A Few (Unfair?) Facts About Women and Men Who Are Aging

You are going through (or have gone through) menopause and andropause. No matter where you live, no matter your race or creed or culture, menopause and andropause affect you as females and males. This new alteration of body, brain, and brain chemistry affects your gender — your estrogen, testosterone, progesterone, and many other chemicals that transform your female body and brain and male body and brain toward the psychological and relational stages in which you will live the rest of your life as a man or woman.

There are some "unfairnesses" in that

gender development now, as you age, as there were before menopause and andropause. Here are a few "unfairnesses," and of course, everything is a generalization, even when it is science-based, and there will be exceptions to everything at any given time. As I share natural gender differences with you, I promise to share with you only the male-female differences (what neuroscientists call "biological tendencies of the genders") that exist between women and men all over the world, in all cultures. They are, thus, "transcultural." This means that they can be expressed differently based on cultural and environmental influences, but the differences themselves exist in male and female bodies and brains everywhere. Scientists have been able to track approximately one hundred of these differences between the male and female brain and body around the world. Here are a few to start our exploration. As we move forward in this chapter, I will share differences that I have found as a mental health counselor to be essential to helping facilitate peace between aging women and men. But first, some physical and neurobiological facts:

- The skin of aging men is about 20 percent thicker than women's. It is also richer in collagen and elastin. Thus, on average, aging men do not develop as many deep-set wrinkles as aging women.

- Women's bones, on average, deteriorate faster than men's, leading to significant bone density issues for older women, as compared to older men. And by the way, on this difference: race does make a difference in quantity of disease. White and Asian men and women are more predisposed to osteoporosis than black and Latino men and women (even though among white and Asian people, women's bones deteriorate, on average, faster).

- Alcohol has a worse effect on women's sleep as we age than on men's, on average. Because men tend to metabolize alcohol more quickly, both women and men may get a pleasant soporific effect from alcohol early in the sleep cycle, but then more women (perhaps because their bodies are still metabolizing the alcohol) have been found to get less sleep in the second half of the night (when REM [rapid eye movement] sleep is essential to health and well-being).

- In metabolism rates in general, there is even more "unfairness" to women. Men's basal metabolism rate (BMR), a key part of weight gain and weight loss, continues to remain higher than women's BMR as the two genders age. For a six-foot-tall man of sixty, the BMR will be around 1,700; for a six-foot-tall woman, it will be around 1,475. She may continue to find it more difficult than a man to keep weight off.

    These are unfairnesses to women. In the vast array of natural gender differences, however, there is actually balance and fairness between genders. Nature loves diversity, it thrives on difference as much as similarity, and it sets up fair playing fields, if we will just expand our glasses to see the large field rather than just one small piece of grass.

- Various parts of men's brains shrink faster than women's as people age, often leading to faster loss of memory for men, as well as faster loss of some thinking and planning functions. Wom-

217

en's brains are more active than men's as we become older, in large part because unless women have Alzheimer's or dementia, they tend to remember more.

• Men do not take in as much sensory detail as women (this includes in all five senses), so it is often more difficult for men than women to savor the sensual moments of everyday life as they age. Women will often find more "meaning" in everyday life than aging men, and men often must reorient the way they find meaning and purpose in order to feel the wholeness and soulfulness of aging.

• For reasons that scientists believe have to do with hunting and gathering differences over the first million years of human development, women's brains tend not to "shut off" like men's brains do. Unlike women's brains, men's brains enter a nearly complete "blank brain" state — a neural rest state — when they recharge, reenergize, or rest at the end of the day and at various stressful times during the day. Unlike men's brains, women's brains remain at least half-active in most brain centers nearly all the time, even when women are recharging their brains. Women often feel a great deal more than men in a given day.

- While more women than men suffer from Alzheimer's disease (AD), still, in a non-AD brain, it is men who tend to lose verbal skills faster than women; similarly, among stroke victims, men tend to permanently lose more language skills than women. As we age, men tend to have less access than do women to the bonds and experiences that come with constant verbalizing.

Gail and I, like Tammy and so many others in our focus groups, joke constantly about gender differences, and also try to accommodate them toward greater relational strength. Humor helps us all notice the basically equal playing field (the long view); accommodation of the other person comes to feel natural.

My brain, for instance, zones out when I have overfilled it, making me "blank" and almost useless for at least a half hour of channel surfing or other "blank brain activity." Gail's brain never gets to rest! Unless she absolutely focuses on stopping her constant multitasking in order to veg out with a book in the evening, she is basically always "on." We joke about this, and we also don't try to talk about deep, emotional things when my brain is blank or when she is distracted by the million things she is doing.

I stumble over my words during a conflict more than she does, and my memory for family and relational details is, basically, terrible. When Gail and I get into a verbal conflict about something, I often end up just saying, "You're probably right," because I cannot remember the ten or so flawed things I have done over the last two months (!), ten or so things she is able to remember and bring quickly and adroitly into our conversation. "You're probably right" has become a ritual between us — for me, a ritual of humility in which I have great respect for Gail's memory.

At the same time, Gail relies on me to help her stay task-focused on things like weight loss. My metabolism is higher than hers, and I tend to be very directed regarding things like exercise. She is not a person who naturally wants exercise or who can easily give up unhealthy sugars and carbohydrates, and she gets distracted from healthy eating habits. So, she teases me about my memory, and our deal of fairness is that I am allowed to point out, "Gail, you're putting so much butter and salt on that huge potato! This is going to kill you." Or "Gail, let's go get some exercise." Gail frowns, even gets a bit angry, but then says, "Damn it, okay!" and pulls back on the unhealthy, fattening food and takes a power walk with me.

A delight of getting older — if we will let this be a delight — can be the decrease in our stressful competition as genders. Now, finally, forgivingly, we can become free to rely on each other more greatly to fill in our "gender gaps." For decades, even if unconsciously, we may have been competing with each other, seeing flaws in the other, trying to change the other, constantly proving ourselves to the other, and trying to get the other to prove himself or herself to us. As we enter a new stage of life, part of becoming an elder involves our concentration on understanding the other gender clearly and lovingly. This maturity can bring with it a new possibility for gender and personal freedom that moves with us as we go deeper into the stages of age and more fully into the pursuit of an attitude of wonder as we age.

## HOW WOMEN AND MEN DO CONFLICT DIFFERENTLY

One of the most important gender differences to work with (not against) as we age is a biochemical difference that applies in many of the conflicts we get into with the other gender. It is a profound difference, and lack of knowledge of it can significantly harm relationships and marriage.

A couple, Marcia, fifty-five, and Sam, sixty-one, came into my counseling practice. They had been married for sixteen years. Of their blended family of four children, only one, sixteen, remained in the home. Sam was stocky and muscular, with balding gray hair and a casual energy — not what I would think of immediately as an "angry" man. Tammy was a bit taller than he, dressed in jeans as he was, but somewhat more elegant, with matching earrings and necklace and a strong sense of self-confidence.

When I asked the couple how I could help them, Sam said, "She thinks I'm a brick, not emotional. And then when I am emotional, she says I'm doing it wrong." Marcia said, "I don't want to spend my life with someone who can't be emotionally open. When any disagreement happens, Sam clams up."

As we talked, I learned that when Sam and Marcia got into a conflict, Marcia would tend to talk the most — she would link memories, feelings, emotions, and desires to words; Sam would start out being able to talk but then, within a few minutes, he would withdraw and go silent. As Marcia kept trying to get Sam to open up ("Sam, don't walk away, talk to me!"), Sam would get angry, snarl, even punch his left fist into his right fist. Marcia would pursue him into another room, trying harder to engage him. Sam would get angrier and, finally, somewhat enraged, go to the garage or out of the house and slam the door behind him.

Because of this repeated dynamic, Marcia and Sam had become increasingly worried about their marriage. Both had been married before, and neither wanted this marriage to end. The couple clearly loved each other, but they were getting into several conflicts per week now; Sam was constantly failing to be emotional in Marcia's eyes, and Marcia was losing her trust in Sam's love of her. At one point in our second counseling session, Marcia began to cry. "I can't spend the rest of my life with a man who won't be there for me emotionally. I just can't!" Sam knew that she would divorce him if she felt she needed to, but he said, "I don't know what to do. I'm just not like her."

While awareness of gender-conflict-style differences do not help every marriage, in the case of Sam and Marcia it turned out to be true that basic gender differences, unrecognized and unaccommodated, were causing significant distress in the relationship. Over a period of time, I helped them understand each other at biochemical and neurological levels, and I helped them reorient the way they experienced marital conflict.

## Baseline Biochemistry and Brain Difference

At any given time, men have more testosterone in their blood and brain than women, women have more estrogen, progesterone, and oxytocin. Oxytocin is a bonding chemical that is female-dominant before, during, and after menopause. You may notice oxytocin at work in or around you when you find that many women are more satisfied in their relationships to *just bond.* They don't need to accomplish something while they're bonding. Just feeling the unconscious rush of oxytocin in their brains while they are building rapport with people or animals or other living things can give them a great deal of joy.

Men, on the other hand — driven by far less oxytocin and far more testosterone — might need to do something or accomplish something or even compete with others in order to feel well bonded. This is true for many men well into Stage 1, somewhat in Stage 2, and dissipating considerably in Stage 3 but not wholly disappearing, ever. (We'll discuss these gradual male changes more thoroughly in a moment.) Testosterone, even after it is basically gone from the male endocrine system by around eighty, has affected male biochemistry and the male brain at baseline levels throughout life.

For Marcia and Sam, oxytocin and testosterone affected conflict in ways they did not yet realize. Because of testosterone (and for various other reasons as well), men can tend to get more "physically expressive" when they get angry, as Sam did. Men can also tend to "withdraw" — check out of stressful verbal dialogue — as Sam did. These responses are fight-or-flight responses: stress signals (higher cortisol levels) in males quickly move to the amygdala (a fear-anger-aggression center in the midbrain) and the amygdala stimulates more brain activity downward toward the brain stem, and thus more quickly into the body. Thus, males may physically move around when they're stressed, or go out for a run, or smash fist into hand as a physical expulsion of the feeling, or physically move away from the stressor (a man like Sam gets up and walks away when significantly emotionally stressed). Testosterone is a fight-or-flight chemical, and its levels shoot up in the brains of men when they are under the stress of a conflict.

In the female brain, more brain activity moves upward from the amygdala toward talking and verbal centers in the brain, in Broca's and Wernicke's areas of the cerebral cortex. Oxytocin levels increase in the female brain and blood, in response to stress, stimulating more bonding function, thus more verbal function. Oxytocin is not a fight-or-flight chemical; rather, it is a tend-and-befriend chemical. Thus, quite often, women will hope to try to move through conflicts with less withdrawal (less walking out of the room), more talk (more words connected to feelings and memories), less physical fight (less hitting fist against hand), more talking, verbalizing, connecting words to feelings. Though, of course, there can be exceptions to this in a given moment or situation, a woman is more likely than a man to say, "Talk to me, don't walk away, stay with me." As the conflict deepens, female oxytocin levels can rise higher and higher, tending to drive a woman to stay connected and physically and emotionally bonded in order to feel better and solve problems.

Meanwhile, a man like Sam is in a state of severe agitation in which he feels his physical and hormonal energy rising to a pitch that can be physically dangerous. He is a big man whose body and brain are flooding with a fight-or-flight chemical more than with a tend-and-befriend chemical. He also senses that his brain is not producing the words his spouse is producing, nor is he able to provide the answers she needs. He becomes over stimulated and agitated, his amygdala swells up, his neural firing moves downward into his body, and he ends up having almost an opposite response to the conflict situation as his spouse. He feels the "fight" mode rise in his body, fights against it, realizes it is time to protectively withdraw (in order to protect his spouse), and does withdraw.

While he is, to a great extent, trying to protect his wife, his wife or friend feels abandoned by this — she feels that he is breaking the bond of love they have — and pursues him, physically, emotionally, verbally. He loves her and tries to stay with her, but his nature and hers are at odds now, and he does what feels safest for her and himself: he moves away from the conflict in order to protect her, and himself, slamming the door, getting in the car, driving away, or going into the den and turning on the TV.

When I worked with Marcia and Sam, I taught them about male brain and biochemistry and helped them look at how they did conflict. Sam and Marcia both took the BBC test, and we found that Sam was very "male" on the gender-brain spectrum and Marcia was very "female." This meant that their gender-brain differences were powerful parts of their relationship. They came to understand what was happening in their conflicts. They realized that, from a nature-based standpoint, the dysfunction in their conflict was twofold: (a) Marcia's pursuit of Sam after he was unable to verbally process created an untenable situation, one in which Sam couldn't trust Marcia to be safe in conflict with him; and (b) Sam's complete withdrawal from Marcia (i.e., he walked away but would never discuss the conflict again) was untenable and created a situation where Marcia could not trust Sam emotionally.

Once the couple understood how their brains and biochemistry worked, they instituted a new approach. When they got in a conflict, and when Sam became physically agitated, Sam walked away; Marcia did not pursue him — she let him go. However, after fifteen to thirty minutes, Sam came back, calmer, able to be verbal again. The couple then solved the problem they had begun earlier, the issue that had previously turned into untenable conflict.

It is so important to understand these differences. They are nature-based — wired into us — because they are neutrally and chemically driven. At the very moment men's bodies are feeling their anger and trying to expel it physically rather than express it in long sentences regarding emotions, the female brain might feel verbally stimulated; she might be saying, "Tell me what you're feeling, what's this anger about?" as Marcia did, and the timing is impossible, given what is happening in the male brain.

While it is true that both women and men have oxytocin (just as we both have testosterone), women have more oxytocin, the tend-and-befriend hormone, and men have more testosterone, the fight-or-flight chemical. The higher the oxytocin levels in a brain, the less physically aggressive the person is likely to be — and the more you'll see the person trying to "talk out" a problem — and that person more often than not will tend to be female. The higher our testosterone, the higher our fight-or-flight quotients will be. The more we understand our brain chemistry, the less stress we live in. Men who understand oxytocin train themselves to push toward keeping bonding rituals strong with women — talking as much as possible, especially at nonstressful times, with women, and often, following a woman's lead in how the

229

bonding relationships are evolving in a family, community, and home.

One man told me, "When I understood this about oxytocin, I saw the 'logic' of what my wife did a lot better. I realized that all those little things she does to bond with the kids, grandkids, and our friends were what gave her brain happiness, and she gave those feelings to others as well. Now I try to support her in these little things and daily conversations more."

Doesn't every woman just want to feel valued for who she is? Women will forgive men just about anything, if men will just find ways to listen, to be present with a woman, and to show that whoever she is, he values her.

— Sa'aana, 49

Especially since the advent of no-fault divorce, research over the last three decades has shown that the primary reason women leave men is that they feel unvalued or devalued by the man. This is important to sit with and look at as we age, because women in the second half of life terminate more marriages than men do (approximately 65 percent of marriages are terminated by women forty-five and older). If we value life partnerships, we have to keep looking from every angle at how to value women at a level of feeling and relationship that men may not have understood before.

At the same time, if we keep saying to males that they are flawed because they leave the room when they are overstimulated verbally in a conflict, we miss the deep, natural protectiveness men are actually practicing in the heat of conflict.

## Interrupting as a Dominance Behavior

The flip side of the Marcia-Sam case is the case of Alberto and Cheryl. The science was similar, but the conflict process differed somewhat in that the "fight" mechanism went on much longer for Alberto than it did for Sam. Sam entered the "flight" mode relatively quickly, and especially when he felt his agitation rise; Alberto did not go into flight mode as quickly as Sam. Instead, he stayed in a fight mode that became dominance and control of Cheryl. He did it by interrupting Cheryl constantly and thus devaluing her. Cheryl reported, "He won't listen. He yells, he becomes harsh, he interrupts. I finally have to give up. I just have to walk away." As we discussed the arc of conflict in this couple's relationship, it appeared clear that as her oxytocin rose, she tried to talk out the issues and process the feelings; she wanted to verbally present memories and explore thought. Alberto's rise in stress hormones, testosterone, and agitation led him to "fight" her by interrupting her no matter what she said.

Alberto risked losing this marriage. He needed to understand what was happening inside him, and to look at how he tried to dominate in order to quiet his own agitation. I needed to work with him to help him catch himself before he interrupts. He needed to let Cheryl express herself for a prolonged period (two to three minutes or more). I taught Alberto to repeat or paraphrase every few minutes, rather than just shut off conflict; meanwhile, we made sure that Cheryl was clear in what she was asking and saying.

Initially, Alberto resisted changing. He said, "I can interrupt if I want, I shouldn't change who I am." He also said, "Anyway, she just keeps repeating herself. Even if I say, 'I got it, okay?' she either thinks I'm too harsh and gets mad or sad about that, or she just keeps saying the same thing over and over and over again. I have to interrupt her!" When I asked Cheryl why she repeated herself, she said, "Because I don't know if he hears me." Alberto shook his head in frustration.

It appeared to me in early observations of this dynamic that Alberto might grant that he did interrupt, but he would not see through his own frustrations to what the couple needed unless we problem-solved a way for him to remain engaged in the conversation even when Cheryl repeated herself. It was not going to work to just say, "Alberto, listen for as long as Cheryl talks." Nor was it going to work to say, "Cheryl, stop repeating yourself." Both people had their own styles and personalities well established by the time they entered Stage 1 of the age stages and walked into my office.

So, a number of future sessions focused on a "listen for the point" solution. This can work with anyone who interrupts (and anyone who tends to talk a lot about feelings, emotions, and memories in ways that include constantly going off into tangents, or not completing one thought before stringing another thought on). The listen-for-the-point technique is a concentration technique by which the interrupter listens for the talker to say the same substantial point a second time. Once the point has been circled back to a second time, the interrupter says something like, "Wait, can I stop you there, I think I get what you're saying," then paraphrases back to the talker the point that the talker made. It helps to repeat or paraphrase the point with as many of the exact words, verbatim, from the talker as you can. "Your point was that I didn't listen to you when you were telling me about your father's new job." Or, "You said you wanted me to talk to Simon about his homework." The "point" can be very simple, but if it has been repeated by the talker, it is important and needs valuing. Alberto gradually learned to use this technique with Cheryl, and Cheryl felt increasingly valued as the interrupting dynamic lessened and she was much better heard by her husband.

## EXPLORING SEVEN DIFFERENCES, AND ENJOYING THEM

In working with these two couples, a subtext of counseling is forgiving differences. As we forgive these differences, we enjoy the other gender at deeper levels of intimacy and even adoration. When we are young, adoration comes from pheromones and hormones and reproduction. The truth of human biology is that, as we age, adoration must come now from more spiritual pursuits in a relationship: enjoyment of each other is linked, to some extent, to forgiving differences and enjoying their many faces. As this adoration grows, stress dissipates.

Here are seven gender differences that grow

from differences in our nature. These are set up, actually, all the way back in the womb, when our X and Y chromosome markers and our fetal hormonal levels format our brains to be female or male. To learn more about the scientific studies that show the genetics and fetal causes of gender differences, check out the Notes and References at the end of this book. I have included a number of intriguing studies and references there.

## The Sit-and-Talk Difference

Because males, in general, do little verbal activity on the right side of the brain, men tend to have fewer verbal centers in the brain (word centers used for reading, writing, and speaking) and, even more dramatic, fewer connections between word centers and emotion-sensorial centers in the midbrain. If you've noticed that a lot of men often use fewer words for fewer feelings than women, you may be seeing this brain difference manifest in your life. In fact, men on average use fewer words than women when reading, writing, and speaking are totaled in a day. "Verbal" means "word use," which includes reading and writing. "Verbal" does not just mean talking: there are a lot of men who talk a lot, but when scientists look at verbal output on average from men and women from all walks of life, in all cultures, they find a biological trend toward less word use across the board for men. A part of this finding is the deeper finding: women have more verbal centers connected to emotion and feeling, and thus rely more on those verbal centers for greater variety of emotion, feeling, and relational content when they talk, read, or write. Most couples notice that women's words show greater variety of memories, sensualities, and experiences to report. Women can spend much of their day talking with their friends, and that talk (and the relationships at all levels) can feed the souls of women in ways that, quite often, men, with fewer verbal centers and fewer connections of words to varieties of feelings and memories, do not have available to them.

Given, also, that males have more testosterone, we can expect them to be more physical or "movement-oriented" even as they age (until their health significantly decreases), especially when trying to relate to younger generations, who are physical and movement-oriented. Men will often substitute actions for words. Women, on the other hand, tend to take in and process more of their everyday lives through more senses than men, and thus may relate to others through a sensorial activity, like drinking tea, that combines fine sensation such as taste and smell with words. Men are of course quite capable of drinking tea, but they might choose these fine sensorial experiences less than women, and competitive bonding (nonverbal) activities more.

As you study these differences around you, you will probably notice that women, more often than men, use questions like "What do you think?" or "Do you agree?" at the ends of their part of a dialogue, so that conversations don't end, but continue. The result is longer conversations with more sensorial and emotional details and memories shared, and relationship time increased via words. You may notice that men tend to ask fewer of these sorts of questions at the ends of sentences or speeches, and thus men tend to have shorter verbal-relationship times than women do.

This "talking" difference can provide us with opportunities to use gender as a form of wisdom. We can learn from each other in order to de-stress relationships. Women can learn to "cut to the chase" with men — don't talk a long time and don't bring in an endless list of details and material that goes off on tangents. You'll lose the guy!

At the same time, a man can be more patient and listen better to what women are saying: nodding his head and otherwise showing her he understood and valued her. And to fully value women, men may need to end spoken paragraphs with open-ended questions like, "What do you think about that?" This may seem like "a small thing," but it is an accommodation that can lead to great adoration in an aging couple.

To live in the present moment is a miracle. The miracle is not to walk on water.

The miracle is to walk on the green Earth in the present moment with someone you love.

— Thich Nhat Hanh

*Why would you alter your face, your nose, your body with sharp tools of man?*
*God adores how you look and will weep when you are gone.*

— Saint Catherine of Siena

## The Relating-Through-Aggression Difference

Men, more than women, tend to joke or mock one another, even hitting each other on the back, arm, or hand (high five) when they want to show agreement or affection, whereas women tend to be less physically aggressive in their affection for another. Women will also tend to use more direct empathy ("I'm so sorry"; "Are you okay?") to help someone she likes through stress but also more behind-the-scenes words to show dislike ("She's just not someone to pay any attention to, believe me").

One thing to always keep in mind is that even as we age, a sixty-year-old man may still tend to be more physical and direct in his aggression than a sixty-year-old woman, who may still tend toward more hidden ways of being aggressive. During their development, men generally gain more training in physical aggression than women do; men are also driven, well into their seventies, by surges of aggression chemistry (testosterone). Aggression becomes a nurturing style for men.

What do we mean? That, actually, men (and boys) are nurturing people by and through their aggression (as long as the aggression doesn't turn violent). The aggressive male nurturing style is quite valuable for raising up the next generation toward strength and high self-esteem. You might notice this aggression nurturance when you see a man of fifty-five or sixty pushing very hard — even yelling at a younger man to motivate him. The older man is trying to nurture the younger man, and often this kind of nurturing will work better than soft conversations or constant praise. It is an overtly higher-risk way of empathy than the more female "direct empathy" approach, and men must be constantly vigilant to make sure they are not destroying the core self of the younger person they are trying to help, but it is a very useful way of nurturing: it keeps motivating, teaching, driving, encouraging, and building character in the younger person. Women often misunderstand this nurturing style in early life stages, but now, as men mellow a little, and as women look deeper into the male psyche, this male style of empathy and care can be studied, understood, and seen as equal in value to the more directly empathic female style of saying, "How are you feeling?"

## Male and Female Biochemical Cycles Still Matter

By the time menopause is complete, the female body will not be sending hormones surging through it like it used to. But the adrenal glands possess some hormonology, and many women will be on hormone replacement therapy. Female biochemistry dissipates in power after menopause but can still affect women in cyclic ways, as we noted in

Less known, generally, is that males have a biochemical cycle that continues, though with somewhat diminishing effect, until very old age. That male cycle is not as clearly a monthly one as the female cycle, but each man does have his own subtle monthly cycle. Males also get testosterone surges every few hours, with testosterone higher in the very early morning, then lower around eight or nine, then higher again around ten a.m., lower in the mid-afternoon, then another surge coming toward later evening. Males get fluctuations in testosterone levels throughout the year as well, often with higher testosterone in October and lower testosterone in April.

Knowing about the male daily hormone cycle can be very helpful in planning when to communicate about deep, emotional things with men. If you want to convince a man of something that is important to you, try talking to him at a lower testosterone moment. He may be less aggressive in arguing or he might listen better. Late afternoon hours are post-lunch/siesta hours, so all of us may become a bit sleepy during this time — male or female — but in men, specifically, low testosterone contributes to lowered competitiveness and aggression during this time.

And adding to the lowered testosterone, at around eight at night, male oxytocin rises — males may be looking to bond right about then. This evening hour is a time when a man — if he's not too tired — might also be likely to talk about feelings. Increased oxytocin in the bloodstream often means a guy will be more malleable.

**The Ruminating and Worrying Difference**
Two brain structures that handle ruminating and worrying look different in scans of women's and men's brains. These structures are the cingulate gyrus and the amygdala, housed in the limbic system of the brain, which is in the middle of our skulls. The cingulate gyrus is an "attention-concentration" center. The amygdala is the "emotion (agitation)-then-action" center in the brain we mentioned earlier.

Brain scans at the Amen Clinics have shown that women tend to have a more active cingulate gyrus than men. Dr. Amen recently told me, "Women can have up to four times more activity in this brain center than men have." One potential result of this particular brain difference may be that women tend to ruminate, worry, and constantly reassess things for more hours of a day or week than men do. Men don't tend to process as much of their lives through this "rumination center" and thus tend to spend less time internally processing or ruminating on relationships, emotions, and past experiences.

This difference can frustrate women (and men) because, as a woman recently put it, "Men don't care about things as much as I do." Men care, of course, but it can seem they don't care as much because they don't spend as much time thinking about certain things and relationships. And while men do indeed worry about things in their lives, differences in the amygdala support the research on the cingulate gyrus. In women's brains that are under stress, more blood flow goes to the left side of the amygdala, what psychologist JoAnn Deak calls "the worrying side," while more men have more activity on the right side of the amygdala, the aggression side, when they feel threatened by someone or feel powerful emotions regarding relationships. This may be another reason, in the brain, that women tend to ruminate and worry emotionally for longer periods of time and men tend to become aggressive and try to problem-solve more quickly.

## Why Do Men Tend to Cry Less Than Women?

While anyone can cry for any number of reasons, women who cry when they are worried often feel relieved. Just as often, men see crying as weak and feel ashamed, not relieved, when they or another person cries. While this difference dissipates somewhat with age, it can still be robust for many people during the stages of age. And while it is certainly true that men in most, if not all, cultures have been trained and socialized not to cry as much as women, have you ever wondered if there's a biological reason men tend to cry less than women, on average, even as we age? There are a number of them. Testosterone is one: it is an aggression chemical that specifically mitigates against tears. Another important chemical involved in crying is prolactin. Women have higher levels of prolactin in their bloodstream throughout life. This brain chemical controls the development of mammary glands (breasts), breast milk, and tear glands. At and after puberty, women's tear glands can be, on average, 60 percent larger than men's. By the time menopause and andropause transform us, the size of tear glands is already well established. This larger tear gland is a biological reason for your observation that, in many cases, women cry more than men. While men older than fifty may tend to cry more than they did when they were twenty, still, on average, tear production of men stays below that of women until Stage 2 or 3, when male testosterone levels decrease, and men may often tear up more than they did previously. Interestingly, still, male tears are more likely to pool in a man's eyes rather than fall down his cheeks, whereas a woman's tears are more likely to stream down her cheeks. Here, too, a biological difference is at play: women's tear ducts are generally narrower and male tear ducts are generally wider, so male tears tend to pool for longer periods of time at the eyes, giving them time to be reabsorbed rather than fall down the cheeks. Women's tears tend to come down onto the cheeks more quickly and copiously.

## The Rest-State Difference

At the University of Pennsylvania, neuroscientist Ruben Gur has shown that men's brains go blank more often and for longer periods of time than women's brains. This can be especially true as we age. We mentioned this difference very briefly at the beginning of this chapter. Let's go deeper into it now. Understanding it can be very helpful in de-stressing relationships between women and men.

A rest state is that state of mind when our eyes glaze over, we zone out in front of the

TV (just channel surfing, and thinking about very little), we stare off into space, or we just try to grab some quick shut-eye on the couch. Sometimes you can tell that a brain is starting to enter the rest state because the person's fingers start tapping pencils on a table or the person entering the rest state interrupts you or tries to get you to talk faster or get to your point quicker. He may feel his brain beginning to go to a rest state or blank out and is trying to stay connected and attentive.

At the end of a long workday, men and women both want to enter a rest state, but while the man's brain actually does rest — it goes nearly blank — women's brains do not go blank. So, the man might truly zone out, while the woman might still try to accomplish a lot during this rest time, multitasking while she does it: cook a meal, talk on the phone, think about six other things.

An important thing to remember about this rest state is the fact that when a man's brain enters the rest state, it is not actively tracking, thinking, storing information, remembering, or processing life experience and conversations around it. So, if you are in a dialogue with a man whose eyes are glazing over, his brain may be going into a rest state. It may frustrate you later that he doesn't remember

246

what you said or value what you said (and thus, who you are) as you wish he would. Given that the rest state is an inherent part of the male brain in all cultures and on all continents, you may need to reorient how you work with a man in order to get what you need. So, if you see a man (or woman) going blank, some physical activity might be needed to get the brain reengaged, or you might need to just let go of the discussion for now and get back to it later. Given that some men, especially males who do not generally tend to be very verbal about feelings and emotions anyway, can go to a rest state if you use a lot of uninterrupted words laden with emotion, you may need to create a new way of talking with this kind of man by noticing where the "word threshold" is for that individual man. Some men can go on and on with words and not go blank. Others can't. Learning where a man (or woman) fits on this spectrum can decrease conversational and relational stress significantly.

## Women and Men Grieve Differently

By now, most of us have been to a number of funerals and helped at least one other person through dying and death. Most of us have experienced significant moments and times of grief. Not surprisingly, women and men often experience grief differently. How we grieve — and understanding differences between how we and our partner grieve — can be like having available to us a beacon into the soul and, seeing through that light, understanding how true it is that no two people grieve the same way.

Gender-specific studies in the United States, Europe, and Asia confirm gender differences in grieving styles. Grieving women, on average, cry more tears than men; they tend to experience the full effects of the grief more quickly (men tend to have more delayed reactions); they tend to want to discuss the grief more quickly and more fully, and for longer periods of time. Women are doing something here that is called intuitive grief, while men tend more toward instrumental grief.

Intuitive grief is quite feeling, emotion, and word focused. It expresses as much inner emotion as possible in a given moment and develops adaptive, transformative self-development through feeling and emotion. Thus, women, on average, "grow through their grief" by processing it as much as possible, and very much through the strategy of verbalizing, writing, talking, and reading.

Instrumental grief is more "doing" oriented. It "thinks out" the situation, including the grief, more with what is popularly called "head" than "heart." It involves, in general, fewer words. This does not mean a man is not feeling a great deal, but the way his brain and body process the grief may be more oriented toward doing an action during the processing, or, when he uses words, talking about the thoughts he is having and about the person who died, rather than his own inner feelings. Men, thus, tend to adapt forward beyond the death of their spouse or friend in the same ways men do so many other things — through "doing" and through withdrawal.

This is one of the reasons that suicide is more common among grieving men who have lost a spouse than grieving women who have lost a spouse. Suicide includes instrumentality in a grieving process. If a man becomes significantly depressed and almost completely withdraws from life, it becomes logical — instrumental — for him to think about "doing something": killing himself.

Neither intuitive nor instrumental grief is better or worse. When an aging man becomes overwhelmed by a woman's ongoing expressions of grief and sadness, he may often try to shut the woman down — he may think "she's weak," or he himself may feel unable to keep up with the emotionality and verbalizations of the woman. He may also become worried that his own emotions will be too overwhelmingly triggered if he is constantly comforting a crying woman. All these responses to intense shows of intuitive grief are within the range of normal for a man who is very "male" on the gender-brain spectrum; they can also feel like betrayals of love. As he ages, a man may need to constantly push through his own fears with embraces and listening, and with helping the loved one spend time with girlfriends and others who can take her emotions into places the man cannot.

On the other side of the equation, a woman will sometimes misread a man's instrumentality, perhaps not realizing its uniqueness and functionality. A woman will sometimes project a "woman's way of grieving" onto a man who is not built for that. She may think he is immature for not talking about his feelings, or she may see him as weak with fear in the face of emotions. She may not see that as he mows the lawn or builds a tree house for a grandchild and uses few words to grieve, he is nonetheless paying his own homage to the dead person, grieving by making something new in the world that will honor the soul who has passed.

## DIFFERENCES THAT DIMINISH WITH AGE

We've looked at a number of gender differences with the intention of understanding one another more fully and richly so that we can protect the wonder of aging. We've emphasized gender differences, but we all sense, also, as we age, that some gender differences soften. We are not as different as we were in adolescence or when we were raising children.

---

Pete and I have both hardened and softened over the years. The hardening factor for him includes the tendency to get stuck in patterns of attitudes and behaviors. For me, it is that now I put on a thick skin or put up a wall to protect myself better against being treated unfairly or with unjust intentions. But Pete has softened, too. I see more evidence of attitudes and behaviors of emotional empathy toward others, including family members and friends. The way I have softened as a woman is a more relaxed attitude toward child-raising attitudes and boundaries, maybe even toward life issues and situations in general. I just don't worry about every little thing as much.

— Deanne, 58

---

After menopause and andropause, some gender differences diminish. You've probably seen the "softening" of gender differences around you.

When we're in our sixties, seventies, or beyond, men who are no longer working full-time often seek out more bonding opportunities than they did — reaching out more to their kids, whom they may not have bonded with during the rushed years as Mom did, or spending more time with grandkids than they did their own kids. Men might also feel less independent, self-motivated, "go get 'em" than they once did. Men may become softer than they once were and might very much enjoy the expansion of their base of feelings and relationships. Their testosterone levels are decreasing, and many of the previous battles they fought seem less important now.

Women might feel more independent, "like I'm getting my second wind," and less dependent on a husband for core-self development and self-esteem. As women's estrogen and progesterone levels diminish, and as children are grown and gone, aging women can sometimes become slightly less conciliatory, more socially ambitious or driven. Many women will start new careers during or after menopause. One woman I know joined the Peace

Corps at seventy-two. She was placed in a program specifically set up for people in the second half of life, people who have found new ambition and purpose, most of whom were women.

Our "new gender selves" as we age are absolutely something to concentrate on and talk about between women and men. They can be game changers in relationships and life. If women don't say, "I'm just not that person anymore — now I need _____, _____, and _____," men won't know what women need now. And if men don't help women see the new man they may now be becoming, they'll try to still be the aggressor they may have been before, but not really have the body and even brain power to discover or delight in what they used to pursue.

It can be a fun activity to do your own "study" of gender differences. With your partner or alone, take a month to observe when and how you see differences manifest in your home, workplace, and neighborhood every day. When you notice that the difference does not happen as I've listed it in this chapter, note that, too. "Exceptions to the rule" can be powerful aids in deepening our understanding of gender. Everyone is an individual, and many things in the brain besides gender are going on at any given time.

## Help the Men Age Well, Too, Will You?

I enjoyed a very pleasant lunch with two friends, Cindy, fifty-four, and Debbie, fifty-seven, of Laguna Beach, California, following a lecture I had given in their community. The subject of this new book arose, and Debbie said, "This is a great idea. You have to write this. And make sure to help men especially." Cindy agreed. "There are a lot of resources for women, but fewer for men. And I think aging actually hits men worse than women. We women have all sorts of relationships and things to do, but men seem kind of lost sometimes. It's sad."

I have heard this kind of comment from both women and men for almost three decades. It is the sense I hinted at regarding therapy: while some men hold very visible, powerful positions in society, there are tens of millions of men who need care and concern from us in ways we don't realize. Our lack of understanding of these men takes a toll on quality of life, longevity, and our civilization. Whether, as Debbie and Cindy suggested, there are more resources in our culture for aging women or whether women simply avail themselves of the resources, as they age, women do tend to work through a great deal with girlfriends and doctors in ways that many men do not. Men are often likely to lose their sense of purpose and identity somewhat dangerously as they age. Men often experience a sense of meaning during their peak work and family years, the building of their legacy, but feel confused about what constitutes meaning and soulfulness when the rush of life is dissipating. These men often make choices that are quite harmful — from leaving a family they will later wish they had not left, to putting off health exams that could save their lives, to suicide as a response to depression.

One crucial area of assistance for men is andropause education. Many men who come to see me between the ages of forty-five and sixty-five do not know that andropause exists, or they think it is a fad or is fake. They do not realize that andropause is a biological and natural transformation that can leave men empty of foundation if they do not greet it with consciousness, patience, and spiritual, relational, and personal transformation. When I and others — such as Dr. Stephen Johnson, founder of the Men's Center of Los Angeles and author of *The Sacred Path* — work with aging men, we try to help them see that the brain changes toward a new slowness and testosterone dissipates; thus "the life of the soul must rise in men in new ways," Stephen notes. He sees the male soul going somewhat underground during the busy years of endless work and child rearing so that, if the foundation of a soulful and mindful life was not well realized by the man earlier in life, he will sense a lack of foundation. He may become, during and after andropause, what the contemporary American poet, Robert Bly, calls "The Man Who Didn't Know What Was His." This man, Bly writes in his poem, will be like a lean-to that is attached to a house — the house has a foundation, but the lean-to does not. Because this man has little spiritual foundation of his own, he may be both kind and angry in the same five-minute period, irritable, inconsistent, the kind of grown man who "leans toward you and leans away." He has no inner measuring standard for how to fully love and be loved. By the time he is in his fifties or later, a hole inside him can create a desperate listlessness in his life and, ultimately, a withdrawal from life, or an angry battle with others, God, family, and death.

Simon, sixty-nine, was one of these men. He came in for counseling. "My wife sent me here," he said. "She says I don't even know how to keep busy anymore. I'm driving her crazy." As we explored his life, he admitted: "I keep going into the office even though I know most of the folks no longer want me there. But I can't play golf every day, and I don't want to just sit around and watch TV." Talking to another man helped Simon, and most of our talking together happened while we walked together. With male clients who are ambulatory, I do a great deal of counseling in the "peripatetic format": walking and talking. This format gives much-needed exercise to a man like Simon, and it keeps the male brain engaged (out of the rest state we talked about earlier). Our time together gave Simon a sense of the hole that was inside him now, and the need to develop a new purpose in life, as well as to just appreciate the small things in life and the joy of *not* working sixty hours a week at an office. But Simon didn't stay in counseling for long, and so I tried to help him set up a circle of male friends so that he would never be alone in his journey as an aging man.

Paul, fifty-nine, and I talked in my office after he was forced to retire due to a motorcycle accident that left him in a wheelchair. Paul told me, "It's all I can do to keep myself from getting angry all the time. I don't have kids or grandkids, my wife left me, I just want to break things." Paul had been at the peak of his career in the high-tech industry, and the accident and wheelchair created a void in his self-development. Paul had contemplated suicide. He was an example of the kind of man Dr. Thomas Joiner, a scientist awarded the Guggenheim Fellowship and the Rockefeller Foundation's Bellagio Residency Fellowship, has studied and discussed in his 2011 book, *Lonely at the Top: The High Cost of Men's Success.* Eighty percent of suicides in the second half of life are males. "Much attention is focused, rightly," says Joiner, "on men's disproportionate share of wealth and power; but too little attention is spent on men's disproportionate share of misery, one index of which is high suicide rates."

Paul needed therapy and new friendship to help him understand the fear and confusion he felt as both an injured, traumatized man, and because he was a man facing pain nearly alone. I worked with Paul for six months; then we drifted apart. When I met him again three years later, he told me he had begun to feel "like a man" again. He had joined a trauma support group in which he found much-needed community — a circle of friends who could understand what he was going through. He also got involved in speaking to Rotary Clubs and at high schools about his accident, and how it had forced him to rethink his whole view of what it meant to be a man.

Men who increase their sense of successful manhood during the first fifty years of life can become men who mainly feel decreased by life in the next decades, unless we show them another way of increasing manhood. In his *First Elegy*, the German poet Rainer Maria Rilke wrote of a time in our lives when we must free ourselves from the self we love even as we keep on loving that self. By this he meant that we are detaching somewhat from the busy ways we used to find meaning — through constant work, attachments, and prowess of body and mind — even as we love self and others; now, we must look at our foundations for meaning and feel them completely, let them send us to new places of soul. Rilke reminds both women and men that we are at the time in life now when "there will be nowhere we should remain." We must make a new life, fly to new phases of life; but if we do not have a sense of who we are *now* as we fly, and if we don't form community and purpose commensurate with our new life, we can get quite lost.

Part of the wonder of aging for men will be found in new, intensive spiritual search during and after andropause. If you know a man who becomes aware of the hole inside, I hope you will help him engage consciously in spiritual activities in nature, faith community, friendship groups, men's groups, and with a spouse or a friend. The wonder of aging for men in the new millennium will come in part from the fact that we now have many more decades in which to grow the soul we may have put off growing in order to protect and provide for our families and build our legacies.

Rilke, again, gives beautiful language for this new journey. In his *Eighth Elegy*, he describes us as being spectators who must reenter the world in a different way now. We have, in the past, entered the world through "the stuff of our lives." But now, if we choose that route, we'll find it unsatisfying, lacking something, not wholly appropriate to our age. We can try to set things in order so that we might gain back the past but, he warns, "that order will fall apart." We can keep trying to "order it again," but finally, he warns, "we will fall apart ourselves."

How beautiful, for both women and men. We must fall apart. That is what transformation is about. The falling apart is the rite of passage men and women must make in our fifties, sixties, and beyond — this is the transformation of masculine identity that is difficult for males, and in some ways very different from the female rite of passage into elder female identity. Men are not used to falling apart — women are more used to it. Now men must look at the order we have created and see what parts can be dissolved. We must look at "the stuff of life" and see what has worth now and what needs letting go of. We must "fall apart" with others who are going through what we are going through — transformations, losses, divorces, remarriages, continued marriages, couple counseling, the fear of not performing as well as we once did at sex, the grief of children leaving us, the destitution of realizing we may possess very little spiritual foundation with which to face death, and the discovery of blessings as we age.

Rilke's words grow from a Christian context, and he was borrowing from Christian theology in presenting a spiritual approach to mortification of the flesh that frees the soul. I asked a Christian pastor and a writing partner, Pastor Tim Wright, fifty-seven, of the Community of Grace Lutheran Church, to tell me more about this "mortification." Both he and I see it as a powerful metaphor for the male journey of aging, especially through the age of transformation. Pastor Tim said: "Mortification of the flesh gets a bad name because it gets portrayed as being about flogging oneself and all that, but the spiritual concept is deeper than that. The idea is that through one's lifetime of the challenges and feelings (life of the flesh) we are gradually freeing our souls to be closer to God."

I have found Pastor Tim's concept powerful in working with men, especially men who are already inclined toward taking a second look, now, at their faith communities, or at least at a spiritual approach to aging. It can be useful to talk with these men about how we have lived, up till now, very "flesh-oriented" lives, experiencing life through our bodies, senses, and physical-social-material accomplishments. Thus, actually, we have been living a spiritual life all along — a life of mortification of the flesh that can now, as we age, be seen consciously as a time of self-reflection.

This self-reflection on mortification lasted three years for Simon and five years for Paul. As these men "fell apart," they looked back on who they had been, all they had accomplished, and repositioned their intentions, read poetry, went fishing, formed a circle of friends, took on new hobbies, found places to volunteer and feel useful. The previous lives each of them had lived, the previous accomplishments, the love given and received, the successes and still-unrealized ambitions, the physical, sexual, social experiences they remembered — everything they knew, both positive and negative, were the foundation of the man each became now. The past was the mortification of flesh and life that built the soul they were now developing in the wonder of aging. The lean-to became for these men a little place to go perhaps to smoke a cigar or do something else that brought a sweet pleasure not appropriate for the house. But the house of each aging, soulful man got built by each of them. Paul fully realized the transformative power of his tragedy in the spiritual love he felt when he decided to serve the world by bringing beliefs, knowledge, and experience — his story — into the world. He felt especially connected to young people who had suffered as he did, and he began to volunteer at a hospital. He became a mentor to those young people. His mortification of the flesh (quite literally) led to a deeper life of his soul, and that deep life became about mentoring.

And so, ultimately, mentoring is, as always, an elder's way. The emptiness men can feel as we age is an emptiness we might turn toward spouses to fill, and spouses will often do their best to help, even when they lament,

"Please, go find a new life!" Or the emptiness may drive us to keep returning to old workplaces or memories of our workplaces, searching for our souls there. Most often, we need a soul's life to be developed now as a gift to young people who, by the nature of their youth, need our wisdom.

Debbie and Cindy wanted the best for men and saw, instinctually, that men are born to father the world, just as women are born to mother it. Until recently, we men did not live long enough to fulfill and complete the part of that fathering that goes beyond our immediate families. Now, this second lifetime gives every man and woman the chance to fulfill the dreams of our ancestors, who did not live as long as we do but suspected that, one day, we would live that long; thus they created legends of elder men, like Moses and Aaron and Abraham and Isaac, who led tribes and nations wisely, even when the men were very old; legends of people like Noah who lived "to be five or six hundred years old." These legendary "wise old men" saw a world that needed them as elder men to care for it. Now, billions of us are living long enough to actually be these legendary people.

How wonderful!

Moved by the force of love, fragments of the world seek out one another so that a world may be.
— Pierre Teilhard de Chardin


There is no place or relationship in which the Beloved is not flowing, though the current's force may not always feel gentle.
— Saint Teresa of Avila


If you find yourself with someone you love . . . kiss the mouth that tells you, "Here, here is the world."
— Galway Kinnell


We cannot know what our life is unless we know what love is.
— Emanuel Swedenborg

## MEDITATION 5: A SPLENDID LIFE

*(I have written this meditation based on Genesis 23:1–25:18, from the viewpoint of Sarah, matriarch of the Jews, wife of Abraham.)*

To live a splendid life then to realize I am aging . . . no, even more, to realize I will one day die like a muffled fall into water — shouldn't this realization change me? To realize I will live thirty thousand days and nights, then drown in one sigh — shouldn't this knowledge change even my way of loving?

In this life, I have been one of those women immersed in life's song, the music and heartbeat, the lyric and echo. I have been guest of many loved ones, host to many souls. Decades ago, I became an adult and felt the trembling of bodies-in-time. That I will lose all this one day — shall I complain? O I must not! Everyone I have loved gave me their cells of light to hold. All a person really owns is every moment of love she has felt in a lifetime.

When I first loved my husband, we promised we would become as one, and we did, and we became at home in the unknown. When we loved with our bodies, we tossed out the maps others had made; we believed we knew more about love than anyone else except God. When we wed, we were two lights lighting one house. Ah, we learned love as did God at Creation — all the possibilities of love became light that cares for the world.

For this, I will never complain.

Some people think: "How much easier it would be if we could just learn Love all at once." That thought is mere desire. Real love is a feeling sung out: "If you have had in your life even a tiny piece of this, you can know freedom." Ten thousand lanterns remain invisible until we learn how to love. Just after, these lights illuminate ten thousand paths of power and peace. This is what it means to say, "They saw the light in each other's eyes."

Let me never complain. With my muffled voice I say, to complain is to drive love away. It takes a lifetime to learn who we are. Love is a changing path. Let me learn everything about love so that, when I do die, I do not complain, "Lord, please give me more time!" Instead, let me sing at my end, "Thank you for the time I had, Lord. 'Time' gave me everyone I loved."

# CHAPTER 5
# THE WISDOM OF
# INTIMATE SEPARATENESS

The meeting of two personalities is like the
contact of two chemical substances; if there
is any reaction, both are transformed.
— Carl Jung

Corinne came into my office for marital
counseling. She said her husband, Eddie,
was not interested in counseling. "But something has happened to us as a couple," she
said. "And I'm not sure our marriage can
survive."

Corinne had an athlete's body, thin and
muscular, and she was comfortable with her
own skin. She wore jeans and a blue sweater.
Winter dropped snow on us that day, and as
she sat down, she removed her wet coat, set
it on the chair where Eddie might have been,
and began to talk. She had the kind of mind
that remembered details of intimacy in easy
sequence, and within ten minutes I got the
basics of her story.

She, fifty-two, and Eddie, fifty-five, had been married twenty-one years. About four years ago, when their two children became fourteen and seventeen, things started changing in their relationship. Eddie lost his job in software design and found another one after a year, but the new job required him to travel for at least half of every month. He was constantly exhausted. Corinne had been a lawyer in another state when the couple married, but once they started having children, she worked part-time outside the legal field while raising her family. Now that the children were independent, she took the bar in this state, passed, and joined a law firm. She still worked part-time but more than before, still mainly responsible for what the children and her husband needed. "Eddie has been a great father," she assured me.

"The problem is," she said, "Eddie and I aren't really the couple we used to be. Eddie never initiates sex; I have to initiate it. He used to always be the one who initiated. And we used to say 'I love you' to each other all the time, like when we hung up the phone, when we got up in the morning, when we went to bed at night. Now, I say 'I love you' and he says 'Thanks.' We aren't intimate very much anymore, he's always tired, I'm trapped in a loveless relationship, and I can tell that he's

269

trapped in . . . life. Life hasn't turned out for him like he thought it would, where he could relax a little after the kids were grown. Life hasn't turned out like I thought it would: our kids are grown, and I have a career again, but I have a bad marriage.

"Finally, after about two years of this, I got up the courage to say to him, 'Eddie, are we okay?' We had a long talk and he was honest when he said, 'I don't know. I still care about you a lot, I'm loyal to you, but I don't know what I think about anything. I'm just doing what I can to survive.' I've come back to this a lot over the last year and he always says he doesn't know where we are or if he loves me like he used to, with all the passion and intimacy. I'm very hurt. I try not to force anything on him, but I'm so unhappy. We aren't in love anymore, at least that's how it feels to me. I want him to get into therapy with me, but he refuses. He hardly even looks at me anymore. When I bring up how unhappy I am, he gets mad or sullen and won't talk. I hate it."

Telling her story, Corinne began to cry. As we paused the conversation, she wept softly, a woman in the third decade of a marriage that seemed to betray the promise of lifelong love. Embarrassed by her tears, Corinne apologized. I offered her tissues and helped her feel comfortable in this safe place to be exactly who she was. Her tears subsided, and we spoke some more, continuing to build rapport. We spoke of her children, of whom she was very proud, and her work; her mother, who was still alive, and her father, who had passed away; her childhood in Florida; her husband's childhood in California. Over the rest of the first session and in subsequent sessions, I learned a great deal about her and about Eddie, and many more details of the marriage clarified themselves. I gave her some questions to ask Eddie, and herself — some "homework." She began to keep a journal and wrote down details regarding her relationship, her own identity, and her needs and wants.

In our fifth session, we were discussing an attempt she had made during this last week to talk to Eddie about the marriage (and his getting irritated and walking out of the house); we talked about how hurt she felt, and how despairing. It was in that moment that I asked her, "Do you think you and Eddie have been too close over the last seven or eight years?" This question stimulated a frown of disbelief. "Too close? No," she corrected immediately. "Not too close. We're hardly intimate at all." I agreed. "Yes. I see that for sure. I wonder, too, though, if you're more enmeshed than you realize, and Eddie's actions are not just about his transformation into what I call the wonder of aging, but also his way of signaling that he wants a new kind of freedom in your marriage."

This was the turning point, I believe, as I reflect on this case, of a new phase of counseling for Corinne herself, and ultimately a way of later getting Eddie to come in with Corinne to work on the marriage. This question — "Are you too close?" — has been a turning point in a great deal of the marital counseling I do, one that becomes especially useful for people between forty and sixty who are looking to rethink and even regain their marriages.

### THE ART OF INTIMATE SEPARATENESS

"To love another person is to see the face of God," the author Victor Hugo wrote almost 150 years ago. We are social animals, wired for relationship and human contact. If we spend some part of our day wondering about sex, we spend even more trying to understand and improve our ability to be intimate. Thus intimacies occur in every workplace, every meeting place, every home. Protecting and developing intimacy is extremely important during the stages of age.

There is healthy intimacy as we age and

there is unhealthy intimacy, and perhaps billions of versions of each. There is certainly no single right way to be intimate, marry, divorce, remarry, choose against intimacy, choose intimacy again, have sex, have sex often, or choose to give up sex altogether. Part of the wonder of aging is the freedom to realize that love, sex, and intimacy are what we make them, and we make them into what we and our intimates need. Desire gradually capitulates its dominant position; deep intimacy gradually takes hold of us. Unless we concentrate on how this is happening, we may not even know it is happening. Wonders, even miracles, in coupled intimacy come from honesty, realistic optimism, and collaboration toward new goals of love.

When I work with couples in marital counseling, I try to flow toward what the couple needs, and often they need short-term solutions to specific issues, such as sexual changes. Sometimes the counseling ends once the short-term solutions are realized. Often, though, counseling continues toward new ways of understanding how to sustain love in the stages of age. Coupled love must now transform into an evolved intimacy system appropriate for love after fifty. The fourth concentration in our wonder-of-aging paradigm is the generous kind of love I call *intimate separateness.*

Adapting a relationship toward intimate separateness can help sustain marriage (or new partnership) through the fifties, sixties, seventies, eighties, and beyond. In this chapter, let's use the term "marriage" for any significant life partnership. Whether you are evolving a marriage of many decades or beginning a new one, your body and brain have matured by the time you are fifty into a self that needs different balances of desire and longing, ideal and real, aggression and conciliation, quietude and passion than before. As you age into and through the stages of age, emotional and sexual intimacy need to transform. "Duh!" we say. Yet few things are more difficult to do, unless we look closely at them. In this chapter, let's look closely at the evolution of both emotional and sexual intimacy as we age.

## Intimate Separateness

When we are young, love is desire plus closeness. When we are raising our children and working sixty hours a week, love is adrenaline and exhaustion, coupled with the million things to do, grabbing a few dates when we can, scheduling sex, and learning to communicate and conflict in ways that can bring out the best (most of the time) in both of us. From adolescence through adulthood and middle age, we perhaps think very little about how important "separateness" is to true love. We think mainly about intimacy.

But when we are aging, true love will not occur unless intimacy and separateness are equalized, in balance. In this equation, by "intimacy" we generally mean the attachment, bonding, and physical-psychological contact we have with our mate. "Separateness" means our own individual identity, free and developing on its own trajectory, coupled with our respect for our mate's individual, free identity, existing in the same life and home, and dependent on each other's common work and love, but not entangled or enmeshed together.

Especially in our modern world, in which marriage is such a fragile institution, true intimacy can't happen without equal parts intimacy and separateness. To see this visually, I like the acronym IS, intimate separateness: the reality of strong relationship, especially after kids are grown, is IS. The reality of love is IS.

I believe our culture as a whole blames the end of a marriage on lack of intimacy, as Corinne did, but that blame is thin. Marriages end as much from lack of separateness as from lack of intimacy. In early stages of love, the marriage goes through the times of "making any sacrifice" to make love last and knowing that "love is very hard work." The married couple knows "we'll destroy love if we selfishly try to hold on to a self too strongly," and the two people know "to have everlasting love, we have to constantly communicate, talk everything out, have no secrets, be close always." All these things are necessary for intimacy in perhaps the first decade or more of a marriage, and they become the focal point of human discussions of love.

Underneath the intimacy all along is the other component of love, the silent partner. The silent partner speaks more loudly as we reach our forties and move toward our fifties. Couples don't have language for it, but they sense that if we try to be too close to another person all of the time, we lose the person. The "too much separateness" (abandonment) culprit to a broken relationship is the one that seems most obvious to us when we first look back at failed love. That's the one easiest to talk about sadly with friends after a breakup. But when we look deeper, especially if we have the help of a counselor or friend, we may also notice that being too close (which usually manifests in control and manipulation of a partner to cover up our own sense of inadequacy) also destroys marriages and relationships. Now as we age, we are able, hopefully, to look back at a relationship clearly — look back before the tumult, before the gradual demise of sexual intimacy, before the constant fear we felt of the relationship imploding — and notice that our love may have been immature, unsturdy, unhappy in its terrifying, clinging adherence to a million knives of closeness. When we were fifteen or twenty-five or thirty-five or even forty-five, these million knives were unclear, but now we can see them if we will let ourselves.

The word in the field of psychology for "too close" or "million knives of closeness" is "enmeshed": enmeshment happens when we can't separate ourselves from our mate, nor can our mate separate himself or herself from us. *Our identities become enmeshed; we are trapped and caged in each other.* Our relationship, in this cage, comes to contradict the freedom of identity we are or have developed outside our marriage; at work, in sports, in other relationships with friends, in volunteer work, in raising our children and grandchildren, we build an identity, but in the marriage, we are having troubles. In the marriage, we are always arguing, or we are utterly withdrawn from the other person's identity. In the marriage, we have to cover up our own identity, for fear that our spouse won't like it, has a too-fragile ego if we assert ourselves, or won't support us if we ask for what we need. In our life outside of marriage, we are a "self," but after twenty years of marriage, we are trapped, unrealized, constantly being hurt by the other (and, if truth be told, we are also hurting the other).

If this is our situation, enmeshment is our psychological condition — we are like a fish caught in a net. Naturally, we will want to escape at some point. Five, ten, fifteen or more years into the marriage, our mate (or we ourselves) will begin making plans for the end of the enmeshment. We or our mate will seek freedom. It is natural, as we age, to try to become free. Eddie was the one who, unconsciously, felt the enmeshment more severely and began to fight off Corinne's attempts to be constantly intimate. Often, this happens — the husband begins the escape pattern, even though, statistically, most divorces are instigated by women. Often, too, the woman begins the escape pattern, and the man never sees it coming. Statistically, as of 2010, among both genders, people in their fifties comprise one-quarter of divorces in America today.

I believe Corinne came to see me because she unconsciously understood that she was actually much too "merged" with Eddie, too enmeshed. She had come to the time in her life when she was unconsciously realizing that she had developed a self over the last two decades by merging with her husband's and children's selves. This had been a courageous and functional self-sacrifice during the first decades of marriage and child rearing (one practiced by billions of people, women and men, in these same years), but now, in the age of transformation, this practice had to be transformed. She and Eddie could not sustain their next decades of happy marriage if her self and identity were merged (and submerged) in children who were grown or almost grown and a husband who was struggling to find a new way of being. Both Corinne and Eddie needed to transform from merged, enmeshed, and distant selves to independent selves able to practice the deep, miraculous love that intimate separateness provides us in our second lifetime.

## Women, Men, and Intimate Separateness

If, in reading this introduction to intimate separateness, you thought, "I bet women lean toward becoming too enmeshed and men probably lean toward becoming too separate," you would be right. This does not hold true in all cases, but still, most science-based relationship research shows that women tend to seek more "intimacy" (which becomes "merging" and "submerging") and men more "separateness" (which ultimately can feel like "distance" and "not loving"). A significant reason for this trend may lie in brain chemistry — oxytocin and vasopressin, as well as estrogen and testosterone, which affect intimacy and separateness.

Sue Carter, a psychologist and researcher at the Brain Body Center of the University of Illinois–Champaign, has studied the impact of these chemicals on both males and females. She has looked at the phenomenon we mentioned previously — how females increase their oxytocin levels when they are under stress. Females tend to seek increased intimacy (bonding) when they are involved in daily stressors. This means: whether the stress the woman feels comes from her relationship with her mate or from work or kids or other people or other experiences, her oxytocin/bonding chemical may rise and compel her brain system toward increased bonding with her spouse or others.

With men, on the other hand, vasopressin rises under stress, along with testosterone. Men will certainly try to increase bonding when they are stressed, but these chemicals can combine to create a greater "fight" (territoriality) or "flight" (independence) approach in men. Men will bond with other people, and sometimes they will bond as women do, but also, quite often, they will bond with cohorts in a competition or fighting group. They will seek others who will "do combat" with them, then remain independent, rather than bond in a verbal-emotive processing group or coupleship that talks about feelings in order to bond. The territorial aspect of men's responses to stress further shows up in outright attacks against people who are "in their space." When a man in a relationship feels stressed out by his partner's attempts to be intimate (especially if she is constantly "in his face, wanting to know what he feels" or "controls his intimacy," in his view), he may "fight her" in ways that hurt her feelings and disrespect her.

For its part, the "flight" instinct shows up in what Carter calls a kind of "brain freeze," primitive, internal state. In these flight moments and times, men try to become separate from the person threatening them or from a person who is trying to be supportive but is "in my face." Carter's research shows that while the female-dominant oxytocin appears to keep the woman's "vulnerable mammalian nervous system from regressing into the primitive states of lower brain-stem dominance (such as the 'reptile-like' freezing pattern with an associated shutdown of higher neural processes)," men, having much less oxytocin than women in general, go into emotional freeze states much more commonly than women, freeze states that cut men off from communication and closeness.

Neuroanthropologist Helen Fisher has confirmed this pattern in both human and animal studies around the world. After studying ten million people on a dating Web site, and matching that information with biological information, she has been able to determine four types of "relationship brains": the Explorer, the Builder, the Director, and the Negotiator. (To learn more about her original research, check the Notes and References section for this chapter.) Not surprisingly, Fisher reports that gender plays a significant role in love and intimacy as we age. For instance, "there are many more women than men in the Negotiator category, as there are many more men in the Director category." Negotiators tend to be deferential. Fisher writes, "Estrogen builds many more connections between the hemispheres of the brain and between the front and back of the brain, [making Negotiators] nurturing, trusting, and using diplomatic intelligence." On the other hand, she reports, Directors tend to be high testosterone, "analytical, logical, direct, decisive, tough-minded, good at rule-based systems, inventive, and not as social as other types. They tend to have only a few very close friendships and are not social butterflies."

The biology-based research of scientists such as Carter and Fisher gives a foundation for better understanding both intimacy and separateness. While both women and men experience both, and "gender patterns" don't always apply — some women are more "Director" than men, for instance — understanding gender tendencies can be one of a number of useful perspectives and tools for gauging where you and your partner are in regard to intimate separateness as you age. It can be a window into asking, "Am I too intimate?" and "Am I too separate?"

The "dark side" of the more "male" testosterone-vasopressin approach to relationships is that it tends toward independent separateness. The "dark side" of the "female" oxytocin approach to relationships is its tendency to overrely on dependent closeness. Our aging brains give us a chance now to build true interdependence, intimate separateness, now that we are fifty and over, but we must reframe and reorient both intimacy and separateness in order to experience the wonder of marriage well into the stages of age. If we

283

continue to unconsciously force too much remoteness or too much enmeshment, our marriages will probably fail. For relationships to flourish in the stages of age, intimate separateness is not a luxury — it is a necessity. Like Corinne and Eddie, we all need to transform the way we love during the age of transformation in order to make love last.

## The IS Survey

Here is a tool by which you can start to measure the degree to which you are now practicing healthy intimate separateness in your marriage.

Take a moment to ponder these points in your journal:

- Do I tend to emphasize intimacy over separateness? Yes ___ No ___

- Do I tend to emphasize separateness over intimacy? Yes ___ No ___

- Am I a "controller"? Yes ___ No ___

- Do I stay distant from my partner as much as possible?
  Yes ___ No ___

- Do my partner and I have weekly or

biweekly bonding rituals in place (date nights, lunches together)?
Yes \_\_\_ No \_\_\_

- Do I praise my partner's separate and individual identity at least a few times a week? Yes \_\_\_ No \_\_\_

- Do I assume my partner "knows I love her" or "knows I love him" (and thus needs few or no words of praise from me)? Yes \_\_\_ No \_\_\_

- Do I always have to be right in my marital conflicts? Yes \_\_\_ No \_\_\_

- Do I apologize to my partner when I hurt his or her feelings?
Yes \_\_\_ No \_\_\_

- Do I forgive my partner for his or her flaws? Yes \_\_\_ No \_\_\_

- Do I know enough about gender differences to value the other gender's way of doing relationship?
Yes \_\_\_ No \_\_\_

- Do I criticize or try to control my partner's behavior once a day or

285

more? Yes \_\_\_ No \_\_\_

- Am I having satisfying sex with my partner, even if not as frequently as before? Yes \_\_\_ No \_\_\_

- Do I like to hear what my partner is thinking and feeling? Yes \_\_\_ No \_\_\_

- Do we (my partner and I) allow each other our own "domains," areas of interests, about which we exert no control? Yes \_\_\_ No \_\_\_

- Do we admire each other's work and hobbies? Yes \_\_\_ No \_\_\_

- Do we compliment each other in public and with friends?
Yes \_\_\_ No \_\_\_

Talk about these questions with your spouse, a counselor, or your circle of friends. See where the dialogue takes you. A picture to keep in mind is of two hands. Enmeshed intimacy (too much intimacy) is two hands clasping each other. Distant independence (too much separateness) is the two hands being held away from each other at arm's length. Intimate separateness is the two hands held in front of you, facing each other, at about three inches apart. This is mature love in the second half of life.

As you discuss the survey, talk about whether you believe you and your partner know how to be both intimate and separate. Ask:

- In what ways am I good at being intimate? In what ways am I better at it than my partner?

- In what ways am I good at being separate? In what ways am I better at it than my partner?

- In what ways is my partner good at being intimate? In what ways is my partner better at it than I am?

- In what ways is my partner good at being separate? In what ways is my partner better at it than I am?

In your journal, list bullet points as answers and write paragraphs and narrative. Tell the story of your relationship, especially over the last five years, and match your own and your partner's stories. Even if your partner will not do this with you, you will still gain from this, and there will be much here to talk about with your friends. At first, Corinne had to do all of this work on her own. Eddie was resistant. Corinne journaled, answered questions, spoke with her circle of friends, rethought intimacy, separateness, and her identity. She began a new course of turning her mind somewhat away from dependence on Eddie to confirm her existence and value, and she began to develop her own discrete value — pursuing more challenging work, working in counseling on her fear of inadequacy in relation to Eddie's quiet, sometimes nonconfirming distance. In the case of her marriage, her "pulling away" from dependence on Eddie created change in the marriage. Eddie began to look at her differently, with more respect and with less fear that she would keep trying to drain him, enmesh him, be dissatisfied with him emotionally, and mirror his failures. It took over a year of Corinne's work on herself before Eddie asked, "Maybe do you think I should go see that Gurian guy with you once?"

One of the best things about a holistic, balanced, IS approach to mature love in the age of transformation is that one of your teachers is living with you. As you focus on the ways your partner is as good as or better than you at being intimate and separate, you can learn those skills, too. It would be best if two partners do this together all the time, but sometimes one partner must take the lead and hope the other will follow.

## How You Will Know You Have Embraced Intimate Separateness

Is there a way to know if you have developed, adapted, and matured your love relationship to become a holistic balance of intimacy and separateness? There is. After taking time (and it could take months or years) to re-evaluate, renew, and adapt your relationship toward the low-stress, high-quality intimate-separateness approach, check in with the following version of the intimacy-separateness survey and see how you are now doing. The more "yes" answers you now have, the better: more yeses mean you have decreased as much chronic relational stress as you can right now, and you have built your own part of a relationship that will help you sustain and protect the wonder of aging over the next decades.

- Have I or my partner let go of control over each other's "domains"? (Do we let each other have areas of focus and daily life over which we exert no control?) Yes ____ No ____

- Do we have a sense of humor together, especially about my own and my partner's foibles, eccentricities, weaknesses, personality quirks, and vulnerabilities? Yes ___ No ___

- Do we have weekly or biweekly bonding rituals in place (date nights, lunches together)? Yes ___ No ___

- Do we praise each other's identity and actions at least a few times a week? Yes ___ No ___

- Do we each allow the other to be right in some of our marital conflicts? Yes___ No ___

- Do we apologize to each other within hours after hurting the other's feelings? Yes ___ No ___

- Do we generally forgive each other's flaws and our own? Yes ___ No ___

- Do we allow for gender differences in the ways we practice intimacy and separateness as women and men? Yes ___ No ___

- Have we cut back on our criticism of each other? Yes ___ No ___

- Are we having satisfying sex, even if not as frequently as before?
  Yes ___ No ___

- Do we enjoy hearing what each other is thinking and feeling?
  Yes ___ No

- Do we compliment each other in public and with friends?
  Yes ___ No ___

If you say yes to most of these, you are moving in the direction of de-stressed and mature love. You are embracing IS in love that lasts. You are moving toward or have accomplished one of the most wonderful and joyful parts of aging: setting a new foundation for sustaining a loving partnership for the rest of your life. You have realized, and acted on the realization, that what was love began, when we were young, as a map of intimacy and a mirror of self that we used in order to seek the other, our partner, our mate, as well as ourselves, our soul; we held on to the mirror and followed the map for many years, even decades. Somewhere, maybe at seven years, or at ten or fifteen or twenty years of marriage, one or both of us experimented with giving up the map we had, giving up the mirror. This was painful, scary. It felt like, before, we knew our best friend well, but now, perhaps, we no longer did; before, we had found what we were looking for in love, but now, as the experiment of age occurs, we have lost love.

Hopefully, somewhere in this pain and fear, we see new possibilities for love. We see that tossing out the youthful map and mirror might bring a new identity, new contentment with self and other, a new way of being safe, loving, true, real — equally attached and detached, equally "in love" and "loving." The biological, social, and psychological changes that happen to us and within us in the age of transformation are generally the concentration point for learning this next stage of human love.

In all this is the miracle of growing older in our time and era: as we've noted, our ancestors had either died by now or stayed married because that is just what people did. We in our new millennium have freedom of choice, and we have many decades in which to exercise that freedom by developing, now, IS. Whether we choose to stay married or choose to divorce, the internal wonder we can now experience for a whole second lifetime is the evolved, mature love of intimate separateness. It is well worth the challenge, and to meet the challenge we may need friendship circles, couples groups, workshops, counseling, marriage encounter workshops, and other structures of love and support that can help us take human love out of the complaints and the deep grief of losing the youthful ways of love and into the deep, lasting joy of new intimacy and new sexuality as we age.

> Jeneene got cancer, and it took her quickly. She was fifty-four. In the final weeks that she was able to talk, she said things to me that have guided me since. She said, "Don't spend the rest of your life worrying about me. I'm going to be fine. I'm going to where you're going, I'm just getting there earlier." And she said, "Love should be stronger than anything. Promise me you'll let yourself love again after I'm gone." And the thing she said that makes me cry eight years later is, "Brad, you always did your best to love me — that and the kids are your greatest gift to me."
>
> — Brad, 59

Jan, fifty-six, and Chris, fifty-eight, came to see me for marital issues. Chris, an overweight man, wore a goatee and had a receding hairline. His hair and goatee were silver in spots, brown in others, giving his face a distinguished look. His eyes, a deep blue, offset against his dark and silver hair so that they twinkled. His face had a few lines at the eyes and cheeks, but not a lot. He was handsome, especially in his kind smile, though clearly self-conscious about his weight.

Jan was equally attractive. Because she, too, was somewhat overweight, she wore loose jeans and a loose blue blouse accentuated by a turquoise necklace and earrings. Her brown eyes were set inside a tanned face and her hair was blondish silver. She later confessed she had once dyed her hair but did so no longer, proud of her looks now. Her smile was somewhat more of a wry grin than her husband's, and her manner more wistful than his.

As we talked together, I learned that this couple was having issues with sexuality. Jan had had a hysterectomy at forty-eight. Chris, who had struggled with anxiety-related issues for much of his life, went on anxiety and depression medications when he was fifty-three. The couple had both gained weight,

Jan now forty pounds overweight, Chris twenty pounds over. Jan and Chris also worked together, which meant they were in contact constantly throughout their days, a circumstance that can deepen intimacy but also destroy it. "Maybe we're together a little too much," Jan suggested immediately. As we talked further, it became clear that this couple had not accommodated the stages of aging. They were not aware of new, freeing directions for their love of each other. They didn't have the passion they had twenty, even ten years ago, and felt an immense grief.

In one session, Chris opened up about their sex life. "I'm just not who I was anymore — I don't know if it's the meds I'm taking or what, but if I'm going to be able to perform, I need more . . . 'help' — from Jan, you know? I need some oral sex, and she says it hurts her knees to do that . . . I don't know, it's embarrassing, but we aren't really intimate much anymore." Before I could ask for timelines, Jan agreed. "My vibrator is my friend sexually now. I love Chris, but sex is tough for us. We love each other, but . . . things aren't what they were, that's for sure." She confessed that they were having sexual intercourse every six months or so.

Sexuality can be a crucial part of intimate separateness: this couple was too separate sexually; sex was out of balance with the needs of love both people felt. In working with Jan and Chris, I worked with a couple whose honesty most probably would not have been possible, at least in such detail, in any previous generation. It is part of the wonder of aging in our generation, the awe and curiosity we can all enjoy, if we open ourselves fully to who we now are. "When it comes to sex at our age," I counseled them, "just about anything is within the range of normal, and we can be much freer now than ever before about all of it, so let's talk about all of it." Jan was somewhat shier about sex than Chris but gradually became equally honest and open. This most probably saved their marriage.

## First, the Truth About Sex After Fifty

How important is sex to the wonder of aging? Where does sex fit in the IS paradigm?

Sex is very important, especially in Stage 1, and sex is especially important to some people more than others in helping balance intimacy and separateness. Though we may have sex less frequently now, our brains still think about and even rely on sex more than we may realize. A recent study conducted by Omri Gillath at the University of Kansas discovered that sexual stimuli "affect mood, motivations, and how the brain responds . . .

296

subliminal exposure to sexual primes even increased positive affect and motivation." Volunteers in the study were exposed to hidden sexual primes via pictures and other stimulants (images of sex in photos or video). Following the sexual primes, they were more likely than without the primes to continue working on or finish even a boring puzzle or anagram (thoughts about sex were that motivating!). Gillath's neuroimaging showed that the sexual primes — even ones people are unaware of — aroused more areas of the brain in both women and men than when no sexual primes occurred. In women's brains, more "control" centers of the brain were aroused than in men; in men's brains, more "arousal" occurred in motivation centers.

This study is one of many showing how important sex is after fifty. Sex can extend life by releasing stress, reducing pain in many cases, decreasing depression and anxiety, improving sleep, strengthening blood vessels and improving our immune system, lowering the risk of certain cancers, such as prostate and breast cancer, and helping people be intimate in new, thrilling, evolving, and healthy ways.

At the same time, we all know that it is normal for sexual drive to decrease. That is one truth we maneuver around as we grow older.

What are some others? Here are seven truths I use with clients. I have found these "truths" to especially affect one's sex life after fifty. Knowledge of them can help you create an agreed-upon baseline for intimate separateness in your relationship.

**Truth #1: There is no single truth that applies to everyone's sex life as we age — just about anything is within the range of normal.** Few areas of human development show more variety than the sex life of people over fifty. Thus, if you or your partner is insisting on one way of measuring sexual intimacy, you or your partner might be using sex to enmesh (or keep distant) the relationship. Sex evolves with the relationship, as a part of mature love, not as a social or cultural ideal to follow.

The latest National Survey of Sexual Health and Behavior (2010) elicited these facts regarding sexuality. The ultimate message of the survey is variety and diversity:

- The majority of men over fifty masturbate, and nearly half of women in this age group masturbate. About five times the number of men over fifty masturbate four times a week compared to women over fifty. Of men between fifty and sixty who masturbate, most do so a few times a month.

- Within the past year, almost 40 percent of men over fifty gave oral sex to their partner, but only 25 percent of women over fifty gave it. Similar statistics were revealed for receiving oral sex: just under 40 percent of men received it and only 25 percent of women received it.

- Within the past year, more than half of men over fifty had intercourse but only 40 percent of women over fifty had intercourse. Very few men and even fewer women had intercourse multiple times per week (10 percent for men, 7 percent for women). The "average" was between one and three times per month for sexually active men and women over fifty, with more men having sex three times per month and more women having sex once a month. (This difference implies that men were having more partners than women were.)

- Anal sex was used by 7 percent of men over fifty in the last year and 4 percent of women over fifty.

- An erectile medication was used at least once in the last year by 8 percent of men between fifty and sixty, 30 percent of men sixty to seventy, 23 percent of men seventy to eighty, and 19 percent of men over eighty.

The bottom line: nearly any sexual pattern you are in right now is shared by someone else in the world. "Normal" when it comes to sex is relative. You and your partner do not have to be ashamed of discussing anything in your sex lives. Everything is real.

**Truth #2: As we age, all of us do end up having less sex than we had before.** A decrease in sexual frequency for both women and men is a fact of life after fifty, even if you are a person who puts off that decrease for a number of years via the use of Viagra or other drugs. Thus, sex becomes a natural way of bringing more healthy separateness into a marriage. If you have noticed a decreased sex drive with your partner in recent years, you are most probably in a very normal decline of sex drive that can be accompanied by greater growth and transformation in emotional, spiritual, and social areas of life. Nature is priming you for the wonder of aging by diminishing a number of the chemicals you need in order to experience sexual desire — testosterone, estrogen, dopamine, oxytocin. Neuropsychiatrist Louann Brizendine has pointed out, "By fifty, men have lost half of their adrenal testosterone and 60 percent of the testosterone produced by the testes." That decline continues throughout the next decade and beyond. For women, the decline in the sex drive chemistry can be even harsher than for men. Brizendine writes, "By fifty, women's levels have dropped by up to 70 percent — leaving them with very low testosterone levels." This does not mean there aren't some women who have a high sex drive after fifty. These are simply averages for you to consider as you look at intimate separateness and the natural transformations that can happen in us all. Both you and your sexual partner are changing physically — your bodies and physiques are becoming less and less nubile (attractive for physical mating and the production of children) — less lean (more fat) and less erect in body posture (more stooped over). Your approach to everyday life is probably also becoming less socially aggressive, thus less sexually attractive to a potential mate. And for more of us than we realize, medications are profoundly affecting sex drive. Medications for blood pressure, anxiety, and nearly any other physical or mental condition can affect sex drive and performance.

Quite often, patients and clients will come into clinical practices like mine with the hope of finding a way to have as much sex as they were having earlier in life. It will feel to them like they are losing a large part of their identity because their sex life is not working as it once did. In counseling, the process of understanding why sex drive is changing becomes a spiritual and self-psychology issue for a person or couple transforming into the second half of life. Some couples learn to engage in discerning the actual causes of diminished drive (medications, body changes, menopause or andropause, psychological issues) and may find themselves, following the discernment, with a rebirth of sexual interest. They may try new things, new devices, new positions and approaches. Some couples — especially those who have tried nearly every experimental sexual device or position already in the last decade — end up finding a deep peace in their diminished sex drive.

If you are experiencing diminished sex drive, make sure to get a medical and psychological assessment and help; talk with people around you, people your age; reach out to trusted women and men. You will feel less alone, and you will find resonance for the truths about sex after fifty that you are learning in your own life. One question regarding sex drive that I am often asked is: "My spouse doesn't initiate sex anymore. Should I worry that my marriage is in trouble?" Corinne did not want to leave our first session without an answer to this.

The answer can be yes if there are other marital problems, but if the marriage is sound, the answer is generally no. This "no" is especially the case if there has been a life change for the noninitiating partner (Eddie was constantly exhausted now, and had very little energy for initiating sex; he was also going through andropause — his testosterone levels had dropped) or if one or both partners have gone through a change that makes them less sexually attractive.

The case of Simon and Melissa illustrates this latter point. Simon was fifty-two and Melissa was forty-nine when they entered a time in which he, who used to initiate sex, no longer did. Simon would have sex, but only when Melissa initiated it. This was a total turnaround from the previous twenty-three years of marriage, and it scared Melissa. As I worked with the couple, it became clear that life circumstances had changed for them both. Simon's job, like Eddie's, had changed, requiring him to commute three hours a day. Also, he was on a low dose of anxiety medication to help with sleeplessness and stress. That medication was affecting his sex drive.

Simultaneously, Melissa, who had been a marathon runner, had developed lower back issues, and cut back on previous athletic activities. She was becoming sedentary, somewhat depressed, and gaining a great deal of weight. She desperately wanted to get back to exercising more, but she wasn't sure when that would happen. Her two children from her first marriage were grown, and she had a grandchild whom she cared for every morning, which gave her great joy, but still, she was unable to interact with this grandchild (chase him, roll on the floor with him, etc.) as she wished she could.

Life circumstances had changed for this couple, and each life change potentially affected sex life and intimacy. Melissa's depression and weight gain were physical and mental factors that diminished her sexual attractiveness to her husband.

Decreased sex drive can be worrisome to a couple, but quite often it is evidence of other life circumstances, not a condemnation or inadequacy in a marriage. And very often, as in the case of Simon and Melissa, a year or two gone by will change situations again: in their case, a year later, Simon's job changed and he was able to work again in his own city; simultaneously, Melissa's physical therapy worked and she was able to develop a new, age-appropriate active life. As both people felt more whole, both de-stressed their lives, and their sex life became more equal in initiation and even stronger for having worked through the adversity it had faced.

**Special Note:** As we get older, our immune system declines, and we human beings very smartly (even if unconsciously) compensate: we seek to have less physical contact, if possible, with people who might be infected or carrying germs that could make us sick. This is another reason we initiate and have less sex as we age. If you've felt a burst of sex drive quickly diminish when your spouse or partner sneezes or shows flu-like or other illness symptoms, self-protectiveness might be the cause of your internal experience. Your sex drive may be quite high at that moment, and you might be ready for lovemaking, but then the decision-making center in your brain (the prefrontal cortex) convinces your sexual arousal centers in the hypothalamus that sex right now might lead to debilitating illness.

**Truth #3: A woman's sex drive is more likely to decrease and stay lower for longer periods of time than a man's.** While for men there is the physical possibility of erectile dysfunction (caused generally by disease, aging, or medications), and while that dysfunction can definitely affect sex drive and performance, for women there are far more physical conditions related to diminished sex drive and performance than there are in men. So, statistically, if a person is going to have decreased sex drive for extended periods of time as we age, it is more likely to be the woman.

The National Survey of Sexual Health and Behavior of 2010 found that for women fifty and over, each year of life, on average, is accompanied by a 5 percent decline of frequency of sexual intercourse and a 7 percent decline in receiving and giving oral sex. Thus, over the time span of the age of transformation, women, on average, will experience a 50 percent decline in sexual frequency.

According to Dr. Susan Reed, a peri- and postmenopause specialist at the University of Washington, women's nerve conduction systems change at around or after fifty (making a woman's sensitivity to touch different than it was); her clitoris size can change; various other chemicals, such as nitric oxide, can change in her bloodstream, decreasing sexual energy; her ability to lubricate sex organs can change. In tandem with menopause, a woman can develop a number of physical, biochemical, and biological issues that further explain her decline in sex drive and sexual activity, such as dyspareunia (pain with intercourse), vaginismus (an involuntary spasm of vaginal muscles), or noncoital sexual pain (genital pain that is induced by noncoital sex).

In a study called SWAN (Study of Women's Health Across the Nation) conducted with 3,302 women aged forty-two to fifty-two, and including samples from the Massachusetts Women's Health Study and three other major studies, women reported changes in these seven areas: desire, arousal, sexual frequency, pain, physical pleasure, emotional satisfaction with partner, and decreasing importance of sex.

Nature is doing stuff to us every day now. As our bodies change, we are challenged by the cause of intimate separateness constantly: to balance intimacy and separateness in a new way by working through sexual changes and making sure to adjust toward new sexual intimacies and, simultaneously, by moving toward other conversations and actions of love that feel independent, soulful, and interdependent without reliance on sex as a baseline for love.

**Truth #4: Men are more dependent on orgasms than women.** According to the National Survey of Sexual Health and Behavior (2010), 85 percent of men report that their partner had an orgasm at the most recent sexual event, but only 64 percent of women report having had an orgasm at that most recent sexual event. This is a difference that appears to be robust around the world. Men tend to think women are having more orgasms than they are actually having.

The study also found that women are more likely to orgasm when they engage in a variety of sex acts, including cunnilingus, masturbation, and use of vibrators. At the same time, a number of studies have shown that women are generally more satisfied with frequency of orgasm than men are — men tend to want more orgasms more of the time. For some women, satisfactory sexual experiences can involve "just being connected" in bed or elsewhere rather than being based solely or mainly on orgasms.

Knowing this and fully inculcating it into our thinking as individuals and couples can be liberating as we age. We can get rid of the "shoulds" we bought into years ago regarding orgasms. We can see other ways of being intimate. At the same time, if your partner (or you) reports agitation or anxiety related to achieving or not achieving orgasm, take it seriously. Unsatisfying sex can damage a relationship. Make sure to communicate with your partner about what you need in order to enjoy sex in general and achieve orgasm in particular. To whatever extent you did not talk about what you needed before, your marriage now needs that dialogue in it if you are to move into new, healthy, de-stressed ways of love that combine intimacy and separateness in balance.

Especially in our fifties, valuing our relationship and protecting it sexually may involve doing things to help our partner achieve orgasm that we did not do before. In this way, adjusting sexually to our partner's needs in new, adventurous ways can become a pathway to making intimacy adjustments in other areas of our partnership. (This will be discussed in more detail later in this chapter.) Leesa, fifty-four, told me, "I just wasn't getting help from Jim in having an orgasm, and even after twenty-six years of marriage, he still couldn't talk about what I needed. But he was in his fifties now and needed more manual and oral help from me to achieve an erection. So finally I just said,

'Look, you need more blow jobs from me now to get erect, so I need your tongue on me. That's just the way it is.' I was scared when I gave him this ultimatum, but because I put it to him as a transaction, he got it. We got some sex therapy, and we take care of each other better now." In this case, communication worked!

**Truth #5: Masturbation is generally good for you, and good for aging.** In the National Survey of Sexual Health and Behavior, most people report having masturbated at some point — among men, 95 percent; among women, 85 percent. Among men between fifty and sixty, 56 percent masturbated in the past month and 72 percent over the last year. Among women between fifty and sixty, the numbers were lower: 28 percent masturbated in the last month and 54 percent in the last year. For men and women both, these percentage numbers decrease about 10 percent per decade as life continues, with masturbation still a key component of sex life well into the eighties and nineties for women and men who can still physically accomplish the task alone or with a partner.

Few feelings can be more easily described as "a feeling of freedom" than the sexual pleasure and release of successful masturbation. Masturbation is embarrassing for people to talk about, but it can be of great value, especially as we age. In fact, pushing beyond our socially conditioned shame regarding masturbation and mutual masturbation may become a key component of a successful sex life and of intimacy after fifty. It may be essential to long-lasting marriage, especially if we need more sexual release than our partner, who may be ill, can be involved in with us. As we age, masturbation is a cure for slow erections (or, even, fears that we can't get erect) for men, and for increased lubrication for women. Masturbation preceding sex can become a pleasant ritual that bonds us together in ways we did not bond before.

My attitude toward sexuality, both my own and my wife's, has changed since I took a class in the truths about sex in our fifties and got rid of a lot of what was in my head. I am 58, a man, brought up a certain way. I never had a lot of male friends that I could talk to, so I wasn't sure what was real or correct in bed. My wife was pretty traditional, too, though we did try a few things back in our thirties.

Things changed for us when I was having constant prostatitis. On one particular visit, my doctor said I should masturbate a lot. During that visit I asked him about some troubles I was having with getting an erection. I had tried Viagra but had side effects from that and just didn't want to go that route, so my doctor asked if my wife gave me oral sex or even manual manipulation to get me going. I said no.

So my doctor said not only should I masturbate a number of times per week to keep my prostate cleaned out, but also that I probably needed to explain to my wife that I needed more help from her now than I had before. I learned that it was normal that I couldn't get an erection as easily as I used to. I went home and talked to Claire about it and she said she had sort of begun suspecting that, but the way we were both brought up kept her from helping out much.

We've both made changes sexually now and we're much happier. We have a deal: she gives me more oral sex and I give her more oral sex. My medical problem and a chance word to my doctor took us down a road we were probably scared to go down from when we were kids in the church. Claire feels like a big weight is lifted, and for myself, I feel better about myself and about being a man who's going to be 60 soon. I didn't realize before how scared I had become of growing older, and how much bad sex and weird ideas about sex played a big part in how scared I was.

— Al, 58

**Truth #6: Pornography can be useful to the aging brain.** Both women and men can enjoy pornography, but men more often tend to enjoy visual pornography, and women tend to enjoy written erotica. Ogi Ogas and Sai Gaddam, computational neuroscientists, analyzed a billion Web searches using a computer model and confirmed that "women are very different from men in how they use online services. All across the planet, what most women seek out, in growing numbers, are not explicit scenes of sexual activity but character-driven stories of romantic relationships." Females in general equally measure three aspects of a man's suitability — physical, social, and emotional — whereas men in general measure the physical over the other two.

When we think of pornography, we don't

tend to think of romance novels — we tend to think of pictures and films, which are visual, so we think of porn as more "a male thing." For women in the age of transformation and older, "porn" can be romance novels. And since pornography exists all over the world and goes back many millennia — think, for instance, of the Kama Sutra — it is difficult to argue, from a scientific perspective, that pornography is inherently wrong or bad. Approximately one-fifth of people over fifty report using visual sexual pornography to enhance intimacy, and far more probably do so but do not feel comfortable reporting their use in surveys.

If you are a porn user or know someone who is, these statistics might be interesting:

- Just over one half of Internet spending is related to sex, and United States porn revenues exceed the combined revenues of all the major TV networks put together.

- On a given day, almost 25 percent of men but only 5 to 10 percent of women visit a visual porn site (this decreases as we age).

- Women buy the majority (approximately 90 percent) of "soft porn" romance novels, insisting on less graphic sexuality than men and more emotional buildup to sexual union.

- Men comprise about three-fourths of porn site users, and many incidents of women's use of porn sites involve women watching or utilizing the site with their male companion.

- Most men and women who visit or use porn sites are not diagnosed with sexual or compulsive disorders (the figure for disorders is around 8 percent for both men and women).

For biological reasons, many aging men often need pornography in order to become sexually capable. As our testosterone, sex drive, and sexual functions dissipate in their aggressiveness, we often need all the help we can get. Women, too, may lose interest in sex for extended periods of time during menopause and beyond but may understand that sexual contact is important to their marriage or relationship; thus they might read or view pornography or read romance novels to get in the mood. These uses are normal and helpful and can create good bonding.

If pornography has entered your life or the life of your spouse or a friend to the extent that other social interactions and social accomplishments have been affected by the use of the porn, it may have become dangerous. It is probably associated with constant masturbation and may have entered the realm of a sexual addiction, which afflicts increasing numbers of people every year. If you, your spouse, or a friend is trying to get sex many times a week or is trying to get many different partners, he or she may have a sexual addiction. If he or she is accessing porn constantly, every day, he or she may have an addiction.

If you are seeing evidence of this addiction for more than two months, consult with a specialist — therapist, psychologist, or psychiatrist — and set up an intervention. This intervention can be handled in the AA model, just as you would do for an alcohol or drug addiction. As much as possible, utilize professional therapists to help you with these interventions. Some people in need of these interventions may require medication.

If, however, you or your spouse are not in a porn or sex addiction pattern, you might want to alter your view of porn somewhat — at least to see that it does have some utility for people over fifty. Visual and erotic stimulation is useful for sexual intimacy in the vast majority of cases in which it is used.

**Truth #7: Sexual fantasies, even "strange ones," can become holistic parts of sexual health.** Men fantasize about the sex act itself more often in a day than women do. One study found more than half of men fantasize about sex several times a day; another found the number even higher. Most studies agree that the number for women's sexually explicit fantasies per day is much lower than men's (though women have many more romantic fantasies per day than men).

Another finding studies generally agree on may be a surprise to many people: sexual fantasies cannot be deemed unhealthy, since they occur as often or more often in people who have the fewest sexual issues and who report highest satisfaction. If you thought your sexual fantasies might harm you or your partner, you might need to rethink that stressor — even if those fantasies involve women or men or images of women or men who are not your spouse or partner. In fact, the images in your mind and scenarios you play out may actually help your marriage or life partnership stay strong in your fifties and beyond. They may stimulate and motivate you to bond even more completely with your partner. Many women and even more men often need these fantasies in order to perform sexually.

That said, all or most of us are capable of having sexual fantasies that scare us or go against our normal morality. If you thought perhaps there was something wrong with you because your fantasies seem contrary to other ethical parts of your life, you might want to focus on whether those fantasies are increasing your stress level significantly. If they are not (i.e., if they, too, are helpful to keeping you sexually active), they may be just fine. If they are significantly increasing your own stress level or the stress level of someone you love, you may want to get help to sort through them.

Studies show that women and men often report similar fantasies, but more women report taking a passive role in their fantasies and more women than men report wanting to be dominated. The phenomenon of the *Fifty Shades of Grey* trilogy illustrates this point. In that set of erotic romance novels, a young woman begins her journey of love with a dominant man by entering a contract of sexual submission. The novel reflects a statistic: more men than women fantasize about being the dominant partner or having multiple partners to dominate. This is true even for monogamous women and men, and it is true also for many women who are dominant in the workplace and for many men who are not.

When sexual fantasy is harmful to another person or to you yourself, it is dangerous, and you can see the danger: the fantasies drive you away from the person you love and toward promiscuous, harmful behavior. They push you toward too much separateness, too little intimacy. The IS paradigm gets out of balance.

But much of the time, sexual fantasy just is: it is not wrong or right, it is just a part of brain chemistry and blood flow in the brain that stimulates us to feel comfortable, vital, interested, and useful to our partner. It gives pleasure and joy. This can even be the case for people who have violent sexual fantasies. Often in counseling, I will hear a story of a violent sexual fantasy in a man or woman who is not a violent person. That woman or man will worry that the violent fantasy is a perversion. While it can be, more often it is not. The etiology of violent sexual fantasies often lies in childhood sexual, physical, or emotional abuse. The man or woman is now in his or her fifties or beyond and has an internal array of fantasies that are sourced in having been spanked frequently or beaten by a parent, or abused in some other similar way. The violent fantasies probably first showed up in adolescence and then developed throughout adulthood, expanding in variety in the brain and retained in the brain's memory centers. The violent fantasies become stimulated when the person becomes sexually stimulated or wishes to be. Quite often, especially as the man ages, he needs to rely on them to get an erection so he can perform for his spouse sexually, but the fantasies generally do not cause any perverted, aberrant, or dangerous behavior. They are just sexual fantasies sourced in childhood that linger (and even help) a person for life.

Having this kind of liberating, realistic, and optimistic attitude about something as private as a violent sexual fantasy is part of the joy of gaining from age all that you need to gain in order to feel whole, adequate, vital, and happy. Making peace with "strange" sexual fantasies may end up a part of one's journey to freedom. As appropriate, it may be a way one can continue growing a sense of adequacy that now replaces a sense of inadequacy sexually. It can even become a part of intimate separateness success, as it helps bond partners through their mutual respect of the other's quirks, eccentricities, and deep, revealing parts of the self and identity that can now be integrated safely into a long-lasting marriage.

## THE MONOGAMY GENE

One of the most asked questions I receive at my lectures and via e-mail regards why some people are monogamous and some are not. Intimate separateness can be very difficult when trust is broken. It is not impossible — I have worked with couples in which either or both people had affairs and those marriages have, nonetheless, succeeded — but few breaches of love destroy more marriages as we age than this one.

Increasingly over the last twenty-five years, scientists have been studying why some people remain monogamous and others don't. While most married people do not stray on their spouses (only 20 to 25 percent of men and 10 to 15 percent of women have extramarital sex), most human beings have more than one sexual partner in a lifetime. Thus, we are not a primarily monogamous species. We are what is called by biologists "serial maters." Premarital sex and divorce are the two life stages most commonly linked to this statistic: unlike monogamous species, such as swans, who mate for life, we humans are *both* "maters for life" and "*not* maters for life," making our intimacy and our separateness complex.

New scientific evidence over the last two decades indicates that we may have genetic and chromosomal markers for monogamy and nonmonogamy. These markers may specifically control our dopamine-oxytocin link when we mate sexually and emotionally with a partner. It may work this way: for all of us, mating (sex and intimacy) activates genetic markers that connect our brain's dopamine-flooded reward chemistry with our sexual and emotional chemistry. For some of us though, those markers may only activate with a single partner once we find that partner. But for others, those markers and that dopamine chemistry may not activate with a single partner but continue to activate with multiple partners. Thus, you may marry someone who promises to be monogamous but who may not be genetically or chemically monogamous; similarly, we ourselves may make the promise, then discover we are not monogamous.

This new scientific evidence regarding monogamy is controversial but can be helpful to us in understanding fidelity and infidelity as we age. I have used this new scientific information to work with couples whose marriages have been shocked by infidelity. When one or both partners have been nonmonogamous during marriage, I ask the couple about family histories — most often, infidelity has existed in the family line, on either the maternal or paternal side or on both sides.

For some couples, isolating nonmonogamy as a biological trait helps to isolate the psychological issues that the couple brings to the marriage. Two comments by a couple in counseling illustrate this. He was fifty-two and she was fifty-one; they had been married twenty-six years and had two grown children.

He: I don't know why I had the affairs. I love my wife. I just never understood. I never wanted to hurt her. When I saw Bill Clinton and Arnold Schwarzenegger and those guys doing it, I thought, "They're not like me, I'm better than them," but I wasn't, and I knew I was doing a bad thing, but I just couldn't understand why I was doing it.

She: I don't know if I can stay married to him now that I know about the affairs, but I am glad to understand about the science of this. If it's true, then I'm not some ugly, fat, inadequate wife that drove him to stray, and he's not an evil person. There's something else going on. If there's any chance I can trust him again, knowing the science helps.

These honest words led to significant growth and transformation for this couple. For many couples, it is not enough help, and for all couples, deeper work in both intimacy and separateness are needed if partners have strayed, but even in a small way, the new science on monogamy may help couples heal the spirit of broken love in the stages of age, especially the age of transformation, when everyone is going through menopause and andropause, and a number of men and women shock their marriages with affairs.

## A NEW WAY OF LOVE

Lao-tzu said, "Being deeply loved by someone gives you strength, while loving someone deeply gives you courage." The second half of life is potentially a time of miraculous love, a love that has shed many skins, transformed into many different forms, and keeps changing, becoming more distinct, and becoming more complete throughout the stages of age. As we grow, we are called on to become courageous about love in ways we were not before — ways of honesty, forthrightness, adaptability, new knowledge, deeper wisdom.

Many of us grow past fifty, sixty, seventy, and come to realize that we can be elders in other parts of life but not in love. We are still not succeeding at love, no matter how hard we try. Many of us are succeeding, and think, "I'm not sure why, but I'll take it. I hope it lasts."

Intimate separateness is, I believe, a kind of freedom and liberation that protects love beyond the first decade or two of marriage. I hope every couple at any stage of love will wonder over the wisdom of this IS paradigm — wonder over it in sexuality, intimacy, monogamy, and even separation and divorce. And I hope every couple contemplating divorce will get professional help with the paradigm in order to develop the freedom to be both intimate and separate.

Ultimately, if we are not free as we age, we will love our mate under gray clouds that never quite turn to nourishing rain or give way to sun. For both of us, every day will be a struggle of duty and anger, and we will glare at each other, blinded by shame. "Where has the radiance gone?" we will wonder, aging now, feeling that we must become free in our relationships or else why stay in them? If we are wondering that, our partner is surely wondering, "How do I open my cage and make a new journey?" A great deal is at stake in this second lifetime of being able to love someone clearly, wholly, with depth, and with beauty. Love cannot be what it was, and that is okay. The new reality of love is our miracle, and that new reality is made of much more than previous ideals of intimacy — it is a kind of freedom no one can give us:

we have to take it by taking our next step in learning how to love another human being with mind and heart in balance.

God enters by a private door
into every individual.
— Ralph Waldo Emerson

Concern yourself not with what you tried
and failed to do, but with what is still
possible for you to do.
— Pope John XXIII

We are shaped and fashioned by
what and who we love.
— Johann Wolfgang von Goethe

A close family is but an earlier heaven.
— Anonymous

## MEDITATION 6: THE TEACHERS

Every person possesses wisdom, but is every person wise? What person, reaching the age of the elder, hasn't lived life in flawed, inept, irritable, impatient, imprecise, enslaving ways? We know we have wandered some days without purpose and given bad advice; we have wasted our life energy in images and idols; we have spent too little time in prayer, meditation, and peace; we have lied, coveted, destroyed; all of us, some time or another, stray into illegal or immoral dens within ourselves or without; and our words are often borrowed, not our own, obscuring codes that confuse rather than console. Who are we, then, to be wise?

Our grandchildren say: *If not you, who?*

If I will not dare to be free, who will? If I will not share my hard-earned flaws, why have I worked so hard to illuminate myself before life's judgment? If I will not give my grandchildren my advice on map reading, how will they discover what I have discovered in my long, frightening, joyful search for love?

It is everyone's calling to interpret the life inside each of us. We carry in ourselves the useful history of generations. We can put into words the lit-up wisdom we have found in our struggles. We see in our lived life the outcomes of our passions. Will we close our bodies around our light so no one sees? Will we withhold what we know?

Let us give our wisdom, and let us give it without judgment, and without becoming a bore — let us make our wisdom confident and humorous; let us not be satisfied until the grandchildren of the world look into our wise eyes with a concentration not only of receiving but also of giving; let us not fear the world's destruction when the young toss our wise books away for a time, and all the other souls we know, even the very old, agree that we may be wrong in our advice.

God sings in each of us, *You can be a teacher, no matter the mistakes you've made, for within you lives a light shining beyond your own inward fears. It shines into the darkness others feel and would ever feel without your wise, flawed love.*

# CHAPTER 6
# THE AMAZING
# GRANDPARENT BRAIN

If you can change your mind, you can change your life. What you believe creates the actual fact. The greatest revolution of my generation is to discover that individuals, by changing their inner attitudes of mind, can change the outer aspects of their lives.
— William James

On July 17, 2012, in a Hampton Inn near the University of Colorado where we were both providing lectures that day, I met the psychologist, author, and PBS documentarian Michael Thompson, sixty-five. It was just a few days after the devastating fires of that summer in southern Colorado. From the front of the hotel and from the back of the university, we could look toward the completely blackened hills and mountains. Though the fires were contained now, just two weeks before, more than three hundred homes had been lost. The power of nature was stunning.

Against this backdrop I was meeting in person for the first time a researcher, thinker, and social philosopher with whom I had interacted remotely in the media for almost fifteen years. Our work and lives had been interconnected during that time because of various books on similar subjects, but somehow, as time and life would have it, we had never met. Today we were finally meeting. Into two intense conversations, woven between conference sessions, we packed a lot of memories, getting-to-know time, and planning for future meetings.

One highlight of our time together came when Michael pulled out his wallet and showed me a picture of his first (and, at that time, only) grandchild, a beautiful five-month-old girl. We had just been talking about research in brain development. Michael smiled and said, "I tell you, Mike, she has changed not only my life, but I think she is changing my brain."

Admiring the picture, I asked him to say more about that.

"Well, we know certain parts of the brain have plasticity, some malleability," he said. "We know this is true even as we age. I'm feeling that plasticity in myself — in my abilities to be more flexible, empathic, connected . . . I feel like these have grown over the last six months or so. My feelings of happiness, joy, they've expanded. There are ways I want to provide for my grandchildren now that I didn't quite feel before I had a grandchild." He pointed to his head and heart: "These both feel different now. Everyone I knew who had grandkids told me there was nothing like it, but I didn't realize what they meant until I became a grandparent. Now I know this beautiful little girl has changed my brain."

If you ever get a chance to hear Dr. Thompson speak, you will enjoy it. He has a mesmerizing style, one that also permeates his books. He is now a grandparent of more than one grandchild, and being a grandparent has most certainly changed his brain. It will change the brains of all of us who engage in the next step in a life, the next grace, being a grandparent.

## THE GRANDPARENT BRAIN

The "Mommy brain," the "Daddy brain," the "economist's brain," "the leader's brain," "female and male brains," "the brain in love" . . . the last forty years have given us deep insight regarding the kinds of brains we possess and the ways they adapt as we engage in new experiences. We have learned that some parts of our brains, such as their gender and basic personality types, are set before birth. We have also learned that templates for development of all parts of the brain are, for the most part, set before we reach three years old. But we have also learned that our brains are formatted to be affected by life experiences of enough intensity and repetition that the brain decides, "I can change this particular way I do things." So, while things like gender and personality don't significantly change, many other areas of brain development do, and they generally do because the environment impresses the brain to such an extent that our neural processing is actually transformed by the repeated experience.

Into this dialogue comes the intensity of experience a grandparent encounters. As a grandparent, Michael Thompson is not changing his core personality or the fact that he is male, but some of his brain processing has altered and will continue to do so. By being a grandparent (as when he became a husband, a father, a psychologist, and so on), he is transforming the way he does some things. The human brain is "hardened" in some ways and "plastic" in others, and being a grandparent is a way of understanding the plasticity of the brain.

Much less has been written about the

"grandparent brain" than about many of the other brain adaptations in our growth. At this writing, in fact, there is no book or even article I know of called "The Amazing Grandparent Brain." This is a term I have coined to help elders enjoy their internal and shared experience from a science-based perspective. Given how amazing the "grandparent brain" is, I offer it as a fifth concentration in our wonder-of-aging journey. I believe it is not an exaggeration to say that being a grandparent constitutes a next stage of the brain's development of social-emotive functioning. Thus, being a grandparent — including any intense, constant mentoring of young people, even if you do not yet have a grandchild — can change your brain. Being a grandparent is, thus, an intense, ongoing experience of life in which we sense that for many decades we as caring adults have touched the world and let the world touch us in order to know our own souls better. And now this knowledge and soul are meant to be shared with the young and vulnerable, who need us — depend on us — for part of their life sustenance.

Grandchildren are great! I feel more free to just enjoy them and indulge them than I did with my own children. We didn't have much money and I couldn't spend what I didn't have. Instead, we cooked, played, read, walked, talked, and camped. Now my grandchildren have toys and electronics I could never have imagined, but they still love reading and all the things we did when my kids were young. I would say I am much more permissive in some ways. Since my income is higher, I care much less about things getting broken and just don't worry about that kind of thing. However, it seems like there is so much violence in the world, I get very protective of my grandkids and worry about them being safe.

— Sarah, 61

My first grandchild arrived when I was raising our seventh child, who was only 9. When I was helping with the grandchildren I only knew one way to "parent." My husband and I believe in discipline when necessary. When we are in charge of grandchildren we have permission from the parents to discipline. Our children agree with us that when you are proud of who your children have become, you must have done something right, so why change that? But there is one thing that we have agreed not to do, and that is discipline grandchildren when their parents are present. We respect our children as parents, and our grandchildren learn that from us. We don't tell our children how to raise their children unless they ask us. It seems to work for all of us. Thank God, we have a beautiful relationship with all of our children and grandchildren.

— Pat, 70

I am not a grandparent yet. However, I am the seventh of nine in my family, so I saw my parents both parent and grandparent. My parents' "grandparenting" changed dramatically compared to my upbringing (their parenting). My father's grandfathering became more tolerant of mistakes, he "treated" more (gave more emotionally, financially), had more tolerance for mistakes of others with fewer expectations; and he laughed more. My mother's grandmothering became more

"closed," however. My mother was very generous and tolerant of me and my siblings when she parented us, but grandparenting was exhausting for her, and so she was very selective with the amount of time she had with the grandchildren.
— Dee, 56

I am more relaxed, yet more aware and able to predict outcomes of behaviors and attitudes in situations and environments. I also am aware that while I'm more patient with myself about attitudes and behaviors, I'm less patient with others. And I definitely spoil my grandchildren. Maybe I am unconsciously trying to make up for past "mistakes" I believe I made with my own children, but whatever it is, I am trying to improve and avoid these mistakes with my grandson. It's about being happy now, and I love it.
— Donnie, 64

## Happiness Plasticity

The amazing grandparent brain is the brain of a person who has taken on the wonderful and liberating task of grandparenting. In most cases, statistically, "grandparenting" will mean grandparenting our own grand-children, but "the grandparent brain" also shines through when we take care of others' children, or volunteer in a halfway house or school, or "come out of retirement" to teach a course in a prison. New scientific research is fascinating in this regard: the actions of grandparenting stimulate brain centers and create neurogenesis in verbal, emotive, and memory centers in particular. Two scientists who have devoted much of their lives to this research are the psychologists Ed Diener and Robert Sussman. Through laboratory work and meta-studies, both scientists have found that the kind of social connection that grand-parenting provides stimulates what are now called, in common language, "our happy hormones": generally oxytocin, serotonin, and dopamine in women and vasopressin, serotonin, and dopamine in men. These chemicals are stimulated in the "happy centers" or "joy centers" of the brain by the caregiving we provide grandchildren — areas in, among other places, the caudate nucleus of our brains (the "reward" center).

Grandparents can actually *feel* the changes in themselves — they can feel the brain centers and chemistry at work.

Beth, sixty-two, a grandmother of three, responded to our survey questions about grandparenting with these realizations of internal changes.

"I have been enjoying the realization of what it means to be 'wise' . . . not just knowing that I have learned lessons but also the blessing of composting the lessons and having creative, fertile ground to continue my own growth and to share what I know with my grandchildren and others.

"I have become 'comfortable in my own skin' . . . letting go of the 'shoulds' and 'oughts' and, like Buddha, making decisions based on my inner authority of right and wrong.

"I have grown to appreciate the power of rituals and the need for rites of passage. I formed a group called 'MATRIX' with four other women many years ago and we focused on the question, 'What is missing in the lives of women?' We used ritual in all our meetings and programming to establish a sense of sacred gathering.

"I work hard and am always busy, but I can accomplish this without a sense of urgency that kept me spinning all the time . . . on alert. The cost of this was burned-out adrenal glands and constant fatigue. It is time to replenish the body and operate at nature's rhythm, which is medium to slow! My body just doesn't act the way it used to.

"In being a grandmother, I am finding the world a wonderful place, and I enjoy my 'saging self' and some of the privilege that goes along with it. I know this may shift as I approach 72 and 82 . . . and my father died at 92, so I have another third of my life yet to go!

"The physical aspect of aging is often the topic of conversations in mixed company. We used to talk about business and children . . . we now talk about body parts and retirement! My husband and I are fairly fit and healthy, so the physical aspects of aging are being embraced with relative grace. As we proceed into our 70s and 80s we may be less graceful!

"I am calmer and more balanced as a grandparent than I was as a parent. What part biological aging plays rather than spiritual development I can't know, but now as a grandparent, I definitely feel different."

## ARE GRANDMOTHERS AND GRANDFATHERS DIFFERENT?

Beth continued, "I think that many women embrace the earlier years of aging with open arms because they have ended the 'mothering' time of their life and have the freedom to explore their own life again. So many women find themselves filled with creativity and begin big projects at this time. I started a school at the age of 52 and am still actively engaged. I don't see a need to retire, nor do I have any interest in ever retiring. I hope to be actively engaged in something until I can't do it anymore.

"I've also found that some men find retirement depressing because they lose their identity. My husband found golf in his 40s, and his retirement is gradual and by choice because he is a sole practitioner. I have friends who have written books, become artists, started businesses, and are embracing this freedom. But I know that my husband has not embraced aging the way I have. I think that when identity is so tied up in an occupation and career, the approach of retirement means 'I am no longer useful,' and there is a great loss. Luckily, being a grandfather does help him feel useful."

As we do with so much of our lives, women and men often experience grandparenting differently. When we asked about this in our survey, we received very insightful responses.

Margerie, sixty-five, said, "We need to allow our grandchildren to fail and let them learn their own lessons. 'Saving them' seems to be the territory of women. Men seem to be more pragmatic and let them fail more."

Tony, sixty-eight, wrote: "Both men and women can have difficulties holding boundaries, but grandmothers are often the chief caretakers when the grandkids come over, so I think grandpas generally just go along with the patterns established in the house."

Sally, fifty-nine, added: "Sisterhood is crucial. My women friends provide a richness and comfort that a man cannot have in the same way because of his gender. Men bond around sports and women bond around relationships. That's not always true, but it's often true. It's true enough that we have to sometimes really encourage men to find ways to bond with the little guys and gals."

Mikhail, seventy, wrote: "The heart can be broken in a million pieces and can mend and be stronger than it was before it broke . . . I want to teach this to my teenage grandchildren, who expect things to be easy. I think women are more likely to talk about the hard things in life than men and share their shoulder and their ear and their wisdom with others who are hurting. But it is okay for men to do this, too."

Gail, fifty-five, explained: "Multitasking and doing too much is something women do way too much: it is a form of martyrdom and high stress and it is harmful to health and well-being. When the grandkids are over, I work hard to not multitask: to just be with the kids. It's very joyful. My husband is always saying, 'Take it easy, don't think so much about everything.' When we're with the grandkids, I can take that advice."

In studying the survey results on aging and grandparenting, I was struck by how difficult it is to posit hard data on absolutes. While the majority of the surveys did fall along the kinds of gender lines you would expect (the kinds of gender lines reflected in the comments above), some did not. But one gender line that seemed quite rarely to be crossed — it showed up in nearly every survey — was the sense women had of feeling more "found" as they got older and embarked on the grandparenting journey, and men feeling a bit more "lost." This result corroborates what we discussed in chapter 4.

Darla, sixty-three, captured it this way:

"My feeling is that the older I get, the more free I am to be who I really am. I have strong emotions about children and what they need: love, physical care, strong models of work and moral character, and the desire to learn every day. I really am so much softer on what's black and white. It seems it's much more about all the tones in between and how we negotiate them.

"Meanwhile, I think my husband is becoming more reactionary and sometimes even fearful in his outlook. He experienced years of incredibly debilitating back pain and resulting drug addiction to prescription pain relievers. He now uses a medical marijuana permit to obtain pot and self-medicate. This complicates things. It all has changed him from the person I used to know, and his moods are sometimes unpredictable. In regards to him and to younger generations, I feel like he understands less and less about everything: relationship, work, and world."

Darla is referring to a kind of social isolation that can often come with the male territory as men age. Dr. Marianne Legato, author of *Why Men Die First*, illustrates this affliction this way: "Harry, a 60-year-old with advanced heart disease and severe arthritis in both hips, is finishing a complete physical examination with me that revealed a stone-hard, irregularly shaped prostate. I ask him to see my colleague for a biopsy. An angry outburst was the response: 'I hate doctors! I've seen enough of them! I'm not going to any more of them!' I wait for him to finish, understanding his fear that yet another threat to his life has arisen and that he simply wants it gone. As he quiets a little, I ask him to think about it. He says he will, but I doubt that I will see him again until some constellation of symptoms once again overwhelms him."

What frustrates many wives of elder men as "denial" about medical things is actually the social isolation Dr. Legato is pointing to in her memory of Harry. Men often isolate themselves from getting assistance when they are afraid. What they are denying is the fear, not the illness. The man understands at many levels that he is ill, but he is confronting profound spiritual and personal fear as he negotiates with his illness. The more the man can get help in understanding his fear of mortality, death, failure, or vulnerability, the more certain we can be that he will come out of isolation and get the help he needs. When trying to get my male clients to seek help, I often have to find leverage. Often I can try to leverage the man's grandchildren. I am a very direct person, so I tend to say directly, "Jim, if you don't get that biopsy, your grandchildren will lose you. Do you want that?" As I help Jim plow down into where his fear of good health comes from, I help him look at his unconscious sense that he is disposable, dispensable, and should be sacrificing himself for the good of others.

All his life he has lived by the edict, "I do for others, I make sure others are safe and happy, I don't take care of myself." To be sick and end up in a hospital and have everyone taking care of him feels alien to him, "not right," "not as it should be." Jim is afraid of being taken care of, and I need to help him see that being taken care of is okay; in fact, it is the service he now needs to provide to his grandchildren.

Ultimately, I learned from the survey on grandparenting that women are much more likely than men to respond to the survey, they are more likely to put words to paper in order to explore grandparenting, and they are just as likely to ask questions back to me, the surveyor, about men as about themselves. As with so much else about aging in our popular culture, resources are constantly being generated to help women, but women feel that resources to help men are less obvious. Men, for their part (when we can get them to respond to the survey!), report feeling somewhat confused about many aspects of aging — and more confused than women at times — but about their grandchildren they feel less confusion than about most other aging issues like health, longevity, work, or death; about their grandchildren they mainly feel, as Michael Thompson described it to me, "a love that is just amazing, absolutely amazing."

*"For Samantha, my granddaughter"*

*You run towards me,*
*An 8-year-old with*
*Arms outstretched,*

*A small loving rainbow*
*Of sweet sensibilities*
*Filled with eagerness*
*And generosity*

*Touching my heart*
*With your welcoming*
*Spirit and innocence.*

*Amazing blue eyes*
*Filled with ancient*
*Wisdom and earnest*
*Consciousness*

*There is nothing*
*Hidden in this wide*
*Eyed vulnerability.*

*I have seen those small arms*
*Comfort your older sister*
*When she was crying*

> *And have been touched*
> *By the tenderness of*
> *Your open heart.*
>
> *You are a small miracle*
> *Of creation and a gift*
> *From life to all of us.*
> — Shirley Aresvik, 87

## THE SACRED STORIES OF THE GRANDPARENTS

One of the joys of grandparenting is telling our stories to the next generation. In our surveys, grandmothers and grandfathers both reported having the urge to be a storyteller and yet not wanting to bore grandchildren. One woman, Judy, seventy-one, said, "If their eyes glaze over, I figure I am boring them. But we have to take the risk of telling our stories. Most times, thankfully, my grandkids don't mind listening."

Often it is elder women who have not spoken much yet about their accomplishments earlier in life, so used to being in the background, especially if they were or are married to successful men; now these women have grandchildren, and the risk of telling their stories is actually an identity- and legacy-building experience. These women are the path their grandchildren are following. Similarly, so often, elder men do not speak often about their hidden lives and experiences but, somehow, with grandchildren, that storytelling might occur.

In my own family, the situation was reversed from the gender situation I just described. My mother talked a great deal about her life, but my father did not. After my mother's passing, my father opened up a great deal more. On one particular visit, Gail and I and our daughters, Gabrielle and Davita, spent Thanksgiving break with him and I quizzed him, in front of the kids, about his experiences in the Depression, World War II, the Korean War, and so on. He just started talking about how he had been born in the first days of the Depression, in 1929, and his parents divorced two years later. By the time he was fourteen, he had gone to fifteen schools, lived in Manhattan, Brooklyn, Hollywood, Las Vegas, and elsewhere. He had met some of the early movie stars and business tycoons because some of his family was in the movie business. His mother, a maverick female lawyer, had argued in front of the New York Supreme Court. And there was much more.

Davita was so mesmerized, she made my father promise to retell the story into a tape recorder soon.

In the blue zones we mentioned as a research base in chapter 1, elders and near elders focus on storytelling regarding the history of individuals, families, and "our people." They understand the psychological bonding and the self-confidence that occurs as elders and near elders decide to focus on the elemental and sacred task of recording the stories, insights, and wisdom of the elders who are moving toward final journeys for the sake of grandchildren.

Whether you are the grandparent in your world or play the role of someone like me — a parent in the age of transformation hoping to support the grandparent in telling stories — you will instinctively know what to do for the sake of storytelling, and you will have tools available to you: tape recorders, e-mails back and forth, holidays when the family is all together and questions can get asked, private conversations if an elder is too shy to share. Your instincts to create a "memoir" of your own elders will generally give you enough direction to get the job done.

As you work, perhaps over a decade or more, to capture the stories of grandparents, you are saying to the elder something very spiritual, very sacred, something like Saint John of the Cross said: "I would like to bow to every suffering and joy that brought me close to God, for the sufferings and joys I knew initiated me into God." Though you may never use words of faith as you tell your stories to grandchildren, they experience you spiritually, deeply, profoundly; they need your stories and your record of life.

They will often not know the right discussion starters, though, and often you will not, either. Here are ways to make sure to get the stories from the elder that grandchildren need. These can stimulate memories and keep conversations and communication open. You will have to be the one to make sure they don't get boring!

Please alter this list if you are the grandparent doing the talking. I am presenting it from my point of view, as the person hoping to facilitate my children's grandparents to speak.

1. Ask about specific places, incidents, and people. This works better, quite often, than, "Tell me about your childhood." Thus, you might ask, "Did you live in an apartment or a house?" "Who were your neighbors?" "Where were you when you heard that Pearl Harbor was bombed?" "Was it daytime or nighttime?" People's memories are generally attached to sensorial details

and details of what is called "geo-
mancy" (details of place and time);
thus, geomantic details of time and
place are good memory stimulators.

2. To keep a story going, make sure to
keep some eye contact, nod, smile, encourage. If the elder is having trouble
remembering, silence is okay. Give
things time.

3. When a "prompt" is appropriate,
prompt your elder with paraphrasing
and verbal directiveness. For instance,
if he or she is straying from remembering, you can say, "So, you were twelve
then, and you moved to Whittier with
your third stepfather, Provenzano. Do
you remember the house you moved
to? What did it look like?"

4. Use and reuse discussion-starter statements whose repetition helps the memory process. For instance, you can say,
"And your mom was a lawyer," or
"Right, and your dad loved to wear
bow ties." As you repeat these memory
prompters, you may hear back, "Yes,
right, and she took me to her office
when I was five," or "Yes, right, and I

remember him showing me how to tie his polka dot bow tie this one morning that turned out to be the morning Pearl Harbor was bombed."

5. As your elder tells stories, there is joy for him or her in just remembering, and that can bring joy to you and your family. At the same time, you might feel that you need more "meat on the bones." So, if your elder is verbally meandering through sensual memories or memories of very small things but you're not getting information and the story about big things, it's okay to return the discussion to "big things." These might be marriages, divorces, moves to different cities, obstacles that were overcome and how they were overcome.

6. Ask for the elder's wisdom and insight. Especially because you are facilitating dialogue for the sake of the grandchildren, look for opportunities to ask the elder, "What did you learn when that happened?" "What insights did you realize?" "What do you want your grandchildren to know?" "How would you have done things differently if you

had a chance?" "What would you not change about what you did?"

7. Throughout the process of asking questions and hearing stories, make sure to ask about your elder's relationship with the mysteries of life, nature, the universe, and God. You'll know best what religious (or nonreligious) language fits your elder or yourself. Use that language to see if you can get the spiritual layers of your elder's story. That spiritual layer is often one of the most moving, impressive, and untapped layers of human experience. Every elder — every single one — has lived a spiritual life. Young people need to hear about that spiritual life.

## STRESS AND THE AMAZING GRANDPARENT BRAIN

This whole chapter is about maximizing the amazing brain of grandparents, and your grandparent brain cannot be engaged if it is under too much stress. The stress that defined you in your youth, middle age, empire building, and family raising is going to kill you now, or ruin your life, if you let it define you in your fifties, sixties, and seventies and while you are grandparenting. You will not be soulfully available to your grandchildren or other young people as you wish you could be. If the material in previous chapters regarding chronic and dangerous stress did not convince you to change your life, let your grandchildren convince you. They are living, breathing reasons to take control of chronic stress.

At the University of California–San Francisco, psychiatrists and neuroscientists have been mapping the psychological effects of stress on aging brains for decades. Professor Wendy Mendes is one of those scientists. She differentiates between healthy and harmful psychological stress. Among the healthy kinds of psychological stress are beneficial or adaptive stress. Among the harmful psychological stresses are threatening or dangerous stress. The stress that is killing you is threatening or dangerous stress, and it has to end as soon as possible. The stress of grandparenting is most probably an adaptive, beneficial stress, even when you help raise the grandchildren in the absence of their parents. You'll know whether this is the case by your own experiences. When you experience healthy, adaptive, and beneficial stress, you feel like you're doing aerobic exercise. Endorphins, dopamine, and other brain chemicals release through your system along with your cortisol (stress hormone) to sharpen your focus, give you a sense of joy, and help you accomplish what you need to accomplish. Your muscles and limbs join your brain in holistically meeting the challenges before you, and even if the challenge taxes you to exhaustion, you feel a relatively unambiguous sense of psychological pleasure and "doing right."

On the other hand, when you experience harmful, life-threatening, traumatic, and dangerous psychological stress, your high cortisol levels correspond not with joy but with anxiousness, irritability, and depression. Christopher Edwards, director of the pain unit at Duke University Medical Center, has shown that blood vessels constrict during this kind of psychological stress. Dizziness can increase as blood pressure increases and even remains high. You might experience bad judgment, your logic might get fuzzy (even though, in the moment, you might think you are making complete sense), and you may even notice your hands and feet getting cooler and your heartbeat becoming erratic, "spiking again and again like a seismograph during an earthquake." As your heart works erratically and your brain is under constant threat, your body and immune system can be negatively affected, to say nothing of your relationships and quality of life. Thus, constant psychological stress depletes your resources and ages you more quickly than you naturally would. Neuroscientist Elissa Epel at the University of California–San Francisco has shown chronic psychological stress to cause premature aging. The higher cortisol levels affect our food intake, our processing of insulin, and the health of specific cells in our body, brain, and immune system. Chronic psychological stress affects cells in our brains as well as blood flow in our brains, rewiring the brain toward self-destruction, depression, constant anxiety, rages, emotional shutdown or emotional blindness, and chronic psychological disease.

Annie, fifty-six, a former business manager, told a story of psychological stress in her life that began in 2006 and has continued for years: "My mother and father live in Florida, and I have two daughters and three grandchildren. My husband and I went through a very hard time, and now we are separated. I lost my job and was unemployed for two years. I was and am constantly traveling to take care of my parents, trying to figure out how to help my children and grandchildren, and not succeeding at anything. I worry all the time and can hardly sleep. Every day, at least once a day, I wonder what it would be like to end it. I don't have a plan in place, but the thoughts of suicide are sometimes so pleasant, I get the most pleasure on a particular day by wondering about what it will be like to just be gone."

While most people are not living in this kind of perfect storm of stresses, all of us might be living some form of dangerous and traumatic stress. Your own psychological stressors are the areas of internal chronic stress that you can and must focus on now, no matter what is happening in the world around you. Your grandchildren will spur you, I hope, to explore changes in your life and protect your amazing grandparent brain.

## Protecting Your Amazing Grandparent Brain

A primary reason we all seem to "lose" brain functions in our fifties is overload of our brains. By the time we enter the age of transformation and may have our first grandchild, we have so much information in our memory circuits, our brains have to start removing what may be unnecessary for survival. Given that our brains are now naturally losing more brain circuits than they did a decade ago, they simply have to drop more memories, forget more words, forget trivia (and, sometimes, people's names —

even people we care about!), and lose other cognitive abilities. Our brains thus allow us to keep and strengthen our wisdom but diminish our mental acuity regarding many of the details of life that seemed so essential to us in the past and now are not.

This scares us or at least worries us for a time. That worry is natural. Hopefully, it can work to our advantage — we can use worry and fear about cognitive decline to spur us toward maintaining the amazing grandparent brain we have. This is a journey of holistic care of the brain appropriate for brains over fifty, and especially as we turn our attention to the sacred act of grandparenting.

I have conducted a literature review of more than one hundred studies on cognitive brain health in middle age and beyond, focusing on science-based studies — studies that look at biochemical and brain scan research — as well as studies that feature actual positive results in brain health. The positive results for brain care in these studies normally occur in two categories:

1. Positive outcomes in the short term (e.g., increased memory functioning, stronger analytic ability); and
2. Positive outcomes in the long term (e.g., Alzheimer's or dementia post-

poned in test subjects, subjects report better quality of life).

While there are many ways to protect your cognitive abilities in both the short and the long term, some universal science-based ways have been observed. Are you doing any of these things? Now is a good time to take out your journal and answer the questions below. The suggestions inherent in the answers should, of course, follow, not substitute for, your being in the care of doctor, psychiatrist, or therapist as needed for crisis assistance or brain health maintenance. Remember, if you have grandchildren, you are doing these things for them!

**Question 1: Are you playing lots of games?** Games are good for your brain. The games can be chess or checkers, they can be word games like Scrabble or Words With Friends, they can even be video games you play with your grandkids. Sometimes people will feel guilty about playing games, as if games are "a waste of time," but unless they become addictive or overbook your time, they can help your brain. For maximum brain health, every grandparent and elder should be playing some kind of game some of the time.

**Question 2: Are you listening to music?**

Music is a "whole brain" activity — it utilizes many of your brain functions at once, thus helping connect lots of circuits. Depending on the kind of music you play, music can also relax your brain, which helps it to recharge its functions and thus perform better at whatever new task is before it. Studies out of the University of Pennsylvania found that musical training or a half hour of listening to music improved memory and other cognitive functions such as the ability to read and speak more quickly and fluently, the ability to pay attention, and the ability to convey emotions in words.

**Question 3: Are you doing what your brain already likes to do?** Let's say you like to read, but you feel like you *should* get on Facebook instead. While Facebook might connect you with someone you haven't talked to in decades, reading words might actually be better for your brain at that moment. With the exception of dangerous, addictive activities, do what your brain likes to do. Your brain is quite smart and is trying to guide you. When we do what our brain wants to do at a certain moment, more circuits open up and more synapses connect with one another. Why? Because the feel-good chemical dopamine washes through reward centers of the brain: we feel good in more places in the brain at once when we follow the path our brain wants us to follow.

**Question 4: Are you reading and writing enough?** Both reading and writing help your brain function better. In the evolution of the human brain, language function was a late arriver (our brains have been evolving for about a million years, but we only started reading a few thousand years ago), yet reading and writing are primary drivers of human brain growth now. Read a lot and write as much as you can. Writing can include typing words, but a little bit of longhand writing instead of typing is also good for the brain — it brings other senses and physical functions into word use and word creation, giving extra physiological stimulation to the brain.

**Question 5: Are you getting the right amount of exercise?** Exercise is a key to everything from heart health to mental health to brain care. When we exercise, we increase our brain function in healing and helpful ways. We also stimulate dopamine and other brain chemicals that help our memory and other brain functions. Of all the advice you get about exercise, here are two pieces of science-based advice to look at taking immediately:

1. Create a realistic daily exercise routine.

If the most you can do right now is to walk somewhere for a half hour a day, do that. Stick with that until you find a way to increase your exercise, but don't go below that unless you are ill.

2. Replace at least one time period of sedentary activity for five minutes of brain-friendly exercise. If you are sitting a long time and your brain is clearly zoning out or no longer functioning well, get up for five minutes and move around. Like listening to music, this "brain break" will get movement/exercise into your brain care so that your brain can work again.

**Question 6: Are you meditating, praying, or relaxing enough?** Prayer, meditation, relaxation in nature, taking vacations, and even zoning out in healthy ways are all important for better brain function. Functional MRI studies, such as those reported by neuroscientist Sara Lazar, have mapped changes in the following parts of the brains of test subjects following meditation: the dorsolateral prefrontal and parietal cortices, hippocampus and parahippocampus, temporal lobe, pregenual anterior cingulate cortex, striatum, and pre- and postcentral gyri. These areas of the brain all help with higher brain functioning. Similar studies conducted by Dr. Andrew Newberg (and reported in fascinating ways in the book *Why God Won't Go Away*), show similar brain-positive results from prayer and other forms of spiritual process.

**Question 7: Are you spending enough time in nature?** Our brains were born from nature and in nature they first learned how to be fully human. When we were babies, we reached out our hands to touch things in order for our brains to grow in the ways they needed to grow. We sought nature's stimulation through our eyes, ears, nose, and mouth so that our brains could experience nature's tools, sights, and sounds. Trees, rivers, dirt, sand, desert, mountain, rocks, and oceans . . . the natural world is our brain's first world, and it is a world we must tap into more than we do now if we are to ensure our cognitive health after fifty. A study conducted on Easter Island, led by McGill University professor Stanley Skoryna, is one of many that show brain benefits to time spent in nature. A team of thirty-eight scientists studied the natural environment there and the effects of that environment on the 949 residents. Studying samples of plants, animals, and human blood and saliva, they found a bacterium called rapamycin, which appears to improve health and life span by 10 percent. Unless grandparents (and everyone!) spend time out in the natural world, we may not live as long as we could with as much health as we could. Nature may be constantly trying to help and even heal us through its natural resources.

**Question 8: Are you sleeping enough, and at the right times?** Sleep is a grandparent's brain's best friend. It can also be one of the most confusing physiological experiences you have right now. Not for everyone in the second half of life, but for many of us, sleep is becoming something more difficult to manage than before. And because our brains depend especially on REM (rapid eye movement) sleep, we need to pay close attention to sleep habits and sleep hygiene. If you (or your friends/partner/spouse) notice that your sleep has become irregular, get help from a sleep specialist as soon as possible. If you feel fatigued more than you used to, ask whomever you live with to tell you if you are snoring loudly and how often you are getting up at night (you might not remember getting up). If your snoring is very loud or staggered, get a sleep study to see if you have sleep apnea. If you are getting up to pee two or three times a night, take that information to a sleep specialist (you may not be getting much REM sleep).

**Question 9: Are you eating the right foods and taking supplements and vitamins when necessary?** Are you eating foods that are healthy for your brain? Perhaps you need more blueberries, other berries, more fish and fish oil. Usually, as you cut out foods that make you fat, you are cutting out foods that negatively affect your brain. As you add foods that help you keep to a healthy weight (such as fish), you are also adding brain-healthy foods.

Along with food intake is supplement and vitamin intake. What foods, supplements, and vitamins are right for you? Which ones best fit the needs, vulnerabilities, and strengths of your brain? A physician can help you find the answer by testing your blood levels and learning whether you might need more testosterone or estrogen or less (and whether bio-identical hormones might be right for you) and whether your vitamin levels are too low. You might need to take more vitamin D, or calcium, magnesium, zinc, or other vitamins. A physician can also give you advice on dietary supplements, and even which spices in your spice cabinet help your brain (some studies show turmeric to be helpful in decreasing the risk of dementia, for instance).

**Question 10: Are you having enough**

**fun, including having enough sex?** Fun is fun, no matter how you get it. Author Larkin Warren, who has cowritten seven memoirs (and is now writing one of her own), told this story of her great-aunt Ruth. "On my great-aunt Ruth's ninetieth birthday, after lobster and a blueberry pie she'd made herself, the birthday girl reached into her blouse, pulled out the soft breast prosthesis she'd worn since a mastectomy nearly thirty years before, and tossed it across the room to my husband's friend. 'Catch this, honey!' Ruthie said, and he did, with that autoreflex guy gesture of intercepting a football midair. When he realized what he'd done, his face flamed, exactly as she'd hoped it would. 'I just wanted one more feel before I die,' she said.'" Ruthie knew how to have fun! And she also tossed in a little sex appeal into the fun. Fun is usually not sexual at our age, but I include the topics of fun and sex together here as a way of reminding us to never forget that the "fun" of sex is good for us at many levels as we age.

Especially for men, sex has been shown to actually improve brain function in aging males. A recent study showed that while a single sexual episode raised brain function slightly, multiple sexual experiences actually increased neurogenesis. Not only was there new cell growth in the brain, but there was also a decrease in stress hormones and anxiety-like behavior, too. One reason grandfathers might initially appear more dependent on sex than grandmothers is that women naturally produce more oxytocin, even after menopause, than men; thus, they more naturally bond with others and get brain care assistance through these bonds. Men may need the bonding chemical boost of sex to help them not only increase cell production in the brain but also bond with others in ways that help them grow, develop, and love.

## YOU ARE IN THE DRIVER'S SEAT

Dr. Mehmet Oz recently wrote, "The secret to living longer might be found in East Patchogue, New York, where there's a little 1966 Volvo that has clocked more than 2.9 million miles, a Guinness world record. How can a car run for almost 50 years and still look as sharp as the day it rolled off the lot? The answer is simple: proper maintenance. Maintenance is also the secret to a long and healthy life in humans, too. Think of your cells as anti-aging mechanics. If you treat them right, by eating well and exercising, they will tune you up on a daily basis. If you don't take care of them, they will go on strike, and you will age faster. You're in the driver's seat."

I love this analogy. It refers to the physical part of what Mark, fifty-five, wrote in this story of a recent occurrence in his life. Let me finish this chapter with his story.

"I recently had a wonderful opportunity to drive my 79-year-old mother and my 82-year-old uncle to a get-together in another city of 14 of their old friends who had all grown up together. Many of these friends had not seen each other in years and in one case with my uncle and a woman, it had been 65 years since they had seen each other! My uncle said to me, 'Gosh, she has aged.' He last saw her at 17, and she is now 82. It was worth a great laugh.

"For me to be a voyeur at this party was special, and in some ways it felt like I was looking 25 years into my own future. When my wife and I were in our 20s and 30s, other than raising great kids and being a partner in a wonderful marriage, I always thought the important things in life were business successes, a beautiful home, the newest kid hauler, and owning the latest and greatest gadgets.

"In a time like I had with these very old people and their grandchildren, I realized there are about three or four things that are really important in life: family, friends, health, and community. Not that there is anything wrong with financial successes and having nice things, but after spending an evening with my mother's contemporaries (who had all been very successful), it becomes clear what really is important in life to all of these older people. There was not one person in that room who wouldn't trade all of their successes to have a loved one still be with them, to not have lost many dear friends, to not be dealing with a loved one who has Alzheimer's or some other dreadful disease, and to not have to be dealing with their own aches and pains, illnesses or disease, and to spend more time with the younger people, their grandchildren, and others.

"I now know that when I am in my 70s, 80s, or, God willing, 90s, the things that will matter to me will be how my children and grandchildren are doing. Have we remained close as a family? Will my siblings still be alive? Will my wife and I still be actively participating in life? Will we feel close to our circle of friends and community? Will we have developed a close spiritual connection? Will we be able to finish this life feeling that we know what is most important in life, and made sure to spend our time with that? What, really, is more important than our children and grandchildren? I can't think of anything more important."

Consider every mistake you have made as an asset.

— Paul J. Meyer


As long as we are persistent in our pursuit of our deepest destiny, we will continue to grow. We cannot choose the day or time when we will fully bloom. It happens in its own time.

— Denis Waitley


Consider the lilies of the field. Look at the fuzz on a baby's car. Read in the backyard with the sun on your face. Learn to be happy. And think of life as a terminal illness, because, if you do, you will live it with joy and passion, as it ought to be lived.

— Anna Quindlen

## Meditation 7: I Don't Live in Jerusalem

I don't live in Jerusalem, Rome, Mecca, or Tibet. Can I still be holy? I don't own a house in London, New York, Cairo, Hong Kong, or Madras. Can I still be considered prosperous? I've been to many places, searched in each of them for love, and heard a voice whispering to me wherever I went: "I will always give you another chance." Chance for what?

Ah well, don't I know? Second chances are always about destiny and love. The painter paints a ceiling in a house that others built. That artist gives the ceiling a second chance to be holy. Michelangelo said, "I saw the angel in the marble and carved until I set him free." The first chance was utility, the second chance is freedom.

So I am on my knees in the dirt behind my little house in Spokane, tending my garden of lilacs and hyssop. Words "either" and "or" are good for the surface work, but "both" and "and" are the digging down. Pondering holiness, angels, and second chances, I kiss the dirt and stone of this earth.

I am aging, so I am reading the Book of Life again, with special attention now to new things I must learn and give, for there is much left to do, and I am keeper of a vineyard smaller than I thought it was in my youth, but larger than I will ever know.

# CHAPTER 7
## A NEW LIFETIME OF
## SECOND CHANCES

If you live long enough, you will get many
second chances. Because of where I came
from, my living to a ripe old age has been a
miracle. I have tried to take all of my second
chances.
— Eva Lassman, 90, survivor of the
Warsaw Ghetto Uprising and the
Maidanek concentration camp

I first met the Holocaust survivor Eva Lassman when she was eighty-one and I was
forty-four. Eva had smallish eyes set close together that were magnified by thick, square-
framed glasses. The eyes and glasses and
Eva's charisma forced a person to look her in
the eyes if possible. I am tall, six feet one, and
Eva was short, approximately five feet two
inches, so I had to bend down to speak with
her. This humility was physically awkward
but soulfully invigorating. Eva's gray hair
was always treated and coiffed toward what

I used to call "poofiness" when I was a boy. Once she said, "Michael, you are staring at my hair. Do you want to touch it?" Her wry grin always disarmed me, as it did with others in her community. When Eva spoke, she spoke carefully, with a fading Polish-German accent, and we listened.

A day will come, perhaps within the next decade, when there will be no more Holocaust survivors like Eva still alive. Her story, like so many stories of one of the nadirs in human existence, could be forgotten, except that Eva, later in her life, has told the story to many people.

Eva was raised in Lodz, Poland, with two brothers. She lost everyone in her family to the Nazis, fled to Warsaw, survived the Warsaw Ghetto Uprising, was taken to the Maidanek concentration camp, and survived that ordeal. Rescued by the Russians, she found her way to a Red Cross station, met and later married another survivor, Zev Lassman, and came to the United States with him in the late 1940s. They raised children and lived the rest of their lives in Spokane, Washington. After she said good-bye to her husband, Zev, who passed away relatively young, she thought of speaking with family and friends about their hardships in the Holocaust, but still she did not. That lack of voice, she told me, gnawed at her, but not enough to push her into talking. Not yet.

Then an incident happened with a granddaughter wherein she began telling her story. This small incident compelled her to go to a conference in Washington, D.C., at which Nobel Prize winner Elie Wiesel spoke. At that conference he said that every Holocaust survivor needed to tell his or her story publicly so that the unthinkable atrocities would have meaning. "That day," Eva told me, "I saw a new thing I must do. I had avoided speaking, but now, in my sixties, this was my second chance at speaking. I came home from the conference and I asked a local elementary school if I could tell my story to the students."

From that moment onward, for approximately two decades, Eva told her story to schoolchildren, university audiences, Rotary and Kiwanis Club meetings, conference audiences, and many other gatherings. For two decades, until her health began to fail, she fulfilled her second chance. For her, this "second chance" was a way to find and give meaning to what, at first, had been a matter mainly of survival. "I had to do more with my experiences now," she told me. "I had to make sure there was no whining about it — I had to tell young people how I understood it, and also the mysteries still in it. What I didn't understand long ago, I had a chance to understand now. Thank God for living so long that I could do something good with the past." Gonzaga University gave stooped, wry, understated Eva Lassman an honorary doctorate for teaching and speaking, and the simple girl from Lodz, as she called herself, ended up having a new department, the Department of Hate Studies, dedicated to her memory at Gonzaga.

I am opening this chapter with Eva and "Eva's Song" because it was from her that I first began to study among elders what I now call "the lifetime of second chances," the sixth concentration of our second lifetime. As I noticed her discovery of her second chance, I began to see the same drive in others who were fifty and over. A man would decide to quit his high-power life and become a schoolteacher; a woman would go back to work after raising her children (and these genders, of course, can be reversed); a person married three times, divorcing for issues of addiction or other self-destruction, would go through menopause or andropause and come into the age of transformation finally ready to end the destructive paths and set a new course. A person who had built an empire would set up a trust or foundation by which to begin giving away a significant part of his or her legacy to the underprivileged. A person who had succeeded already at business or raising a family would begin a new artistic career of writing romance or espionage novels. Parents who had raised their children one way would now talk with joy about the second chances they got in raising or helping to raise their grandchildren.

As I began studying my own clients and available research from this context, I saw that there was some but, in my opinion, not enough actual study of this phenomenon going on (yet more evidence, unfortunately, of our culture's lack of concentration on aging). However, many people in the second half of life at some point experience moments where their psyche directs them toward "seeing my life now as a second chance" or completing the "things I have put off." Everyone I observed seemed to need to make an inner journey of second chances during various times in each of the three stages of age in order to fully discover, or rediscover, their sense of wonder at being alive.

Thus, as a mental health counselor and philosopher, I began to help aging clients focus on discovering this journey more fully. It was clear to me that some people had an easier go of getting to their second chances than others. My job became to help frame the second chances and to suggest resources and ways to pursue them. This led to my working with a new frame for the journey, which evolved into framing the *completion spirituality* I introduced in chapter 3. I would like to go deeper into it here with you, and I begin that journey of deepening the topic with a case example housed in "Eva's Song."

### "EVA'S SONG"

Part of my own completion spirituality — and, I believe, a small part of Eva Lassman's — took place as we worked together on a public rendition, in poetry and oratory form, of her story. I began interviewing Eva for this piece when I was forty-nine years old and she was eighty-seven. We met many times over the years and completed early versions of it, but the final piece did not emerge until after her passing (she died in February 2011, at age ninety-two). By then, I was fifty-four. I believe this five-year act of service to her became for me a beginning of my own completion spirituality and a part of the end of hers. For both of us, it was a part of our lifetime of second chances, and we discussed this a number of times, hopeful that this record of her legacy would move others toward their own second chances and their own completion.

Find a quiet place now and sit comfortably. If you are willing to read this aloud, please do so. I have read it aloud, as Eva Lassman speaking from the beyond, in a number of public gatherings. One of these readings took place at our home synagogue, Temple Beth Shalom, in which the piece was performed with musical accompaniment. For this rendition, click www.youtube.com, then "Michael Gurian," then "Eva's Song." The piece takes seventeen minutes to read or listen to. This speech is called "Eva's Song," but it could just as well be called "A Lifetime of Second Chances."

**Eva's Song**

> 1.
> My friends, I speak to you from
>     beyond your dreams,
> an old woman whose hands no longer
>     tremble with love.
>         My voice once spoke of six million
>         candles
>             that rose to the sky, and now I
>             sing again.
> You who gather here, good people who
>     have all you need —
>         your families, your friends, your city

of lilac and rose,
>your boxes of blue light in your
>>living rooms,
>>>your Internet with its endless
>>>poems —
now, at this gathering, what gift have
>I left to give you?
>>I have my last song, my memory
>>of another time,
a question of the eternal soul like a
>light, still, inside me,
>>>"Did I do enough with my
>>>life?"


2.
When I lived among you, I was known as
>Eva Lassman,
>>born Eva Bialogrod, in 1919, that
>>old time
>>>of horsemen, valor and
>>>trains.
In Lodz, my Polish home, evening skies
>burned
>>>electric red like a beating heart,
>and every map that was ever vague
>seemed clear.
In their black coats and hair curls, our
>Hasidic men
>>>*davened* at *shul,*
rocking back and forth on their invisible

boats of glory,
    while our women held the
    wanderer's moon
        in their busy hands.

My family of Jews carried thirty centuries
  of sorrow
        off a few small stands of joy.

My *Ojciec,* my father, held me on his lap,
        and talked of the great light.
"Eva," he said, "God will keep His
  promises,
        though not always how you
          expect."
My mother, my *Matka,* taught me to knit
  curtains for our windows
        and light candles for
          Sabbath.
    When my brother, Chaim, was born,
    she smiled,
        "Eva, be grateful for this world,
        and always love the
          children."
When my older brother Moshe's
  daughter was born,
        I held her tiny fists in mine:
    "Lord," I smiled, "she will be our
  butterfly!"

Can you see my family there? I once had
   photographs.

   There are no photographs anymore.

   Much happened to my family, and
      the Jews.

I learned: there is a light so infinite it
   cannot be seen
               until it flickers.


      3.
My friends, did you know: everything can
   be taken from you?
      The world can hate itself with the
         fury of love,
            while you wander in the thick of
            it.

      Throughout my life in America,
         people asked,
"Eva, how could the Jews not know what
   was coming?"

My answer: hate happens slowly, near
   firelight and singing,
      while children, playing in the snow,
         breathe air white as a loaf of
         bread,

and old people sit together,
    comparing their wings.
The radios fill with loud lies, the streets
    with tyrants,
        but we say to one another,
    "When have the Jews not known a
    bit of hate?"

When the Nazis ordered, "Wear the
    yellow star!"
    we raised our heads in pride.
When the police took our bicycles, we
    thought,
        "It's better to walk anyway."
When a young German soldier, blond
    fuzz on his cheeks,
        ordered me to clean the sidewalk
        with my underclothes,
        I refused. He beat me with his
        black stick
until the flower of my body became no
    more than flesh
        attached to his brutal rapture —
    yet, still, I did not think I would have
    to become
        other than myself.

How could we not know what was
    coming?
There are questions a Jew asks

384

for which all the answers are dead.

4.

The Nazis broke down our doors. *Juden,
Schnell!*
    They chased us through the grainy
        fields.
"Eva, hide!" my family cried. "Eva, save
yourself!"
    My *Matka,* who sang me awake to
        this life,
        lost her heartbeat to the fleeing.
My *Ojciec* died retching and pockmarked
with disease.
    Moshe and his wife and daughter . . .
        shot dead;
Chaim, little Chaim, held on to his
ragged clothes
    until, a naked boy at Auschwitz,
        he burned to ash.

I fled to Warsaw where the days of time
closed to me.
    In that ghetto of grief, I became a
        woman.
    I learned to read the maps of God's
        silence.

Friends, when you cannot save your own
family,

forgiveness of yourself becomes
    the worst cruelty imaginable.


5.
When the Nazis set fire to our
    ghetto,
we who survived were herded into cattle
  cars.
    In the iron moan of trains, we rode
      to Maidanek.
A rabbi near me whispered, "We must
  remain brave —
    but Lord, what trail is the Jew
      following?"
We arrived at walls of echoing screams, as
  if God
      could make a hateful symphony.
    I begged the soldier at the garrison,
"Please! Let me keep my last family
  photograph!"
    He put his gun to my head, he said,
      "You may keep it in death."


In the falling snow, I watched the last
  paper of my life
        turn to ash.


    People have asked me:
"Eva, how did you few souls survive the
  camps of terror?"

386

My answer: We decided the footprints of
   the Jews
            must not disappear from this
               earth,
         so we moved rocks from one wall to
            another
               to prove we were alive enough
         to move rocks from one wall to
            another.

      We breathed just enough air each
         day
            to hold in our small hands each
               night
         the beating heart of shattered things.


      6.
My friends, what would *you* have done?
Would you have given up on the world?
      Would you have hated God?
Would you have closed away your love?

I tried to hate God, I tried to close myself
   away,
      but I was a Jew who had lived for
         many years
            in a garden of the beautiful sun,
      and though I lost my family and my
         home, still,
            an ancient poem returned to me,

still, a light appeared in the crack of an
    old doorway,
        still, shadows promised mysterious
            truths
                of that light.
*Matka* whispered, "Eva, will you sing a
    song for us?"
                and *Ojciec:*
"No matter what, Eva, you must carry
    God's stars
                in your trembling hands."
                So, I prayed:
"Lord, if I die in this place, please make
    my bones
                into wax for Your lit candles."

People ask me: "Eva, how could you keep
    your faith
                in that dark and godless time?"

Friends, I do not know why God brought
    us to the grave
                of a thousand spectacles,
but in the name of all who once touched
    my baby skin,
                I could not blame that light.

People say: "But Eva, God abandoned
    you!"

I say: God was the presence of light
     even in the darkest dark.

People say, "But Eva, that God is not
     enough!"
          I say: there is no greater God in the
          universe.


          7.
When the dying mothers with their empty
     arms,
          and the dying fathers with their
          darkened eyes,
and the children sobbing before their
     burning
               commanded their angel of God,
          "Young woman, you will survive," I
          heard also:
               "Young woman, what promises
               will you keep?"
Twenty-five years old, rags for skin, I
     promised all I had,
               the eternal lightness of seeds:
that ash rising from smokestacks would
     carry with it
                    weightless births on other
                    shores.

When the Russian soldiers came, their
     faces sordid and grim —

when they gave us back our freedom,
that dull magnificence regained at the
    cost of everything —
                I promised to live.

My dears, I have seen paradise:
        it is wherever you breathe freely.


8.
I walked half-dead from Maidanek to
    Lodz,
        saw *tefillin, tzitzit,* and hair curls
        again,
                saw a Torah again.
I met a skeleton from Buchenwald who
    still breathed.
Zev Lassman and I learned how to eat
    and drink again,
            we tasted milk and candy.
    At an altar of broken glass, we
        married.

There are six million reasons to love,
            and no reason not to.

Holding hands at the rail of our ship
    to America,
Zev and I watched wind slide across the
    waves. How beautiful!
        Eternal light wrinkled the water

like jewels.
In America, we had three sons, Iro,
  Joel, and Sylvan:
    they became the stars God gave
    us to carry
      in our trembling hands.


9.
And our boys grew into men and
  married,
    and I became a grandmother,
a bent lily with a slight accent, butterflies
clinging to my stem.
    One day after Zev had gone, my
    granddaughter
      helped me hang curtains on my
      windows,
for I could no longer lift my thin arms;
  with her kind voice
    she asked me why I had no
    photographs of my childhood.

I told her my story.

Her eyes filled with angry tears, and we
  held each other.
    We talked a long time of the old
    worlds.
Finally, she asked, "*Bubbe,* should I hate
  the Germans?"

I spoke my truth: "Jews must never
        hate —
                we must use that ash for our
                flowers."

O my friends, O my dears, this is my
        song:
                I am a Jew, and Jews were born to
                plant flowers
                        even in the garden of a thousand
                        sobs.


        10.
        Do you understand, then, do you
                understand
the beauty of being here, in *your* time, in
        *your* place?
                Will *you* choose to see what *you* must
                do?

                You don't have to walk through
                fire —
we did that for you, so that, now, you are
        free to dream.
                You don't have to love as if the death
                of love
is all you'll ever have. We did that for you,
        too.
                But what you must do is keep your
                promises.

                                392

Care for your family as a promise, and
  take photographs.
      Let them become your
        masterpiece.

  And when your life is hard and
    tiring,
      promise, still, to cherish it.

And when your marriage does not fulfill
  you,
      promise, still, to practice mercy.

And even when God seems to disappear
        into His own thoughts,
      promise, still, to choose between
        the sweet and the bitter.

And you who always want more . . .
  more . . . more,
      promise to love what you already
        have.

And you who sit complacent in a gilded
  cage —
          find your journey, and a star.

    11.
And when terror comes knocking on *your*
  door,

say, while you're cooking in firelight
and your children play in the
snow —
when hate hisses on your Internet or
television or radio,
"*Your* God is not the right God,
*Your* children are not as holy as *my*
children" —
promise to fight that hate with every
breath you have.

No matter your creed or color, never let
the ash of hate
cover our human footprints.

And when in your lives, you lose sight of
God's stars —
when you think, "I cannot have
faith anymore" —
remember why the first flower
opened its petals
to show its fragrant heart:
it felt encouraged by a light so vast, such
an infinite, blazing eye,
it sought truth even in darkness, and
flickered there,
a piece of creation ever
reborn.

12.

I am the voice of Eva Lassman, born Eva
    Bialogrod, in 1919.
I was a Jew who survived the excesses of
    God's masterpiece.
        When my life ended at 92, I knew
        "the truth."
        Truth is not some loud answer to a
        human fear;
truth is a question as fragile as the world's
    most fragile child,
            "What will we do with our
            lives?"

        I gave everything I had to mine,
            so it would not merely be taken.

Now I end my last song with love for you
    and your homes,
            with reverence for my life and
            yours,
I end my song with hope that you will
    now and always ask yourself,
            "What will I do with *my*
            life?"
in a voice so loud and clear your
    children's children will hear
            your determination long before
            they're born.

My dear friends, I hope you will feel the
freedom of being alive,
as I did,
and may you learn the lesson I
learned:
no matter how much you suffer in a
human lifetime
nor what mistakes you think
you've made;
when in *your* life, God opens *your*
soul and asks,
"Will you keep the promise I made
to you at Creation?"
you answer,
"Yes, Lord, Yes, I will: to my last
heartbeat,
to the last action of my last breath, to the
last flickering of my light,
my *life* will be the promise
You kept."

## COMPLETION SPIRITUALITY

Spending five years writing this lyrical oratory with Eva helped me posit and study
the completion spirituality I hope you will
consider as a sixth concentration in your life
after fifty.

Eva entered her lifetime of second chances
and began honing her completion spirituality
in her sixties; you might enter it in your fifties

or seventies, or slightly earlier or much later. It appears to me that there is no set time, though it will affect us most powerfully in the second half of life.

Our sense of soul's growth premenopause or pre-andropause — that is, in the first half of life — is different, biologically and socially, from this completion spirituality in our second half. During our first half of life, we are making our sacrifices for our children or, if we decide not to have a family, for our ambitions. Our biology and our culture, no matter where we are on this earth or what role we play, drives us in the first half of life to "begin our lives" and "pursue our dreams." We are thinking of first chances as we move from drive to drive, focus to focus, crisis to crisis, and goal to goal.

Something begins to shift, though, as we approach or transcend fifty. We begin to "look back." Our ambitions slow (though they do not end); our focus moves more inward than before. We begin to sense the possibility of second chances as our souls clarify themselves to us. Family configuration can reflect this. Individuals who remarry while in their forties or fifties and start second families often discover their second family to be a significant part of their dialogue regarding "getting a second chance to do it right." A number of male clients and friends especially have said, "I made mistakes in the most important part of my life, my family, the first time around, but I am more mature now; I get a 'do over' now." They may have profound regrets about the past, and much healing and work to do, but even that is part of their second chance. For these people, a second chance to understand themselves as parents occurs.

This is an example of our ability during the second half of life to get a second chance at identity development. A woman will return to school and get a PhD at sixty or sixty-five. A man will give up his intense moneymaking career and decide to become a teacher. Of course, the genders can be switched here. And for some people, the new identity occurs in the way it did for Eva. It can involve speaking up in ways we have not before, telling a necessary story in order to survive and thrive.

The time of second chances is the time when children (at least those children who come from a first family) are grown or nearly grown; our financial obligations to them and even to ourselves may be subsiding; our workplace relationships may not be what they once were; our intimate relationships may involve more intimate separateness now than they did before. Whatever our life circumstance, we feel pulled to adjust to new physical realities and our emotions to new emotional realities, and the desire to get a second chance becomes primary, if it feels needed in our lives and family and community.

All this can feel like the wonder of aging rather than a scary sense of loss if we see it all as a cumulative new beginning, a rebirth. In that vein, we can ask, "Have I fulfilled my purpose? If not, what now? If so, will I have a new purpose?" Even the debilitation of our bodies, inevitably a companion of aging, can feel liberating if we spend time (even a few years) digging deep into the self in order to decide what our second chances need to be. These second chances can happen in the relationships we are in or in our awakening to new passions and a new sense of adventure. They can happen as we enjoy our rites of passage into new stages of life and focus on becoming spiritually whole. Where we have regrets, we can make peace with them (see them as part of who we are) and work to change them. We may become activists, do a bucket list, go to a new country, or, at a certain point, let go of all our accoutrements. These second (and third and fourth) chances will be more than themselves in that they will also provide a new layer of foundation to our completion as individual human beings. They will ground our completion spirituality throughout the last decades of our lives.

If you gave up everything, including your family, for your career a decade ago, you now have a second chance. If you have lost your family to an addiction, you now have a second chance. If you forgot to love someone, you can now begin again at love. It is soul-freeing to see second chances as a sacred task: to right former wrongs, end former feuds with family members, or ensure that our lifework is protected and constantly of service to others. It is freeing at life's core to do as Eva did — face her deepest inner fear, of speaking about the atrocities she suffered, and come out the other side with a story of hope. There is no single correct way to get a second chance, but part of the wonder of aging today is that we get the time to discover our second chances.

Will we take that second chance? Will we do what Eva Lassman did and live a new lifetime of second chances? Will we ask, "Have I done enough with my life?" and realize that, until the last action of our last breath, our answer must be, "What's next? I'm ready."

## Asking: Have I Done Enough with My Life?

Frances Spielhagen, 66, teaches at Mount Saint Mary College in Newburgh, New York. She and I have worked together on a number of occasions, and on one of these, Fran, a Catholic by upbringing, happened to read and view "Eva's Song." This reading coincided with her students' graduation in May 2012. She wrote:

"I just got home from the college, having celebrated life with my graduating students who are just starting on their journeys, their faces full of promise and fear. This is such a daunting and challenging time for young people and just in these moments, I read 'Eva's Song.' It brought tears to my eyes. It is so much about picking up our socks and getting on with the business of living. 'Eva's Song' brought back memories of the elders I grew up with in Brooklyn, when no one spoke of the Holocaust, but the shadow was there. I remember one man, who ran a candy store in our Brooklyn neighborhood. One hot day he was dishing up ice cream (I was about 6 or 7 years old at the time), and I noticed numbers on his forearm, because he had rolled up his sleeves. I asked him, 'Bernie, why do you have numbers? My daddy's tattoo has a word on it.' He replied, 'You should never know of it, and we will never speak of it.' When I got home and asked my mother, she scolded me for being nosy. That was Brooklyn in the 1950s, and yet we knew that some great evil and sadness permeated their lives. They, too, got on with the business of living, only too aware of how fragile that quest can be. Eva decided, obviously, to change that. This is how I hope I will always be. As I face the second half of my 60s, I am continually reminded that we are only promised today and that we must reach out to each other each day."

In Fran's e-mail (and from knowing Fran personally), I sense, as I hope you do, the push to constantly ask, "Have I done enough with my life?" In that inward push will be, so often, the push to reach out to others in some way. If we are not sure how to answer "Have I done enough with my life?," we need only look toward our family and community with open eyes, and we will see something that needs doing. Relationships house needs, always; people live unfinished lives and need us to help them. Some of our second chances will be utterly personal and independent, done "just for me." Some will become twenty-year adventures, as was Eva's, because once the people around us see and feel what we are doing, the vision expands to fit the needs, and the needs are relatively endless.

## The Pain of Taking Second Chances

A new client, Sam, walked into my office. He was sixty-four and had been married for thirty-one years. His children were twenty-four and twenty-eight. He was a lawyer who had initially been a social worker. Near tears, he said, "I cannot stay married anymore. Carole and I have tried and tried, but we can't do it. We have no intimacy — we haven't been physically intimate in three years — and we just don't feel any joy with each other. It's been ten years, I think, since we've felt joy together. I don't want to die in this relationship, and neither does she. We both want to go farther, find more, become more, discover more. We don't want to just stop our lives here, in emptiness and a meaningless marriage."

Sam was a short, thin man with silver hair, wearing a well-pressed suit. His blue tie matched his blue eyes. His face wore a look of both wiry intensity and deep sadness. Seeing that he was a man once filled with passion for his wife, I talked with him now in realization that his disappointment about his marriage was as much about his own inabilities as his wife's to fulfill intimacy. Over the weeks, as we walked and talked, I saw that his divorce was finalizing, and he did not need help from me in rehashing the marriage right now. He needed help from me in discovering joy again, dealing with emptiness and meaninglessness, and, in the terminology I asked him to consider, "discover where his journey of second chances would take him." We talked together about how "incomplete" he felt as his divorce became final and he set up a new, small apartment. We talked about how important it was to become inspired, not defeated, by the inward feeling of incompleteness. That feeling of incompleteness was going to hold the key to his development, now, of a completion spirituality.

Throughout our work together, we talked about pain. He talked about how much joint and arthritic pain he was in now, and we used that feeling of his body to inspire a review of the most painful moments in his emotional life: when he was rejected from the air force for eye problems (his dream had been to be a pilot); when his first marriage failed; when he realized he was in the wrong career and needed to change careers; when he and his wife had separated the first time, fifteen years ago; when his daughter had lost a leg as the result of a car accident. His list of painful times was long, and it wasn't possible to work through his present pain without his feeling the trail of that pain, both physical and relational, in his growing and developing soul. We walked and talked about pain and stress and transformation and distinction and completion. We spent many weeks and months helping him rebuild a self that could take on new challenges and find new options.

By the time we had finished working together, Sam felt some peace at being alone. He felt that he would most probably find a new companion for his old age but preferred to be alone now. He became more involved in grandfathering his grandkids than he had been before. He decided to "succumb to getting a cane, and using it." This had been something he had stubbornly avoided but now felt would empower him to walk faster and better. He also reported feeling more joy than before — some of that joy a kind of relief to be free of a painful, empty relationship and some of it a powerful push to provide volunteer services at a local prison. When he was younger, he recalled, he had worked as a clinical social worker in a prison, and now he felt the pull toward that again, a second chance to fulfill the drive, still in him and emerging fully again, to help incarcerated women and men to rebuild their lives. Articulate regarding his inner life, Sam said to me, "I am attracted somehow to the pain of these people. It is almost as if my body is magnetized back toward the prison. I feel like I've gotten some of my own issues with my own pain out of the way, and now I can see more clearly where I'm needed. I'm needed in this work, I'm needed with these people. This is some of the work I want to do for the rest of my life."

## Rethinking the Soul's Location

Eva went back into her physical and psychic pain in order to begin teaching the life philosophy and story that would become a prominent part of her own completion spirituality. Sam went back into his pain — adjusting to the physical pain better than he had and plummeting again the psychic pain — in order to feel what he described as a magnetic pull toward where he was needed as he moved into second chances. These two people took time during their stages of age to search for the magnetic pulls, the places they were needed. Many times we may not realize that people who do this are discovering directions for their completion by exploring pain. Actually, in most of the cases I have helped with, the pain a client experiences in the past and present can leave them emptied or it can become the confronted pain and history that inspires them to push further into the life of being an elder. These clients see their aging souls as vital, and they take action to give that soul the kind of voice that gradually completes them. This taking of action depends somewhat on looking at pain clearly. It also depends, I believe, on now fully understanding, or at least now reimagining, what the soul actually is.

In his final book of poems, published just before his death, the Israeli poet Yehuda Amichai wrote that the soul is not merely "pilot of the body" but something that changes shape as we grow. It is not static, but active, adapting, evolving. "Sometimes," he wrote, his soul is "my hair in the wind," sometimes it is "my aching feet as I walk," sometimes it is "my cheerful feet skipping," sometimes it is "my eyes, my eyelids, sometimes even my eyelashes — all these are my soul." As it was for Aristotle, the soul for the elder Amichai was not a single energy force separate from the body but something that actually inhabits every cell of the body and thus grows and adapts with it.

This kind of thinking is important for "second chances" thinking. When I was in the first throes of my severe, constant pain, all this talk of second chances and completion would have been ludicrous. But as the months passed and I concentrated on discovering meaning in the pain, I needed to embrace pain-as-soul and body-as-soul. It was for me just as it was for Eva with her stooped back and painful memories, or Sam with his arthritis and joylessness, and everyone who has worked through trauma. Our body pain is not separate from our souls — our pain is part of our soul. From our pain comes inspiration and a lens to look inward and beyond; to see what has been and then see meaning in it; to inspire ourselves toward new work, new passion, new elements of completion. The brain research we discussed earlier regarding stress powerfully illustrates this point. Stress and trauma can kill us if we allow chronic stress to continue to rule our lives. But healthy stress — healthy pain — pushes our souls toward quality of life. Taking control of stress is not removing stress but adapting our lives toward healthy stress — stress that gives us meaning, power, passion, and joy.

There is no one fifty or over who has not experienced or is not experiencing some form of trauma and pain. Thus, there is no one who does not have a way of embracing soul through stress and trauma. Part of the wonder of reaching our age lies in guiding trauma and pain toward helping us become fulfilled human beings. I remember my father-in-law, Dean Reid, who had never spoken to his family about his near fatal year in a Nazi POW camp in World War II until the movie *Saving Private Ryan,* in 1997, triggered a post-trauma growth response in him. Pulled toward completion, and inspired by the movie, he began talking in his seventies about his experiences in the past, including his misshapen toes, which had become frostbitten from treks through snow at the front end of Nazi rifles in near-starvation conditions. As he worked through his myriad health issues associated with aging now, he tried to work out ways of healing between him and his wife of fifty years; he opened up his soul as a grandfather; he joined a veterans' group to talk about the past, make peace with it, and tell its story in communities. After *Saving Private Ryan* opened his soul, he took his freedom and made his past trauma into a healthy stressor that led to enhanced relationships. You never know when or how a second chance will happen.

So we are saying that something often missed in second chances is the role of bodily pain in the development of the soul. By that we mean: we need to see the soul in the second half of life as it truly is, a part of every part of us, energy-of-body inside us that moves as we move, directs itself to whatever we direct ourselves toward, and supports all of our efforts to do those things we have not yet done, enjoy the relationships and people we love, and engage in a long second chance to become the person we had always hoped to become. The body is the soul, and pain is the root element of new joy. The soul is everywhere in you; the parts of yourself that you lose (a limb no longer working) have not destroyed soul but rather, like a sense that stops working, directed your attention to the other parts of yourself that now contain even more soul and energy located in the working parts.

This new logic of soul might also be understood as applying to old and new passions. When we were younger, we had myriad passions and directions, goals and ideas of self. Many of them are now fulfilled, and we may have somewhat less passion for a certain person or for the kind of love we practiced in our youth. This can feel utterly like "loss" unless we move toward a "second chances" attitude, a new spirituality in which, now, the loss is a flow toward new areas of interest, hobbies, ideas, and evolved senses of love and relationship that will complete us. We surrender the variety of passions we once had for the spiritually freeing opportunity of honing and refining a smaller, completing set of passions, for now we are looking not at constantly expanding the self in order to grow the self, but contracting the self in order to fully discover soul and God in the self. As our bodies decay (which they must and will so that we can complete ourselves through illness, dying, and death), how else should we see life as we age except as a life-time of second chances?

If we don't take charge of the spirit of aging — if our mission is to always look backward for our standards of growth — we will not understand soul. We will not take the great opportunities of the second half of life. Bereft of new vision now, we may not ultimately complete the self, which is the felt sense that soul is all of us, the whole of us. We may face illness, dying, and death as yet more constant loss rather than an invitation to be complete and free before the next part of the journey. The pains we experience in our first stages of age are real, and they are also rehearsal.

Thus, making peace with our bodies' gradual vulnerabilities as we age is a spiritual act, a second chance at becoming spiritual in the way we may not have had the time to become before. Even if we were good at practicing our religion before, knowing all the rote elements of it, we might now become better at practicing its spirituality, for now we can "get" what the masters have always been trying to teach

411

— Self, Soul, Identity, Grace, Service. If we enter a time of making spirituality a part of our lifetime of second chances, we can stop spending a great deal of our second half of life in low-grade sadness, depression, anger, even rage at what is happening to our bodies (our souls), but instead see how miraculous the life of the soul is as it flows and adjusts within even our illnesses.

**Finding Your Haven**
To feel your whole body as soul, and to fully live the second chances, you will most probably need to find, build, or return to a haven. The haven might be a cabin in the woods, a spiritual community, a place in the home of your children and grandchildren, a room you take as your own in your house. It can be any of these, or any other place where, when you enter it, you feel that your soul expands to encounter the heavens. You feel that you have "arrived," you are safe, you are awake and yet dreaming, you are a free spirit.

My haven is a rustic cabin in the woods where I go to meditate, pray, and write. It is a bit ramshackle; it constantly has problems, as water leaks through the foundation into the basement, mosquitoes attack the house in the summer, woodpeckers make loud sounds in the spring, snow pushes the limits of the roof in the winter. Like my own body, different parts of the cabin are constantly in need of some repair. My cabin and I are mirrors of each other, and in the light of the mirroring, spirit is always present.

Near the cabin is a stream that makes the most wonderful sound of life. No matter what is happening in my daily doings, the sound awakens my spirit. Neurologically, as it is for all of us when sitting near water — the sound of the water triggers negative ions to flow through brain circuits, which create a dopamine-charged "feel good" in the brain, then throughout the body. The word "negative" in "negative ions" is actually a misnomer (referring more to the neurophysics of the experience than the thought experience): the feeling is very positive indeed.

In this description of my haven are three elements you can find in your haven (or build and make in it): a place in which you can be quiet and away from the busy world; a place that is "yours," that is, it mirrors who you are; a place that includes some form of nature (water is always good). For you, your haven might be a room in your home where you can meditate, a room that has "you" in it through your books, objects from your travels, an altar, a desk, a chair that fits you, and a small fountain, perhaps, or a sand tray, or flowers and plants.

Without a haven, you may not be able to activate spiritual life, feel your soul throughout your body, and enjoy the decades of completing yourself. One reason this is the case is that without a haven, it may be very hard to stick to some form of spiritual discipline. For me, for instance, my mornings are my meditation and writing time — my "discipline time." And while I can meditate wherever I wake up, in whatever city or country, it is easiest to do so in my haven. In my haven, I am undistracted; I feel immediately and effortlessly at home in spirit.

Another reason you may need a haven in order to complete yourself is that the haven supports your widened thinking and feeling: your contemplation. The haven is your place of contemplation regarding the self, your relationships, and the soul within you. It is the place in which you can completely trust your insights regarding what you should do, whom you should forgive, what relationship you should repair, and how. While you can become reflective wherever you are, sometimes it is hard to trust insights you have in the middle of your busy day.

In your haven, you feel a sense of trust as in few other places on earth.

## The Place You Have Found

By the time we realize we are in a lifetime of second chances, we have been called to the place we have found. We may see that our children and grandchildren have risen or are rising out of our shadow, and these accomplishments of theirs can make us prouder than we ever thought possible. As we live our second chances, we may also realize we learned a high quality of love, one in which desire is no longer as immense as comfortable joy. Enough of the world's resources may now be ours, so that we may become an example of the world's completed truth. We may now be the sage who has or will soon find what we are looking for. Most powerful, perhaps: this place in the self we have found will be our home.

As you live your second chances, I hope you will review your life, see what is unfinished, make a plan to finish it, even if you don't accomplish every new goal you set. Second chances are about setting new directions, not about arriving at perfect destinations. How wonderful to be aging and fully understand what the cliché means: "it's all about the journey, not the destination." If ever you need direction or inspiration, go hang out with young people to get their energy into you, and go hang out with old people to hear their stories. While getting what you need, you'll be admiring the young, who desperately need your admiration (even if they pretend to resist you), and you'll be listening to the old, who need your admiration, too, as they tell the stories of their lives. Soon you will become one of these very old people who have, in a sense, become their own story. Even that act of contrition and glory, telling one's life story, is a second chance.

Death is one of the most intimate acts
of the body.
— Rabia, eighth-century poet

Thus I conform to my divinity
By dying inward, like an aging tree.
—Theodore Roethke

Now it is time that we were going, I to die,
you to live; but which of us has the happier
prospect is unknown to anyone but God.
— Socrates, in Plato's *Apology*

## MEDITATION 8: THE HORN OF DEATH

Before the horn of death blows, we are meek, not humble; harsh, not strong. Before the sound of wailing begins, we are mean, we gossip, we estrange. Before the last breath of a friend: what is best in ourselves, we hoard away. After our loved one dies, we want only to collect the treasures meant for us. After a death appears in our community, we have a chance to take off our masks, and feel God's greatness. After the horn of death blows, even dying is less frightening; even our dead become evidence of our freedom. How can this be? How can one person's dying change us?

Because some events sing of truth. Thunder on a mountaintop, and an angel interceding; the crashing of waves on an ocean shore; listening to our loved one's last breath . . . hearing these sounds, we can choose to open our souls to God's magnificence.

Friends, I don't know what you mean by God. I can't tell you what I mean, without argument. I just know: when a loved one has died, it is time to end all our pursuits, and let the Great Breath shatter our complacencies.

It is time to put down our carving knives and blow the horn of wailing.

It is time to listen to instructions deeper than our own ambitions.

It is time to feel the One who is in-comprehensible enter our inwardness through sounds of grief.

# CHAPTER 8
# THE MIRACLE OF DYING AND DEATH

We fear dying until we know the truth of ourselves. When we know who we are, dying is not frightening anymore.
— Saint Teresa of Avila

One day what Elisabeth Kübler-Ross called "the final stage of growth" will happen: you and I will live the wonder of dying and death. Along with the miracles of birth, growth, and relationship, every living organism shares the journey of dying. It utterly equalizes us, rich or poor, young or old. It is the final challenge and concentration in this life. It drives the human spirit to great heights and great depths; it completes us in a way unique to each of us, no matter who we are.

If we die suddenly, at the peak of our faculties, we don't feel the aches of death coming gradually into us. We don't witness our own souls as they gradually rise from deep within us to the surface of our skin, organs, and tendons to bring us ever-new pains and diseases. If we die suddenly, we don't experience the miracles of relationships that happen, sometimes over decades of our illness, as others come near to care for us through illness. If we die suddenly, we experience the wonder of death but not of dying.

If, however, we die slowly, we experience dying fully, its breathing into the void, the gradual rising of the soul to an occupancy of every nerve ending, and then its gradual shrinking inward, away from the surface, until our body can no longer find it and our breath ceases. If we die slowly, we witness ourselves disappearing into the inner vastness that opens its doorway to the ethers of the whole universe, where we join the overflow of energy and matter in search of new directions.

The Chilean poet Pablo Neruda wrote some of his best later poems about the final stage of growth. In one such poem, "October Fullness," he writes of how life happened to him as much "little by little" as in great leaps. He confesses that he hoped he has lived his life in such a way that "nobody who crossed my path did not share my being." He recalls embracing adversities and the sufferings of others, for his business, he says, was spiritual fullness and wholeness. And now, as he is moving toward death, he thinks of himself as the sum of all his previous and present actions. His heart is like the unwinding of foam on the ocean shore, "an essential spasm dying away as it seeps into the sand."

The best words poets and songwriters write about death are some of the best words about anything we will ever read, for death is miraculous, and thus inspires utter truth. Throughout our lives, especially if we know we have lived well, death is not the final end; rather, we realize that our life has been like a canyon over which a fragile bridge we have called "a life" extends. As we have walked that bridge, death has held our hand all the way across. The situation we face now is called "death," but in the wonder and miracle of the universe, it is actually a rebirth. Neither energy (soul) nor matter (body) can be destroyed; they can only be transformed. Dying and death are a transformation.

Near our end of life, so many things become clear: death and life are never severed; what we do in a life has been about many things, including communicating with death itself — being inspired by death to express our passions, care for others, accomplish our legacy, give back to others who needed us — for we always knew, at some level, that our death would come. The knowledge that we

will seep into the sand one day can be enliv-
ening and a part of the wonder of aging if we
look back and realize that we have also been
the wave and foam of a lifetime, a piece of
the eternal embodied and real and beautiful
and of use.

### There's No Right Way to Die, but There Is a Better Way

In discussing her studies on death and dying,
Dr. Kübler-Ross wrote: "People who are in-
formed that they have a limited time to live
react in different ways. Some seem to be able
to cope adequately with the psychic pain
that may come in the form of anger, depression, fear, or inappropriate guilt. They adjust
emotionally to the point that they are able to
live the final weeks and months of their lives
with inner tranquillity. Other patients seem
unable to handle this pain. The terminally
ill patent, by definition, cannot be helped to
regain physical well-being. However, he can
be helped to live his life as fearlessly and fully
as possible until he dies."

Two elders in my life died within a year of
each other, and both provided two different
templates of end-of-life reactions to dying.

My wife's father, Dean, eighty-five, died
quietly and without complaint. As he was
dying, he cleaned out his room, organized his

things, told his wife, Peggy, and his daughter, Gail, and son, Mike, how he wanted things dispersed. Just before his eighty-sixth birthday, he went into the hospital for yet another heart operation, expecting to live through this one as he had the others, but just as fully expecting that he would not. For two weeks after this operation, he remained in the hospital, his organs failing. We held his hand, spoke with him, let the hospital staff care for him, helped as we could, and, when necessary, left the hospital in shifts to live our lives, which was exactly as he, unable to master even a sentence now, wanted it.

As a fighter pilot in World War II, Dean was shot down over Germany. He had spent the remainder of the war in a German POW camp, experiencing significant suffering and near starvation. He survived and returned home to the United States to devote his life to farming, farmers, and his family in Nebraska. A stoic man of his generation, he had not, during his life, expressed much of his inner world to his family or friends, protecting them from his own past traumas, "just going forward." He had raised three children, loved his wife, buried his firstborn son when that son was thirty-three (Tom Reid died of a stroke caused by a congenital heart defect), lived quietly, and now lay in a bed ready to go into the next unknown. He feared death, as we all do, but not so much that his fear led him to be angry with the living.

My own mother, Julia, eighty-two, died differently than did Dean. Her years of dying were longer, her pain level more severe, and her anger more ever-present. While Dean spent approximately six months in the actual dying process, she spent more than five years in the dying process. She spent her last year of life with shingles across her abdomen. There are few experiences of pain as severe as shingles. As she gradually lost the ability to speak or care for herself, her final utterances were "No!" Her mind, once prodigious, became reduced to a one-word negative with which, I assume, she hoped to dominate death. On and off over her last years of life, she lived out her personality as Dean had his — not the quiet person Dean had been, she died a louder person whose angers surfaced more fully and constantly than did Dean's.

Two different lives, personalities, and life experiences: two different ways of dying. You will know people who have died slowly or quickly, as they lived and as they loved, with their personalities intact, or with their minds effaced; you will have seen many scenarios for dying and death. By now, you will know that there is no right way to die. Everyone dies in his or her own way.

That said, I am betting you have wondered: "When it happens to me, what will I do?" and, perhaps: "Is there a 'better' way to die than the way I just saw?"

How, indeed, will we each approach death? Let's ponder it now, together, so we can live our dying as we have lived life and age: to its fullest. Let us look at a "better way" — not morally better but experientially better (emotionally and soulfully most satisfying for us and those we love) — so that dying and death can feel like an integrated part of our lives. The wonder of aging is about freedom, and so can death be. A primary standard of a society's maturity lies in how well elders in that society die in service of the people they love.

## COMPLETION SPIRITUALITY AND DYING

Our dying and our death complete us; thus they are by nature a part of the completion spirituality we are developing (even if unconsciously) in our last decades of life, and then, in deep concentration, the final years or months of life. This completion involves our seeing the self as the sum of its parts — an accumulation of relationships, memories, and accomplishments in our life — a "sum" that still has a purpose: service to others. I believe we become most free in our dying and death when we remain in service to the world, to the very end. In this concentration and devotion, our personal feelings are ours, as sacred and private as we wish; and we do not either withhold them too much or show them so much that we manipulate and overwhelm others with our fears.

That said, there can be no doubt that dying and death can be terrible and upsetting. It can truly stink. There may be little or no nobility in it, and very little dignity. We lose control of ourselves and lose everything we have gained and loved. With the longevity we are living in the new millennium, there comes, also, the possibilities of decades of decline, self-destruction, and dreadful dying. Not everyone can or will welcome death, and that is just reality. If a person lives the process of dying without in any way welcoming or realizing the richness of death and dying, he or she is just living his or her process and is not somehow flawed. While in an ideal world, perhaps, dying and death would be understood by every person as natural and freeing, in the real world dying and death will not be understood by all, for sometimes dying and death just do not feel freeing. In fact, it is fair to say that most of the time dying and death feel terrible.

I make this point here because dealing with dying and death is a humbling experience, and though I have some points to make in this chapter, insights that I hope will help you and yours explore the life of the soul as dying and death enter your world, I want to say with vigor that I am, ultimately, humbled by working with those who are dying. I offer my insights in that spirit, and without judgment. One of the people who kept me honest about this was a client, Trudy.

**Trudy's Story**

Trudy, seventy-nine, stricken with cancer, came into a session carrying these lines from the poet Rabindranath Tagore. "On the day when death will knock at thy door, / what wilt thou offer him?" She had been battling cancer on and off for six years, and had been told there were no more interventions — medications, chemo, radiation — and it was time for her to make peace with the fact that she was terminal. My job was, she said, "to help me mend fences with my kids." That is what Trudy wanted to offer death. So I met with Trudy and her two grown children, in hopes of helping Trudy and her children to say the things that needed to be said between them.

Trudy had a personality somewhere between my father-in-law, Dean, and my mother, Julia. Trudy was quite capable of getting angry and, in the words of her son, fifty-two, "unreasonable." She was also quite capable of withdrawing and being silent about much of what she felt. By no means was Trudy "perfect" at dying — she admitted that she was not very proud of some things she had said and done.

But one thing she did till the very end was to live in service to her family, friends, and others. Never did she withdraw from wanting to make sure her family knew she loved them, heard her apologies for past mistakes, and felt connected to her via clear documentation of her wishes — durable power of attorney, living will, health directives, will and testament, and scrapbooks and other documents of her legacy and love. As much as possible, Trudy tried "not to drain" her family. She asked me to help her "explain to them that I don't mind if they let me go." This was a significant issue for Trudy's daughter, Tamara, who kept pressing her mother to find a new treatment in order to prolong her life at all costs.

"Let me go," Trudy begged her daughter angrily. "Go live your life."

"I can't, I can't, I want you to live," her daughter cried.

"I have lived," Trudy responded. "Now you

go live. Don't spend your life trying to keep me alive."

As I helped Trudy and Tamara, I asked Trudy if this reframing of her comments was helpful: "Are you saying, Trudy — please, Tamara, let me serve you by dying"?

Trudy thought about this for just a second, then nodded her head. "Yes. Let me serve you by dying." The rest of our session was spent on this idea, and there were a lot of tears for mother and daughter. Trudy desperately wanted to be let go of, but not just as a withdrawal or from cancer fatigue; she wanted to be let go because she believed her time to die had come, and that her death should be of service to her family.

The word "serve" is resonant, I believe, because to serve is our lifework even in our last days. There is no time in our lives when service is secondary; even as we die, it is liberating to perceive ourselves as being on this earth in order to serve others, especially those we love. This concentration — service — clarifies our dying, keeps it meaningful (even through the pain and fear), attaches death to sacrifice for others, and allows us to leave this life and enter whatever awaits us with feelings of completion, of giving. Feelings of taking, ultimately, do not complete us. We have lived long enough to know that we will be measured not by what we took in this life, but what we gave; not by how we ruled others, but how we served others. "Service in death" is a very freeing concentration as we die, and one we can explore in the frame of the wonder of aging. That exploration will require us and our culture to think differently about death: to reframe death from "death is bad" and into "death is a journey of freedom."

**PROTECTING THE MIRACLE OF YOUR DEATH**
When I was in such pain that I thought I should kill myself, I reached out to a friend, Lloyd Halpern, MD, an anesthesiologist in Gail's and my circle of friends. Even before he helped me to get care and surgery for my spinal condition, he and I had been involved in Jewish spiritual life together, and we had engaged in a number of professional and personal conversations about dying and death. We had developed a certain point of view regarding our own future dying. Lloyd put his position this way while discussing memories of his grandmother, who had been forced to live for nearly a decade with Alzheimer's.

**Lloyd's Story**
"My earliest memories of my grandmother are her pinching my cheek as a small child,

kissing me on the cheek with the wettest kiss I've ever had in my fifty-two years, and calling me Lloydeleh. (No one else has done that since.) I remember trying to find the right moment when she wouldn't see me wipe the kiss off my cheek and smearing the lipstick off my hand, but I loved the kiss. I also remember borscht, and trying to understand her broken English accent; she learned English as an adult after fleeing persecution in Romania. I remember being amazed at her attempt at writing English in the letters she would write to my dad after we left New York.

"But the image seared in my memory is my grandmother at the end of her life. I was a teenager by then, and I will never forget visiting her in the nursing home with my dad. She was restrained in a chair, being wheeled in the room to see us. She didn't know who I was or even who my dad was. She just kept asking us for ice cream. I remember seeing my dad try to hold back tears and talk to her like a child. He had no choice but to put her in a nursing home after she had been found wandering the streets in her nightgown on a cold winter night in New York City.

"I decided then that this wasn't going to happen to me. I realized then that Alzheimer's disease robs us of the person — without memories we are only a shell of the person we

432

were. I realized that taking care of a person with Alzheimer's is a tremendous emotional and financial strain on the family and on society. And finally I realized that I didn't want my grandchildren's final, seared memory of me to be of a toddler, restrained in a chair and asking for ice cream.

"I decided then that if Alzheimer's strikes me, I would have the wisdom to take my own life in a planned, serene ceremony with my family there at my side. I wanted to be able to say good-bye to my family, and them to me, with meaning and understanding. I wanted to teach my children and grandchildren that death is a part of life, and that dying with dignity is a choice we can all make."

Lloyd's point of view, like Trudy's, I believe, has its roots in a completion spirituality that our biology actually creates: we are hardwired to serve our loved ones by protecting and providing for them. Those of us who have decided to fight for the freedom to choose our death are guided, in general, by the drive to protect and provide. We have built a legacy of emotion and resources over many decades of work and love. It is natural for us to build this legacy and to want to pass it to our children. If we come to feel that our illness is destroying that legacy — destroying its memories, invading our family's good life, destroying

433

our children's inheritance — it is natural for us to want to end our lives to provide for our family and to protect our family from years of suffering.

Lloyd continued:

"So I told my family that if I get Alzheimer's, I am going to end my life in the beginning stages, while I still can. My family was unhappy to hear this, but I saw my grandmother gradually lose herself to Alzheimer's, and it was terrible for everyone involved. If she had known who we were, she would have been mortified to know that our family resources were being used up on her. She would have hated knowing that the people who loved her were in constant stress trying to keep her in care. She was the kind of person who would have walked out into the woods in the old days to die once she saw the need for that sacrifice. That's the person I want to be.

"I live in Washington State, and physician-assisted suicide is possible, so I might go that route, but since I am a physician, I think I will finish my life myself if possible. This is a right any of us should have, not just physicians. We should all have the right to learn from mistakes of the past — in my case my grandmother's last years of life — and evolve and grow as human beings toward the freest, most helpful course possible for society.

"In every culture, when sacrifice of ourselves will help others, especially others who are dependent on us, it is right to be able to sacrifice ourselves. Certainly it is assumed we will do this in war, if we become soldiers. Why shouldn't we be able to sacrifice ourselves for others when we are old and sick?"

I agree with Lloyd, and I have joined with Lloyd and another friend in our circle of friends in a promise to help one another choose this kind of death. I have used the phrases "service death" and "free death" for what we seek. Hopefully, one of those phrases will be helpful to you in your thinking and conversations. Lloyd, I, and others like us feel that our death should be both of service and a free choice.

We have come together as a physician and a mental health counselor to posit a "three times rule" for determining whether a person is ready to be assisted in suicide: three conversations of significant depth need to take place with the person at the outset of a disease or during a disease. These conversations need to take place over a three-month period. If after these three (or more) conversations over three months it is clear that this person consistently asks for assistance in a free, service-oriented death, then we should be free to assist.

One reason I believe so fully in this position is that I watched my mother during her last years of chronic pain. She wanted to die but was not able to find social support for this choice. She kept saying, "I'm staying alive for your father" (they had been married fifty-nine years). She also said, "I want Jack to help me die, and maybe I'll let him, but the legal consequences could be severe." She and I also discussed my helping her die, but, again, the legal consequences were ultimately deleterious to my family and me.

Throughout these last painful months, my father was constantly ill as he tried to take care of my mother (they kept Mom at their home for as long as possible). He got pneumonia more than once during this stressful time; he fell a number of times; he had both brain surgery and heart surgery during my mother's last years. My mother yearned for a service death and a free death, but she worried that the consequences for my father would be terrible.

After my mother died, my father's health improved. He did not resent her the years she hung on to life, but he said honestly, "We agreed many times it would be better for her to die. I didn't beg her to stay alive. I knew many years ago that I had basically lost her to the pain and the drugs. She was kept alive by a society that didn't know her. Her own needs and her family's needs were distorted and not heard. I wish I could have helped her do the thing she wanted: die when she chose. She would have been happier. Her soul would have been free much sooner, too."

Every happiness in the world is the child of a separation it did not think it could survive.

— Rainer Maria Rilke

If I had my life over again I should form the habit of nightly composing myself to thoughts of death. I would practice, as it were, the remembrance of death. There is no other practice which so intensifies life. Without an ever-present sense of death life is insipid. You might as well live on the whites of eggs.

— Muriel Spark

As quickly as the world changes, like clouds racing across the sky, everything that finishes falls home to the ancient source.

— Rainer Maria Rilke

> Now I'm beginning to come apart . . .
> I'm getting detached and curling into
>    myself.
>
> — Yehuda Amichai

Detachment becomes a greater norm now than it was before. It is not that we separate from life completely. It is more that our daily lives take on the tone of a symphony in its final movement. If we do not learn the art of detachment now, in this final movement, we shall be running counter to the nature of time and life. Few things create more sadness and pain than trying to fight against detachment when detachment is what must naturally occur.

> — Reverend William Harper Houff

**Curtis's Story**

Curtis was a businessman and educator for more than thirty years before being diagnosed with ALS (amyotrophic lateral sclerosis, or Lou Gehrig's disease). As the years of his disease progressed, he was unable to move limbs, even "pick up my iPhone." He is now able to write only by tapping one finger on a key; he became "trapped inside a motionless body, a living mummy, a burden to those around me . . . my core is almost gone, and soon my arms and legs will become completely detached. Most of my muscles vibrate 24/7. All that constant (muscle) contraction causes perpetual fatigue and tension headaches."

Curtis wrote an article recalling the monarch butterflies in Pacific Grove, California. Every February, they die there. "They have no choice," Curtis noted. "I do." Curtis decided to choose the moment of his death. He decided to choose freedom over "hanging on," and he wished to utilize the assisted suicide that is legal in Washington State (he was unable to physically cause his own death himself because of his ALS symptoms) as a way of being of service to others. His goal during his completion was to donate his organs to others. "Every day," he wrote, "18 people die while waiting for a transplant of a vital organ such as a heart, liver, kidney, pancreas, lung, or bone marrow." For Curtis, providing these organs gave meaning.

However, he was caught in a bind. It is legal in Washington State to effect assisted suicide, but it is not legal to donate organs except in a hospital; simultaneously, it is not legal to effect euthanasia in a hospital. So, if Curtis chose freedom he could not be of service.

If he died at home, his organs could not be harvested, but he could not be assisted to die in the hospital, where he must be to donate his organs.

In the face of this situation, Curtis concluded all that he could conclude: his bottom line. "Dying is hard — it would be a little easier if I knew I was saving others. Isn't it time we changed our laws to reflect our true humanity — and shared the gift of life?" As I write this, Curtis is still struggling with exactly what he should do. His message is clear, though: the call to service during our time of purest completion is absolutely natural to us. It is our highest calling in death as it has been throughout life. One of the best things we can do for ourselves and our families is to die well. How shall we move forward in our culture, and in our individual families, to follow this calling?

**CONFRONTING OUR FEAR OF ABANDONMENT**
For millions of people there is an inner conversation about these things, even if we don't speak aloud as much as we should. All of us are experiencing dying and death, as Curtis is, or watching dying and death of others and wondering about our own. Many of us want to move forward with dying on our own terms. The critical mass of these people — us

— will only keep growing because so many of us will be hit, during our second lifetimes, with major, debilitating illnesses, and medical miracles will keep us alive for years, even decades, in the throes of these illnesses, often to our own and our family's detriment.

An example: thirty-five million people lived with dementia in 2010, according to the World Health Organization. That number is conservatively expected to rise to 66 million by 2030 and 115 million by 2050. The agency's director general, Margaret Chan, recently put these statistics into context: "The catastrophic cost drives millions of households below the poverty level." In America specifically, 16 million people are projected to have severe Alzheimer's disease by 2050. It is America's sixth leading killer. There is no cure for Alzheimer's, and treatment only temporarily eases some symptoms. While mild Alzheimer's can be managed well, severe Alzheimer's can take an immense toll on everyone involved.

And whatever the disease or condition we might face in our last years, months, weeks, or days, specific costs for hospital stays just on their own are devastating to families and communities. *Newsweek* reporter Amanda Bennett lost her husband to kidney cancer and recorded the financial consequences of just a few days of his care in *The Cost of Hope:*

- $33,382 for a four-day hospital stay
- $43,711 for a second hospital stay
- $14,022 for the last three days of life.

His costs of care over the years of battle were far larger than these, making this nearly $100,000 for just a few days of care the tip of the iceberg in financial terms. Amanda was immersed in her husband's life and death, so much so that she reports not really understanding until later that many of the nurses, doctors, therapists, and others in the hospital wished there were ways to support her husband's smoother death; they could see that he was ready and could not gain from additional expenditures. Yet the oncologist and the system of care required the expenditures and the interruptions to her husband's free death.

Bennett writes: "We could have done better. We all should be doing better to adjust the focus on the needs of the patient and not on the business model of the doctors, hospitals, and insurance companies. . . . More and more people are beginning to think that some intelligent and neutral counselor may be able to help guide our choices of when to treat — and when not to." Dr. Joan Teno of Brown University, who studies end-of-life care among cancer and dementia patients, says that the "more intensive care a patient received, the more the family felt that the patient hadn't been well cared for." Part of the reason for this emerged in a study published in *The Journal of the American Medical Association*. As it had been in Bennett's case, the focus of the medical community and the social pressures on the dying patient united around "cure" or "medical care" rather than on other aspects of service, insight, and communal and family conversation. In the model practiced in Bennett's case and the majority of cases today, the *JAMA* study reported research from a group of Boston-area hospitals that concluded that six months after their loved ones died, the bereaved caregivers of such patients "experienced worse quality of life, more regret, and were at a higher risk of developing a major depressive disorder."

The dying patient, in this model, becomes a person destroying his or her family rather than serving it, a person crushing a life legacy rather than passing it on courageously. The dying person and his or her family see the time of life that is naturally set up for completion of love, happiness, and life's work altered toward destruction, denial of completion, lack of loving conversation, immense confusion, intense regret, and enslavement to systems that focus on experiments on a dying body rather than care of that person's and his or her family's living souls.

## Abandonment Anxiety

What stops us as a culture from moving forward with the freedom to choose our death? Many things, obviously — denial of death, possible liability, unclear definition of what constitutes a "sound mind," the argument that "If we let old and sick people kill themselves, won't depressed teenagers see that modeling, and kill themselves too?" Each of these is worthy of its own study, but behind them all, I believe — especially behind our society's denial of freedom in dying — is a root psychological cause we must deal with: lack of maturity regarding our fear of abandonment. It is a lack of maturity that correlates with our highly individualistic, industrial approach to life in general. Let me explain what I mean.

All through our lives, even if we never named it, we have been confronting a lifetime of abandonments and, within that lifetime, our own individual fears of abandonment. A thousand times in our lives, we have felt abandoned and felt guilty for abandoning someone else. Perhaps we have actually, literally, been abandoned by a parent or spouse. Perhaps we have abandoned the people we love, lost in an addictive behavior or other long-term confusion. Even if no tragedies have occurred in our lives, abandonment is a part of our days. A mother feels abandoned by a child who is growing up. A child "abandons" the mother, feels guilty, but must keep pushing away in order to become an adult. A father pushes a child away but feels guilty for forcing maturation too soon. A grown child, angry at a parent for past wrongs, decides not to even visit his dying parent and then, at the funeral, breaks down in tears for having abandoned the parent.

Karen, sixty-two, told me of another way of abandonment that was touching in its depth and subtlety. "I have a ninety-year-old stepdad. In his late eighties he'd had both knees replaced and surgery for arthritis on his back. He lives alone, is very active, goes to the gym to work out with weights, winters in Florida, which he drives twelve hundred miles to all by himself. To deny him any medical procedures because of his age sounds ludicrous. He is not dying; as he likes to say, he is living, and medical care, he says, is well spent on him.

"But what about my friend's mother, who is ninety-four, not doing well at all, and has bad knees? If the quality of her life isn't going to change, and if she isn't going to become more active from knee surgeries, shouldn't she be denied the surgery? She is much closer to the end of her life, in terms of physical age, than my stepfather, and it would be wrong for the whole system to spend tax dollars and other monies keeping her alive and her body repaired; this would rob other people, especially younger people, who need these resources.

"But all of us (including me) are so afraid of 'giving in' to death, dying, or even aging, that we feel like we're abandoning her if we don't spend resources on her. It's very complicated, I know, and I have no easy answer, but I wish we could as a society get beyond feeling like we can somehow put off the inevitable abandonment we will feel when our elder dies by 'falsely,' in some cases, keeping the body parts and even the body of the elder alive."

There are infinite ways to abandon and feel abandoned and feel guilty about abandoning others, and we will each participate in circumstances of abandonment in our own lives. There are, indeed, no easy answers. But the truth is also plain: Dying is a time of abandonment. Dying brings up all of our emotions of abandonment in a long-term inward explosion of fear — this is true whether we are the one dying or the caregivers, family, and society. If we have not — individually and culturally — understood and confronted our fear of abandonment in a significant way earlier in life, we will have greater difficulty dying freely, in service, and greater difficulty allowing others to do so. We will be confused about what life and death are; we will "selfishly" try to hold on to a person, and not be able to respect the wishes of people who are dying. We will not give them their freedom — we will enslave them in our own fear of abandonment. So afraid of being abandoned by them, we will use every argument possible to keep them alive.

Hopefully a time will come when individuals and cultures will see the wonder of dying and death: the service and freedom that can occur. To work through the fear and anger, though, let's all look at previous abandonments. Let's make peace with them and atone and complete them as we can, so that they do not hover over our lives during our illness and dying, or the fearful illness and dying of those we love. If we don't look at our abandonments, we may operate out of a painful fear of abandonment until our dying breath.

## Death as Reunion with God

Many religions in the world treat death as a reunion with God; this is a theological way of quieting our human fear of abandonment. I do not know of another way to feel complete at death than to transcend abandonment, and I can find no research that provides a way more universally successful than to focus your mind during your quiet hours of dying, and the dying of your loved one, on what you believe reunion with God will be. Your religion may teach you what it is, but just as likely, you will imagine something that fits your personality, your life experiences, your ability to create an amalgam of all that you have learned and hope for.

The act of imagining your own or your loved one's reunion with God is a freeing act, one lived in hundreds of "acts" — hundreds of conversations with others, visits to the hospital, quiet times spent beside a river or fountain, loud times near grandchildren who are curious about death, if they are old enough to talk about it, or just delighted to feel you close to them, if they are very young.

You know from your most joyful life experiences what your after-death experience will be. At the end of every quest on earth is a love story. Think about every fairy tale you've ever read; every religious or spiritual tract;

every story of quest, perseverance, death, and rebirth. Every quest ends, and it ends with some kind of wedding. This is how it will be and feel for your loved one and for you — the abandonment will be worked through; death is like your most intimate, close, freeing, and completed moments in this life.

As Moses approached the end of his life, he thought back on his brother Aaron's death and said, "Happy is one who dies that kind of death: his family by his side, his people there to show their love, and the final moment coming painlessly, with a kiss from God." What a beautiful phrase for the moment of death: "a kiss from God." Modern medicine and science have developed to the point where transportation has become so routine, one's family can come from anywhere in the world to be by our side, showing their love. Hospice, palliative, and pain-management care can help us to at least approximate "the final moment coming painlessly."

And no matter what our circumstance, we can experience our final moment as a kiss from God if we concentrate on our own fear of abandonment — how it has manifested in our lives; how we've made mistakes because we thought we were being ruefully abandoned, when in fact we were just living our

449

present part of a dance of life. If we are the caregiver who is angry or afraid as our loved one says, "It's time for me to be free, I am going to end my life," we will feel the fear of abandonment utterly and we have a choice to make: Will we be ruled by it, or will we help our loved one to become free, complete, and die? To help our loved one, we will need to see the love story waiting for him or her, a love story we will not be part of until we die and join that loved one, but a love story nonetheless.

Life is a quest whose last days can be lived in conflict and fear, even loneliness, for both the one dying and the family and culture around the one dying, or it can be a quest whose last days are lived in the purest love. It can be a few timeless moments of family history lived together, charged with energy, that help us all realize life's great plan: love. It can be a time of resolution when the one dying is allowed, through the support and ease of his or her family and society, to see that what we give in our lifetimes has been substantial. This resolution can make our death very beautiful. In this beauty, we who will survive the dead are already grieving, but the grief is beautiful, too, for it opens our souls like intense therapy, naturally accomplished.

In the case of both the dying and the caregiver, the idea of "reunion with God" can unite with the role of "service" to quiet the fear of abandonment. If both parties concentrate on visions of reunion with God and discuss these, and if they serve each other through the process of life and vision, the closeness they develop can experientially quiet the fear of abandonment they both have. They can become two intimates for whom no topic is off-limits, and even death can be joked about. Their closeness in this time of grief, fear, joy, and love becomes an antidote to abandonment. They can feel, in the last days of life, the completion of body and soul that this one life had been building toward all along.

## TEN CONCENTRATIONS

Whichever side of this interaction you are on — the one ill and dying or the one doing the caregiving    here are ten concentrations to focus on, ways to make closeness happen, embrace a sense of reunion with God, and to help quiet the natural fear of abandonment.

1. Open yourself to everyone who will help you, however random their appearance might seem in your life. Your illness and your dying will give them gifts of love, and it will give you the op-

portunity to make many new friends, and love and be loved by many people you might not have met without the miracle of illness in your life.

2. As you are ill and dying, give comfort and kindness to others, even to the end. Be easy to care for, as much as you can be. Complain less, and if you see people in mental, emotional, or even physical pain, ask them how they are doing. This does not mean you don't advocate for yourself in the health care system — nor does it mean you roll over and die. It means you target your complaints very specifically, and your concentration is on helping yourself by helping others.

3. Ask for the death you need. Choose the moment of your death, especially if your quality of life becomes irretrievably harmed. This should be your right and freedom. It should be your way of protecting and providing, even though your body is failing you and you can't "work" anymore in the larger world to provide and protect: you can still serve, provide, and protect by choosing your time of death and by making

sure your paperwork is in order. This will mean both a will and a living will. The living will should be customized, not vague (check out agingwithdignity .org for some useful forms), one that appoints a health care agent (perhaps your spouse or a grown child), one you discuss with your doctors and family. If you are having trouble starting conversations about this, check out american bar.org and click "Consumer's Tool Kit for Health Care Advance Planning."

4. Work to atone, forgive, and be forgiven. Say everything you have to say to everyone, including by e-mail, letter, and video, and in legal documents. Call people together and tell them how much you love them and are proud of them. Don't let this go unsaid.

5. Give your remaining strength to caring for your friends and family. If you have children, you know that once you have a child, all your strength must go to helping a child grow up well. Now, perhaps, your children are grown, but that instinct is still a good one. As you feel strength remaining in you, and you see some piece of that strength needed

by your family and friends, give that strength to them.

6. Review your life and complete your legacy. If you can, write things down. At the end of this chapter is a lyrical oratory called "Kathy's Song," which I adapted and wrote with and for my good friend and business partner, Kathy Stevens, in order to help her give voice to her life philosophy and legacy. I read it aloud at her funeral. Work on your own statement together with others, or write it yourself. Make sure your people know where to find it when you are gone.

7. Protect your family's assets with your life. See the moment of death as a sacrifice you make for others. If you are beginning to seriously drain your family's assets or your legacy assets to your family, and if you can sense that your life has passed its point of spiritual completion, end your life as you can. In planning beforehand for this eventuality (many years before), purchase life insurance policies that do not penalize your family for your final actions.

8. Inspire others with your wisdom, humor, and stories. Bring young people to your bedside or into your life as constantly as you have energy. Young people need to experience dying and death. They need to see human beings in utterly vulnerable states of being. That witnessing can inspire them to grow well and live in service themselves.

9. Give away what you have as much as you are able. Have a will that fairly divides your assets. Feel fulfilled and meaningful by giving away some of what you have to charities. We can hoard who and what we are — our life energy — as we are dying, or we can give parts of ourselves away. The latter feels the most freeing.

10. Make peace with becoming an infant again. You are in the process of being reborn. Your reunion with God will be as a child reuniting with nature itself. You will be completely vulnerable after death, completely open, completely ready for the next adventure. To some extent, the long illness has been a rehearsal of vulnerability for death itself,

which will be pure vulnerability. Make peace with becoming utterly vulnerable again, as you were when you were born and your loving parents and caregivers cared for you.

If we do these things, our society is more likely to understand what "completeness" is and will not fear letting us go. If we do not do these things, everything feels unresolved. For our family members and for policy makers, the fear of death controls even our own dying, legally and morally.

But if we live in concentration and completion as we are dying, perhaps our family members and our policy makers will see that we are fine and that we do not need to be overprotected, overmanaged, infantilized, caged by others' will, and kept physically alive longer than our souls wish to be alive. If we live well in our final months, years, and days, we will feel (and show to others) that we are truly relevant as elders. Our dying and death will be seen as the opportunity for unconditional love that it is — the miracle of living long enough and dying slowly enough that we and others can complete our goal in life of learning how to love without conditions. This way of dying allows elders to complete themselves and teaches lessons of love to the young for whom the dying one is making room: the next generation needs and wants us to complete ourselves so that they can fully begin their quest, their journey, their next stage of life.

Thus, we are saying that the "better" way to die is the freest way to die. The wonder of aging is freedom, and in dying and death that freedom is also what we make it, our responsibility to make happen in our world, our gift to protect as we die, and our song to sing to others, especially those younger than us (who tend to think they should make policy about us even though they have not lived what we are living), so that our whole society awakens finally to the fact that my dying, like my sexuality and my other individual rights, is not someone else's to determine; it is my own individual right.

### "KATHY'S SONG"

This memorial oratory is an example of helping dying family members and friends to give voice, ahead of their deaths, to their legacy, life philosophy, and completion spirituality. Feel free to use this form, if you wish, and modify it to fit your life and the life of your loved one. If it is appropriate, you can have a loved one read your oratory at your memorial service as I did at Kathy's.

## Kathy's Song

*— for and with Kathy Stevens (August 28, 1949–April 1, 2012)*

1.

My family, friends, from my new home,
  where everything is music,
      seated beside Jesus who died for
      me,
         I call back to you my tender
         song.
I was a driven, honest woman who took
  life so seriously,
      she gave herself young.
Mother of Kevin and Mike, I changed the
  world my small portion.
    With Don, I found a love measured
    only by eternity.
Grandmother of eight grandchildren, I
  met the God of wonders.
    A traveler with a big heart, I saw into
    all your chests:
      in each of you, a rose grows from
      God's beauty.
You may gather to weep for me now, you
  may not think to envy me,
      but I have my song!

2.

All who love me, make no mistake: my

death has come.
The great bear climbed to the top of the
small plum tree —
forgetting life's weight, she broke my
fragile branches.
My death has come.
The irascible old man at the door, up till
now my refuser,
stepped aside to let me pass. He held my
hand
through the opened doorway, into the
sleeve of light.
My death has come.
By fault of none, threads of yarn flew out
my garden window.
A cat gave chase, chasing them far away.
What was left to say?
I said, finally, "Go, my little soul, make
friends where you can."
My death has come.

3.

My friends, my family, how will you greet
my death?
All of you who helped me through my
years of illness —
will you remember only my sick bed?
My children, at your births you flew onto
my strong limbs
with newly opened wings —

please don't live now just to glue back my
broken branches.
Don, with you I learned a love greater
than any book —
you knew: my body hid holiness
inside.
Don, don't argue too long with the old
man at the door.
Mother, I know you didn't plan on my
dying before you —
dear mother, chase only my lightest
threads
back from oblivion.


4.
All who love me, no matter what you do,
remember my song!
For sixty-two years, a blue-eyed girl
collected spring rain in a bowl,
then tripped and tipped her
water into the sea:
help me climb now into my boat of
beautiful memories;
sprinkle the sparkles of my life's joys
over your grief.
During my illness, you saw human life
become cold and painful,
so I said to God, "I will die to remind
them of their loveliness."
Please, friends, always remember

your own loveliness.
You are the wave sunlight seeks on the
    water; your bodies,
        no matter their pain, echo the sound
        of oceans.
Be generous like light, and easy to care
    for —
        hear God's heart in your own beating
        hearts.


    5.
And when you leave this place today, love
    your children
        to their completeness; love your lover
        without envy;
hold an old person's hand — each of us
    wants only to be loved.
And you who run between calamities, run
    no longer —
            the God you need is always
            beside you.
        And you who rush from ambition to
        ambition —
know what I know now: rising in our
    throats, wherever we are,
            is God's voice.
Friends, when you leave here today, grasp
    your own fragile soul
        in your strong hands until you are
        grasped by it,

even to your breaking point, even to the
   tipping of your water
                  into the sea.


      6.
I know this truth from my life — fear
   disappears at the doorway
      if you have sung to the world
              the song you were born for.
Not even a sapling now, nor breath
   chasing anymore after breath,
      I know what I was: the body of God,
      breathing.
From now on, my dears, please
   remember me as glistening threads
              in the float of the sun.
It was me who tossed my life out the
   garden window, into the wind;
              it was time I go back out to play.
O my dears, don't wait another heartbeat
   to make your own lives beautiful and
   brave.
      Your death will come.

I praise what is truly alive,
what longs to be burned to death.
— Goethe


Well, I find the older I get, the more intense
my appetite for living and for appreciating
life gets. I think I was heedless when I was
younger. I thought it was endless. But I
just lost two really close friends in the last
two years, and, man, you realize you've got
just seconds. I just — oh! I mean, my kids
wouldn't dare say they were bored to me.
I would kill them! How dare you! You have
the gift of life. You've got to get out there
and eat it!
— Meryl Streep, 2012


I come into the peace of wild things . . .
I rest in the grace of the world, and am free.
—Wendell Berry

# Epilogue

Every day, no matter how old you are, and even if you think you have done everything you could have done, you still have the chance to do that one other thing you were born to do. Even on your last day of life, you are still changing, transforming, growing, because even in your last moment of breathing, you are changing someone else, helping them transform, helping them grow. We are alive until we die, and even after we die, we are still forces to be reckoned with in the world.

— Jim McNeill, MD, author of twelve
book-length journals recording his
spiritual life during his sixties,
seventies, and early eighties
until his death in 2008

Jim McNeill was a friend and mentor who, like me, loved words. We sat for hours, over a period of years, reading aloud and talking about the journals he began to write after his wife, Vicki, died of lung cancer. These journals were his spiritual companions for almost two decades. As he wrote them, he enjoyed his retirement, caring for his home and land in the mountains, being with his children and grandchildren, supporting numerous important causes, and mentoring young people. I met Jim and Vicki when I was in my midthirties, said good-bye to Vicki when I was in my early forties, then said good-bye to Jim in my early fifties. As Jim's journey of life was ending, he gave me a great deal of his soul to carry and helped me begin my own journey of conscious mortality.

I hope as my journey of this book ends with you, your journey through the wonder of aging will just begin. I believe deeply in the power of the book — I believe a book is a greater power than a blog, article, or sound bite; a book carries soul in a way that only a larger work can. A book is a long, communal time you and I have had together that carries a force by which we have and can celebrate, even protest, the terms of existence. The poet Robert Hass, at sixty-eight, put it this way: "It would be good if that force were felt by readers coming to this volume as an instance of the force with which human beings seem to need to represent themselves, to make symbols out of their experience, to say what it is like to be themselves, to make things that have not been made before and to bring them into the world and alter the world by doing so, to protest or celebrate the terms of existence, or at least not to go through it mute."

As three generations in one, assessing and understanding our decades of age in the new millennium, we who are over fifty are certainly not mute. We have voice, should we choose to take and celebrate that voice. We are elders of great worth, and much of that worth is not material, it is spiritual, a triumph of world-sustaining visibility rather than mere material hegemony. As elders, we now can be as interested in mercy as in success. As elders, we are gradually losing strength in the vessels of the body, but we can sense the richness of wine carried in the vessel as we never did before.

I hope you will go forward from this moment on with a new intention, one beyond having a midlife crisis, then, after that crisis, wandering aimlessly through the decades between midlife and death; miraculous age and the wonder of aging are something more than youth, and much more than a midlife crisis attached to an amorphous, distended nothingness. Earlier, I quoted Meryl Streep who, in her interview for her movie *Hope Springs*, discusses renewing intimacy while aging. Elsewhere in her interview for the movie, which appeared in *AARP Magazine*, the article's young author refers to Streep, at sixty-three, and her costar, Tommy Lee Jones, at sixty-five, as a couple "in midlife." When I read this reference I wanted to say, "Really? Sixty-three and sixty-five are midlife?" By the time they made that movie, Streep and Jones had entered, I believe, the stages of miraculous age — in their case, the age of distinction. Why not enjoy that? Why hide it by pretending these beautiful, distinguished people have not yet discovered the wonder of aging?

As we go forward, forming everywhere we go a community of committed elders, I hope we will agree not to see our age just as one "midlife" crisis that is a last gasp of youth, then many decades of getting old; rather, I hope we will now see our transformations throughout the stages of age as wonders of life and spirit. We are living through rites of passage that are baptisms by both fire and ice, a spiritual falling and rising, replete with crises of family, economy, love, loss, disease, pain, joy, appetites, renunciations, and death. These rites of passage constitute a journey in which our relationships are tested and cleansed, and through which our real worth on this earth is clarified.

As we emerge at various times in the journey to journal or define our insights, stories, and reminiscing, let us see the life we have lived as a kind of peaceful, glorious song, and watch how our self emerges, now, more or differently free than before. "Midlife crisis," "old age," and broad phrases of this kind are good words — they are not ruiners of spirit. On the other hand, though, we deserve more than these words for our story. They are somewhat trivial words in comparison to what we are going through.

You and I are becoming or have become spiritual elders. We are becoming or have become the people our own elders — my mother and father and your mother and father — hoped we would become. Let us celebrate this, without apology for getting older, and with a sense of freedom and love. Medical miracles keep us alive longer than any previous generation; a sense of wonder itself gives us the deep, beautiful life we deserve. By the time death comes for us, may we know that we have found the treasures of this lifetime and passed those treasures on to the next generation, as nature calls us to do, from the deep inward soul, no matter our pain or suffering, delight or joy, and no matter our place and time in our twenty-first-century journey of wonder and age.

# ACKNOWLEDGMENTS

My work in aging could not have occurred without the work of many others, whom I would like to mention gratefully: Elisabeth Kübler-Ross for her understanding of the stages of grief and loss that helped our culture redefine the end of life, and Gail Sheehy, whose work inspired millions of people to look much more carefully at the stages of middle age. The area my book covers lies between midlife and end of life, in those many decades so many of us are now living. Thank you, Christiane Northrup, for changing the way women think about menopause, and Jed Diamond for helping integrate the science of andropause into men's lives. Thanks also to Ken Dychtwald for *Age Power*, which helped define the way that aging baby boomers affect economics, politics, and everything else. Michael Roizen's *RealAge*, Roizen and Mehmet Oz's *You* books, Andrew Weil's *Healthy Aging*, and Daniel Amen's *Use Your Brain to Change*

*Your Age* provide insights and practical strategies for continuing to feel young and vital as we age. My thanks go out to all of the individuals, teams, and resources for your pioneering approaches. This book could not have been written without your work.

For insights, conversations, and correspondence regarding the subject of this book, thank you, Nancy Snyderman, MD; Daniel Amen, MD; Michael Thompson, PhD; Jed Diamond, PhD; John Ratey, MD; JoAnn Deak, PhD; Ruby Payne; Louann Brizendine, MD; Adie Goldberg, LCSW; Harold Koplewicz, MD; Phon Hudkins, PhD; Tracey J. Shors, PhD; Gregg Jantz, PhD; Rabbi Jacob Izakson; Reverend William Houff, PhD; Pastor Tim Wright; Lloyd Halpern, MD; Marny Tobin, RN; Tom Tobin, MD; Pam Brown, MA; and Jeannie Corkill, MSW. Your research and insights inspire me to keep pushing the envelope.

Thank you also to the women and men who have responded to my surveys and joined my focus groups. Your stories, questions, and challenges have made possible my own thinking and service. To my clients, I extend my profound gratitude. By letting me serve you, you have taught me more than you know.

To all those who have aided us in the Gurian Institute's wisdom-of-practice research over the last fifteen years, thank you for your time and wisdom. We could not conduct our research without your help. Kathy Stevens, our former executive director, passed away during the writing of this book. She appears in these pages. Many others in the Gurian Institute continue her legacy, including Don Stevens, Dakota Hoyt, Kelley King, Beth Black, Janet Allison, and all our team members.

To my literary agent, Bonnie Solow, and the wonderful people at Atria and Simon & Schuster, especially Sarah Durand and Judith Curr: thank you for your confidence and wisdom. It is a joy to be on your team.

To Gail and our daughters, Gabrielle and Davita, I extend the kind of gratitude that can barely be expressed in words. Thank you for guiding my work in your generous and powerful ways. We grow together, one book at a time!

# NOTES AND REFERENCES

**INTRODUCTION: THE WONDER OF AGING**

Administration on Aging, www.aoa.gov/prof/Statistics/statistics.asp. United Nations Report, United Nations Populations Division. These statistics change every year, but constantly show an increase in the size of the aging population.

Haya El Nasser and Paul Overger, "1990–2010: How America Changed," *USA Today,* August 10, 2011.

Some of my original meditations and other spiritual poetry have been published in *Ancient Wisdom, Modern Words* and *The Sabbath.* To learn more about these books, please visit www.faith-communities.net or www.amazon.com.

**CHAPTER 1: TOWARD A NEW SPIRIT OF AGING**

"The Layers," by Stanley Kunitz. See *The Collected Poems* (New York: Norton, 2002).

"The Journey" is quoted from Marilyn Sewell's *Cries of the Spirit* (Boston: Beacon Press, 2006).

Denis Whately's words were sent to me by my friend and colleague Kathy Stevens.

## The First Concentration: Forging a New Spirit of Aging

D. Bulettner, *The Blue Zones* (Washington, D.C.: National Geographic, 2010).

J. Robbins, *Healthy at 100* (New York: Ballantine Books, 2006).

## Stress as the Catalyst of Spirit

Bruce McEwen, PhD, "The Brain Under Stress." Bruce S. McEwen, PhD, Alfred E. Mirsky Professor, head of the Harold and Margaret Milliken Hatch Laboratory of Neuroendocrinology at the Rockefeller University, spoke at Fong Auditorium at Harvard University on September 27, 2011, as part of the center's Distinguished Scholars Lecture Series.

Steve Cole, PhD, is a professor of medicine and psychiatry and biobehavioral sciences in the UCLA School of Medicine. His research studies the biological pathways by which social environments influence gene expression by viral, cancer, and immune cell genomes. See "Social Regulation of Human Gene Expression," *Current Directions in Psychological Science* 18, no. 3 (2009): 132–37.

Tracey J. Shors, PhD, is Professor, Department of Psychology and Center for Collaborative Neuroscience, at Rutgers University. She has been generous in sharing the neurogenetics research with me. A number of her authored and coauthored articles on the subject appear on www.traceyshors.com.

For a number of years, Phon Hudkins, at the Human Ethology Institute in Washington, D.C., has been a source of information regarding stress in American children and adults. He is constantly informing my research, and I want to thank him for his passion.

## Embracing Our Age

Nancy Snyderman, MD, has been generous in sharing with me her insights on aging. As medical reporter for NBC News and the *Today* show, she has traveled the world interviewing and observing leading-edge medical and human researchers.

My observations linking happiness to aging are based on integration of the work of Ed and Robert Diener, Martin Seligman, and Mihaly Csikszentmihalyi, among others. This area of research is becoming vast, and rightfully so. To access some of it directly, a helpful Web site is www.happycounts.org. Also see the Center for Positive Psychology's Web site, www.ppc.sas.upenn.edu.

S. Beilock, *Choke* (New York: Free Press, 2011).

Beilock is quoted from "Master Class," *Tennis* (July–August 2012): 50.

## A Circle of Friends

John J. Ratey, MD, is an associate clinical professor of psychiatry at Harvard Medical School and has a private practice in Cambridge, Massachusetts. He's also the author of *Spark: The Revolutionary New Science of Exercise and the Brain* (New York: Little, Brown, 2008). He and I spoke at the Gurian Institute Summer Institute at the University of Colorado–Colorado Springs in July 2009.

J. Ratey, *A User's Guide to the Brain* (New York: Pantheon, 2001).

## Becoming an Elder

J. Fuller, "What's a Blue Zone, and Am I Living in One?" *Discovery Health* (August 12, 2011). See Howstuffworks.com.

D. Winterman, "The Towns Where People Live the Longest," *BBC News Magazine* (August 14, 2011). See newsvote.bbc.co.uk.

J. Wall, "Blue Zone Longevity," *Hartford Health and Science Examiner* (August 15,

2011). See examiner.com.

W. Cockerham and Y. Yamori, "Okinawa: An Exception to the Social Gradient of Life Expectancy in Japan," *Asia Pacific Journal* 10, no. 2 (2001): 154–58.

### CHAPTER 2: THE AGE OF TRANSFORMATION

From Rilke's Ninth Duino Elegy, *In Praise of Mortality*, trans. Joanna Macy and Anita Burrows (New York: Riverhead Books, 2004).

*The Essential Rumi*, trans. Coleman Barks with John Moyne (San Francisco: Harper-SanFrancisco, 1995).

From *Zen Poems*, selected and edited by Peter Harris (New York: Alfred Knopf, 1999).

### A Time Like No Other

Debra Gore, MD, is a family physician at Group Health Cooperative in Spokane, Washington. I spoke with her in Spokane.

Daniel Amen, MD, is a neuropsychiatrist and founder of the Amen Clinics. I spoke with him at the Gurian Institute Summer Institute at the University of Colorado–Colorado Springs in 2010.

### Stage 1: The Age of Transformation

Julie Taymor is quoted from *Newsweek*, May 28, 2012. See Jacob Bernstein, "Julie

Taymor Roars," 82.

A. Singh-Manoux, "Cognitive Decline Can Begin as Early as Age 45, Warn Experts," *British Medical Journal*, (January 5, 2012). 33 (0)1, http://bmj.com/press-releases/2012/01/05/cognitive-decline-can-begin-early-age-45-warn-experts.

J. L. Steiner et al., "Exercise Training Increases Mitochondrial Biogenesis in the Brain," *Journal of Applied Physiology* 111, no. 4 (October 1, 2011): 1066–71.

## Menopause and Andropause as Spiritual Quest

For more detail on the medical and psychological effects of menopause and andropause, see:

Christiane Northrup, *The Wisdom of Menopause* (rev. ed.) (New York: Bantam, 2012).

Jed Diamond, *Surviving Male Menopause* (New York: Sourcebooks, 2000).

Mickey Rourke is quoted from *Newsweek*, November 1, 2011.

Mary Oliver's poetry is, like Rumi's or Rilke's, a life companion for me. All art is at least as much a matter of taste as objective standard, and I know that. You might not find in her poetry the sustenance I do. But I hope you will at least look at her selected poems. They provide a powerful aid to morning writing meditation. And as works of art, I believe they will stand the test of time very well.

Mary Oliver, *New and Selected Poems,* vols. 1 and 2 (Boston: Beacon Press, 2005, 2007).

## Developing Fearlessness in Our Fifties

A. Maslow, *Toward a Psychology of Being* (New York: John Wiley Publishers, 1998).

J. S. Moser, S. B. Most, and R. F. Simons, "Increasing Negative Emotions by Reappraisal Enhances Subsequent Cognitive Control: A Combined Behavioral and Electrophysiological Study," *Cognitive, Affective, and Behavioral Neuroscience* 10 (2010): 195–207.

Jason Moser and David Nussbaum are featured in Jonah Lehrer's "The Art of Failing Successfully," *The Wall Street Journal,* October 28, 2011.

## CHAPTER 3: THE AGES OF DISTINCTION AND COMPLETION

A powerful Hikmet anthology is *Poems of Nazim Hikmet, Revised and Expanded Edition,* trans. Randy Blasing and Mutlu Konuk Blasing (New York: Persea, 2002). I have adapted Hikmet's lines.

See Marie Howe in *Cries of the Spirit,*

ed. Marilyn Sewell (Boston: Beacon Press, 2000).

D. H. Lawrence. *The Selected Poems* (New York: Penguin, 1989, reprint).

## Stage 2: The Age of Distinction

Rabbi Jacob Izakson lives in Spokane, Washington. He is the former rabbi of Temple Beth Shalom.

R. Housden, *Risking Everything* (New York: Harmony, 2003).

Rumi translations in this book are generally mine from the Turkish. I began working on translations of Rumi from Turkish when Gail and I lived in Ankara from 1986 to 1988 and I was learning the Turkish language. Translating Rumi has been a nonprofessional, spiritual experience for me, as have been my attempts to translate Rilke from the German. I translate these poets as a part of my morning reunion with God. Because I am not a trained or professional translator, I know that my translations are more projections of meaning than pure translation.

For actual translations of Rumi, I especially recommend Coleman Barks's beautiful volume, *The Essential Rumi.* For translations of Rainer Maria Rilke, the Barrow and Macy volumes, such as *Rilke's Book of Hours*, are some of the most powerful.

## Identifying Your Distinction and Legacy

I have quoted a few lines of this work from an e-mail sent to me by a friend. You can find the full poem and the full work of Michael Josephson at the Josephson Institute of Ethics in Los Angeles and at josephsoninstitute.org.

The studies at Stanford University appeared in Lewis Timberlake's *First Thing Every Morning* (Vancouver: Sim Publishers, 2010).

## The Elder's Love

Nazim Hikmet is my translation from the Turkish. Hikmet is virtually unknown in the United States, but if you can read him, you will discover a treasure. He writes of many things, including aging and, especially, freedom. Persea Books has put out very fine volumes of his poems.

Pablo Neruda, "There Is No Clear Light," in *The Essential Neruda: Selected Poems,* ed. and trans. Mark Eisner (San Francisco: City Lights Books, 2004).

Robert Bly et al., *The Rag and Bone Shop of the Heart* (New York: HarperPerennial, 1990).

## Women, Men, and Distinction

See Womensphilanthropyinstitute.org.

Helen Fisher's very readable brain-based book, *Anatomy of Love* (New York: Ballantine Books, 2000), joins with David Buss's *The Evolution of Desire* (New York: Basic Books, 2003) to provide a strong foundation for understanding how the past still affects us as women and men.

A. Quindlen, *Lots of Candles, Plenty of Cake* (New York: Random House, 2012).

## Stage 3: The Age of Completion

Reverend William Houff's remarks in this chapter are composites of a number of conversations, though most of the content of this section occurred in two specific conversations in 2009.

W. H. Houff, *Infinity in Your Hand* (New York: Skinner House, 2001).

D. Friedman, *Don't Ever Get Old* (New York: Minotaur Books, 2012).

Shirley Aresvik lives in Spokane, Washington, and is at work on a number of volumes of poetry.

## The Spirit of Completion

D. Amen, *Amen Solution Newsletter,* July 2012.

Galway Kinnell's *A New Selected Poems* (New York: Knopf, 2000) is a powerful volume of "real life" at its most tender and beautiful, yet without sentimentality.

The Riversong group was called to my attention by Rebecca Nappi of the *Spokesman-Review*. See Rebecca Nappi, "Ensemble of Note," *Spokesman-Review,* June 2, 2012.

T. Roethke, *Collected Poems* (New York: Anchor, 1974).

C. Milowsz, quoted in Robert Bly et al., *Rag and Bone Shop of the Heart* (New York: HarperPerennial, 1990). This whole volume, collected and commentated by Robert Bly, James Hillman, and Michael Meade, can act as a companion throughout a man's life journey. It is the kind of volume one comes back to year after year. It is for men what something like Marilyn Sewell's anthology *Cries of the Spirit* (Boston: Beacon Press, 2000) can be for women. A number of the epigraphs in this book come from Sewell's anthology. I highly recommend it for daily reading and book groups, if you have them, in your circle of friends.

James Earl Jones is quoted from *Newsweek,* May 14, 2012, 56.

Elisabeth Kübler-Ross, *Death: The Final Stage of Growth* (New York: Scribner, 1997).

## CHAPTER 4: HOW MEN AND WOMEN AGE DIFFERENTLY

Marilyn Sewell, *Cries of the Spirit* (Boston:

Beacon Press, 2000).

Adrienne Rich, *Adrienne Rich's Poetry and Prose* (New York: Norton, 1993).

William James, *Principles of Psychology* (London: Dover Publications, 1950).

This chapter is the outgrowth of more than twenty years of integrating science-based studies into working with women and men. Here are just some of the studies that ground this work. I have divided them into subject areas for you. You'll recognize some of the topic areas in direct relation to the points I made in this chapter; others I am including so that, if you are someone who likes to read the science yourself, you will have a number of places to go. By my count, there are more than five hundred studies worldwide that look at various parts of male/female difference.

## Scientific Studies on Gender Differences

Arthur Wunderlich et al., "Brain Activation During Human Navigation: Gender-Different Neural Networks as Substrate of Performance," *Nature Neuroscience* 3, no. 4 (April 2000): 404–8.

Ruben Gur et al., "An fMRI Study of Sex Differences in Regional Activation to a Verbal and Spatial Task," *Brain and Language* 74, no. 2 (September 2000): 157–70.

N. Sandstrom et al., "Males and Females Use Different Distal Cues in a Virtual Environment Navigation Task," *Cognitive Brain Research* 6, no. 4 (April 1998): 351–60.

M. Eals and I. Silverman, "The Hunter-Gatherer Theory of Spatial Sex Differences: Proximate Factors Mediating the Female Advantage in Recall of Object Arrays," *Ethology and Sociobiology* 15, no. 2 (March 1994): 95–105.

I. Silverman and M. Eals, "Sex Differences in Spatial Abilities: Evolutionary Theory and Data," in J. Barkow, L. Cosmides, and J. Tooby, eds., *The Adapted Mind: Evolutionary Psychology and the Generation of Culture* (New York: Oxford University Press: 1992), 487–503.

D. Saucier et al., "Are Sex Differences in Navigation Caused by Sexually Dimorphic Strategies or by Differences in the Ability to Use the Strategies?" *Behavioral Neuroscience* 116, no. 3 (June 2002): 403–10.

**Gray and White Matter Processing**

Ruben Gur et al., "Sex Differences Found in Proportions of Gray and White Matter in the Brain: Links to Differences in Cognitive Performance Seen," study, University of Pennsylvania Medical Center, May 18, 1999. http://www.sciencedaily.com/releases/1999/05/990518072823.htm.

Maria Elena Cordero et al., "Sexual Dimorphism in Number and Proportion of Neurons in the Human Median Raphe Nucleus," *Developmental Brain Research* 124, nos. 1–2 (November 2000): 43–52.

Marian Diamond, "Male and Female Brains," lecture for Women's Forum West Annual Meeting, San Francisco, California, 2003.

R. C. Gur et al., "Sex Differences in Brain Gray and White Matter in Healthy Young Adults," *Journal of Neuroscience* 19, no. 10 (May 15, 1999): 4065–72.

**Structures in the Brain**

Thomas E. Schlaepfer et al., "Structural Differences in the Cerebral Cortex of Healthy Female and Male Subjects: A Magnetic Resonance Imaging Study," *Psychiatry Research: Neuroimaging* 61, no. 3 (September 29, 1995): 129–35.

Tracey J. Shors, "Significant Life Events and the Shape of Memories to Come: A Hypothesis," *Neurobiology of Learning and Memory* 85, no. 2 (March 2006): 103–15. http://www.rci.rutgers.edu/~shors/pdf/ Significant%20life%20events%202006%20 Shors%20article.pdf.

M. de Lacoste et al., "Sex Differences in the Fetal Human Corpus Callosum," *Human*

*Neurobiology* 5, no. 2 (1986): 93–96.

L. A. Kilpatrick et al., "Sex-Related Differences in Amygdala Functional Connectivity During Resting Conditions," *NeuroImage* 30, no. 2 (April 1, 2006): 452–61. http://today.uci.edu/news/releasedetail.asp?key=1458.

S. Hamann et al., "Men and Women Differ in Amygdala Response to Visual Sexual Stimuli," *Nature Neuroscience* 7, no. 4 (April 2004): 411–16.

William Killgore et al., "Sex-Specific Developmental Changes in Amygdala Responses to Affective Faces," *NeuroReport* 12, no. 2 (February 12, 2001): 427–33.

W. D. Killgore and D. A. Yurgelun-Todd, "Sex-Related Developmental Differences in the Lateralized Activation of the Prefrontal Cortex and Amygdala During Perception of Facial Affect," *Perceptual and Motor Skills* 99, no. 2 (October 2004): 371–91.

Thich Nhat Hanh, *The Miracle of Mindfulness* (Boston: Beacon Press, 1999).

Saint Catherine appears in Daniel Ladinsky's *Love Poems to God*.

## Brain Chemistry: Our Neurochemicals and Hormones

H. E. Albers et al., "Hormonal Basis of Social Conflict and Communication," in D. W. Pfaff, A. P. Arnold, A. M. Etgen, S. E. Fahrbach, and R. T. Rubin, eds., *Hormones, Brain, and Behavior,* vol. 1 (New York: Academic Press, 2002), 393–433.

Lynda Liu, "Keep Testosterone in Balance: The Positive and Negative Effects of the Male Hormone," *WebMD,* January 2005.

K. Christiansen, "Behavioral Effects of Androgen in Men and Women," *Journal of Endocrinology* 170, no. 1 (July 2001): 39–48.

J. C. Compaan et al., "Vasopressin and the Individual Differentiation in Aggression in Male House Mice," *Annals of the New York Academy of Sciences* 652 (June 1992): 458–59.

K. Alexanderson, "An Assessment Protocol for Gender Analysis of Medical Literature," *Women and Health* 29, no. 2 (1999): 81–98.

**Men and Women React to Stress Differently**

Gwendolyn Wood and Tracey J. Shors, "Stress Facilitates Classical Conditioning in Males, but Impairs Classical Conditioning in Females Through Activational Effects of Ovarian Hormones," *Proceedings of the National Academy of Sciences* 95, no. 7 (March 31, 1998): 4066–71.

Tracey J. Shors, "Stress and Sex Effects on Associative Learning: For Better or for Worse," *Neuroscientist* 4, no. 5 (September

1998): 353–64.

Tracey J. Shors and George Miesegaes, "Testosterone *in Utero* and at Birth Dictates How Stressful Experience Will Affect Learning in Adulthood," *Proceedings of the National Academy of Sciences* 99, no. 21 (October 15, 2002): 13955–60.

Lauren A. Weiss et al., "Sex-Specific Genetic Architecture of Whole Blood Serotonin Levels," *American Journal of Human Genetics* 76, no. 1 (January 2005): 33–41.

Rossana Arletti et al., "Oxytocin Involvement in Male and Female Sexual Behavior," *Annals of the New York Academy of Sciences* 652, no. 1 (June 1992): 180–93.

Andrea Decapua and Diana Boxer, "Bragging, Boasting and Bravado: Male Banter in a Brokerage House," *Women and Language* 22, no. 1 (Spring 1999): 5–11.

**For More on Men and the Biochemical Cycle**

Deborah Blum, *Sex on the Brain: The Biological Differences Between Men and Women* (New York: Penguin Books, 1998).

Gabrielle Lichterman, "Men's Room: The Male Hormone Cycle." Available online at http://www.hormonology.info/malehormone cycle.htm.

## Verbal Communication Differences

Bennett A. Shaywitz et al., "Sex Differences in the Functional Organization of the Brain for Language," *Nature* 373 (February 16, 1995): 607–9.

J. D. Bremner et al., "Gender Differences in Cognitive and Neural Correlates in Remembrance of Emotional Words," *Psychopharmacology Bulletin* 35, no. 3 (Summer 2001): 55–78.

Michael Phillips et al., "Temporal Lobe Activation Demonstrates Sex-Based Differences During Passive Listening," *Radiology* 220, no. 1 (July 2001): 202–7.

Frank Schneider et al., "Gender Differences in Regional Cerebral Activity During Sadness," *Human Brain Mapping* 9, no. 4 (April 2000): 226–38.

R. Salomone, *Same, Different, Equal* (New Haven, CT: Yale University Press, 2003).

Elizabeth Sowell et al., "Development of Cortical and Subcortical Brain Structures in Childhood and Adolescence: A Structural MRI Study," *Developmental Medicine and Child Neurology* 44, no. 1 (January 2002): 4–16.

Elizabeth Sowell et al., "Mapping Cortical Change Across the Human Life Span," *Nature Neuroscience* 6, no. 3 (March 2003): 309–15.

**Nonverbal Communication**

J. A. Hall, *Nonverbal Sex Differences: Communication Accuracy and Expressive Style* (Baltimore: Johns Hopkins University Press, 1984).

J. A. Hall et al., "Status Roles and Recall of Nonverbal Cues," *Journal of Nonverbal Behavior* 25, no. 2 (2001): 79–100.

T. G. Horgan, "Thinking More Versus Less About Interpreting Nonverbal Behavior: A Gender Difference in Decoding Style" (unpublished doctoral dissertation, Northeastern University, 2001).

R. F. McGivern et al., "Gender Differences in Incidental Learning and Visual Recognition Memory: Support for a Sex Difference in Unconscious Environmental Awareness," *Personality and Individual Differences* 25, no. 2 (August 1998): 223–32.

D. McGuinness and J. Symonds, "Sex Differences in Choice Behaviour: The Object-Person Dimension," *Perception* 6, no. 6 (1977): 691–94.

S. J. McKelvie, "Sex Differences in Memory for Faces," *Journal of Psychology* 107 (1981): 109–25.

S. J. McKelvie, L. Standing, D. St. Jean, and J. Law, "Gender Differences in Recognition Memory for Faces and Cars: Evidence for the Interest Hypothesis," *Bulletin of the*

*Psychonomic Society* 31, no. 5 (September 1993): 447–48.

S. Nowicki Jr. and M. P. Duke, "Nonverbal Receptivity: The Diagnostic Analysis of Nonverbal Accuracy (DANVA)," in J. A. Hall and F. J. Bernieri, eds., *Interpersonal Sensitivity: Theory and Measurement* (Mahwah, NJ: Lawrence Erlbaum, 2001), 183–98.

P. A. Powers, J. L. Andriks, and E. F. Loftus, "Eyewitness Accounts of Females and Males," *Journal of Applied Psychology* 64, no. 3 (June 1979): 339–47.

L. Seidlitz and E. Diener, "Sex Differences in the Recall of Affective Experiences," *Journal of Personality and Social Psychology* 74, no. 1 (January 1998): 262–71.

P. N. Shapiro and S. Penrod, "Meta-analysis of Facial Identification Studies," *Psychological Bulletin* 100, no. 2 (September 1986): 139–56.

J. A. Hall and D. Matsumoto, "Gender Differences in Judgments of Multiple Emotions from Facial Expressions," *Emotion* 4, no. 2 (June 2004): 201–6.

Hara Estroff Marano, "The Opposite Sex: The New Sex Scorecard," *Psychology Today* (July–August 2003): 38–44.

E. B. McClure et al., "A Developmental Examination of Gender Differences in Brain Engagement During Evaluation of Threat,"

*Biological Psychiatry* 55, no. 11 (June 1, 2004): 1047–55.

J. F. Thayer and B. H. Johnsen, "Sex Differences in Judgment of Facial Affect: A Multivariate Analysis of Recognition Errors," *Scandinavian Journal of Psychology* 41, no. 3 (September 2000): 243–46.

## Memory Differences

D. A. Casiere and N. L. Ashton, "Eyewitness Accuracy and Gender," *Perceptual and Motor Skills* 83, no. 3 part 1 (December 1996): 914.

P. J. Davis, "Gender Differences in Autobiographical Memory for Childhood Emotional Experiences," *Journal of Personality and Social Psychology* 76, no. 3 (March 1999): 498–510.

R. W. Doherty, "The Emotional Contagion Scale: A Measure of Individual Differences," *Journal of Nonverbal Behavior* 21, no. 2 (Summer 1997): 131–54.

Terrence G. Horgan et al., "Gender Differences in Memory for the Appearance of Others," *Personality and Social Psychology Bulletin* 30, no. 2 (February 2004): 185–96.

A. Herlitz, L. G. Nilsson, and L. Backman, "Gender Differences in Episodic Memory," *Memory and Cognition* 25, no. 6 (November 1997): 801–11.

D. J. Herrmann, M. Crawford, and M. Holdsworth, "Gender-Linked Differences in Everyday Memory Performance," *British Journal of Psychology* 83, part 2 (May 1992): 221–31.

Also see: Archana Singh-Manoux, "Memory, Mental Function Begin Slipping as Early as Age 45," *Neuroreport* 11, no. 7 (May 15, 2000): 1581–85.

**Gender and Clothing**

H. M. Buckley and M. E. Roach, "Clothing as a Nonverbal Communicator of Social and Political Attitudes," *Home Economics Research Journal* 3, no. 2 (December 1974): 94–102.

L. L. David, "Clothing and Human Behavior: A Review," *Home Economics Research Journal* 12, no. 3 (March 1984): 325–39.

H. Douty, "Influence of Clothing on Perception of Persons," *Journal of Home Economics* 55 (1963): 197–202.

R. A. Feinberg, L. Mataro, and W. J. Burroughs, "Clothing and Social Identity," *Clothing and Textiles Research Journal* 11, no. 1 (September 1992): 18–23.

B. H. Johnson, R. H. Nagasawa, and K. Peters, "Clothing Style Differences: Their Effect on the Impression of Sociability," *Home Economics Research Journal* 6, no. 1

(September 1977): 58–63.

S. Kaiser, *The Social Psychology of Clothing* (New York: Macmillan, 1990).

M. L. Knapp and J. A. Hall, *Nonverbal Communication in Human Interaction* (Belmont, CA: Thomson Learning, 2002).

Y. Kwon, "Sex, Sex-Role, Facial Attractiveness, Social Self-Esteem and Interest in Clothing," *Perceptual and Motor Skills* 84, no. 3 (June 1997): 899–907.

J. K. Lundberg and E. P. Sheehan, "The Effects of Glasses and Weight on Perceptions of Attractiveness and Intelligence," *Journal of Social Behavior and Personality* 9, no. 4 (December 1994): 753–60.

E. W. Mathes and S. B. Kempher, "Clothing as a Nonverbal Communicator of Sexual Attitudes and Behavior," *Perceptual and Motor Skills* 43, no. 2 (October 1976): 495–98.

S. L. Sporer, "Clothing as a Contextual Cue in Facial Recognition," *German Journal of Psychology* 17 (1993): 183–99.

## Gender and Body Image

S. E. Cross and L. Madson, "Models of the Self: Self-Construals and Gender," *Psychological Bulletin* 122, no. 1 (July 1997): 5–37.

D. M. Driscoll, J. R. Kelly, and W. L. Henderson, "Can Perceivers Identify Likelihood to Sexually Harass?" *Sex Roles* 38, nos. 7–8

(1998): 557–88.

S. Gabriel and W. L. Gardner, "Are There 'His' and 'Hers' Types of Interdependence? The Implications of Gender Differences in Collective Versus Relational Interdependence for Affect, Behavior, and Cognition," *Journal of Personality and Social Psychology* 77, no. 3 (September 1999): 642–55.

M. B. Harris, R. J. Harris, and S. Bochner, "Fat, Four-Eyed, and Female: Stereotypes of Obesity, Glasses, and Gender," *Journal of Applied Social Psychology* 12, no. 6 (December 1982): 503–16.

L. A. Jackson, L. A. Sullivan, and J. S. Hymes, "Gender, Gender Role, and Physical Appearance," *Journal of Psychology* 121, no. 1 (January 1987): 51–56.

S. Jobson and J. S. Watson, "Sex and Age Differences in Choice Behaviour: The Object-Person Dimension," *Perception* 13, no. 6 (1984): 719–24.

**Gender and Grief**

K. J. Doka and T. Martin, *Grieving Beyond Gender* (New York: Routledge, 2012).

T. Martin and K. J. Doka, *Men Don't Cry, Women Do: Transcending Gender Stereotypes of Grief* (Philadelphia: Taylor & Francis, 1999).

P. Rosenblatt, R. Walsh, and D. Jackson,

*Grief and Mourning in Cross-Cultural Perspective* (Washington, DC: HRAF Press, 1976).

A. Wolfelt, "Gender Roles and Grief: Why Men's Grief Is Naturally Complicated," *Thanatos* 15, no. 30 (1990): 20–24.

## Competition and Cooperation

M. Van Vugt, D. De Cremer, and D. P. Janssen, "Gender Differences in Cooperation and Competition: The Male-Warrior Hypothesis," *Psychological Science* 18, no. 1 (January 2007): 19–23.

J. Van Honk and D. J. Schutter, "Testosterone Reduces Conscious Detection of Signals Serving Social Correction," *Psychological Science* 18, no. 8 (August 2007): 663–67.

Shelley E. Taylor, *The Tending Instinct* (New York: Times Books/Henry Holt, 2002).

Judith E. Owen Blakemore, Steve R. Baumgardner, and Allen H. Keniston, "Male and Female Nurturing: Perceptions of Style and Competence," *Sex Roles* 18, nos. 7–8 (April 1988): 449–59.

## Men and Family

P. B. Gray et al., "Marriage and Fatherhood Are Associated with Lower Testosterone in Males," *Evolution and Human Behavior* 23, no. 3 (May 2002): 193–201.

"Daddy's Brains," *Parents Magazine,* January 2006. The Princeton study discovered that connections in the male prefrontal cortex (executive decision making) increased, as did male bonding chemicals, when males parented (and grandparented).

Brian Braiker, "Just Don't Call Me Mr. Mom," *Newsweek,* October 8, 2007, 53.

Stephen Johnson, *The Sacred Path* (Los Angeles: Sacred Path Books, 2012).

See also Wendy S. Harman et al., "The Psychology of Voluntary Employee Turnover," *Current Directions in Psychological Science* 16, no. 1 (February 2007): 51–54.

And Helen Fisher's very readable brain-based book, *Anatomy of Love* (New York: Ballantine Books, 2000), is a classic.

Anita Barrows and Joanna Marie Macy have translated *Sonnets to Orpheus, The Duino Elegies,* and many other volumes. Translations by Stephen Mitchell of the same Rilke books give yet another translator's perspective.

Pastor Tim Wright can be reached at www.faceofgrace.org. Community of Grace is in Peoria, Arizona. Pastor Tim and I also wrote a rite-of-passage program together, which can be accessed at www.heroicquestforboys.com.

## Chapter 5: The Wisdom of Intimate Separateness

Teilhard De Chardin, *The Phenomenon of Man* (New York: Harper Perennial Modern Classics, 2008).

For Teresa of Avila, see Daniel Ladinsky, *Love Poems From God.*

Emanuel Swedenborg, *Divine Love and Wisdom*, trans. George F. Dole (West Chester, Pa: Swedenborg Foundation Publishers, 2009).

See Galway Kinnell's *A New Selected Poems.*

### The Art of Intimate Separateness

David Buss, *The Evolution of Desire* (New York: Basic Books, 2003).

Sue Carter is quoted from Sue Carter, "The Love Hormones," *Family Therapy Magazine*, May–June 2012. This article includes endnotes of some of the most compelling primary studies available regarding the topics of sex, love, and stress, as well as some studies that discuss monogamy research.

Helen Fisher is quoted from "The Brain, How We Fall in Love, and How We Stay Together: An Interview with Helen Fisher" in *Family Therapy Magazine,* May–June 2011.

See also Brett J. Atkinson, "Reconditioning Emotional Habits," *Family Therapy Maga-*

*zine*, May–June 2011.

## Sex and the IS Paradigm

Omri Gillith is quoted from "What's Love Got to Do With It," *Observer* (Association for Psychological Science) 23, no. 6 (July–August 2010): p. 23.

For original source material and for more depth regarding sexuality facts, see the National Survey of Sexual Health and Behavior at Indiana University. I have used the 2010 version, and the links provided from it (www.nationalsexstudy.indiana.edu). Sexual health and behavior statistics are fluid, and one of the best ways to see their evolution is to go to the Indiana University Web site and browse through the postings and links. I thank the team at Indiana University for bringing together this information in such a compact and powerful way. Their work allows me to draw some of the conclusions I make in this chapter. See also L. Brizendine, *The Female Brain* (New York: Three Rivers Press, 2007).

Susan Reed's work and the SWAN study were provided to me by Debra Gore, MD, from the Group Health Cooperative, "Healthy Aging CME for Primary Care," continuing education course, October 5, 2011, SeaTac, Washington.

Ogas and Gaddam are quoted in "The Online World of Female Desire," *Wall Street Journal,* April 30–May 1, 2011.

See also T. D. Conley et al., "Women, Men, and the Bedroom," *Current Directions in Psychological Science* 20, no. 5 (October 2011): 296–300.

## The Monogamy Gene

H. Walum et al., "Genetic Variation in the Vasopressin Receptor 1a Gene (AVPR1A) Associates with Pair-Bonding Behavior in Humans," *PNAS* 105, no. 37 (September 16, 2008): 14153–56.

J. Lammers et al., "Power Increases Infidelity Among Men and Women," *Psychological Science* 22, no. 9 (April 13, 2011): 1191–97. This article includes endnotes that provide further scientific studies regarding monogamy.

You will find additional information regarding the monogamy gene in the following: Louann Brizendine, *The Female Brain* (New York: Three Rivers Press, 2007); Helen Fisher, *Anatomy of Love* (New York: Ballantine Books, 2000); David Buss, *Dangerous Passions* (New York: Free Press, 2011) and *The Evolution of Desire* (New York: Basic Books, 2003).

## A New Way of Love

Here again, Daniel Ladinsky has worked with the writings of Saint Francis, Catherine of Siena, Teresa of Avila, Kabir, Rabin, and many other spiritual poets of history to create translations that fit the language of the new millennium. I hope you will look at Daniel Ladinsky, *Love Poems from God* (New York: Penguin Compass, 2002). Many of the epigraphs and quotes from historical spiritual figures that appear in this book are beholden to Ladinsky's approach to translating and adapting the spiritual poets' words.

### CHAPTER 6: THE AMAZING GRANDPARENT BRAIN

See www.appleseeds.org, which provides inspirational quotes such as Pope John's. The site is associated with Franciscan University.

For Emerson and Goethe, see Robert Bly et al., *The Rag and Bone Shop of the Heart.*

## The Grandparent Brain

You can learn more about Michael Thompson and his work at www.michaelthompson phd.com.

The June 2012 issue of *Success Magazine* includes a number of articles on happiness. I highly recommend this issue, including "Why Happiness Matters" by Patty Onderko. Diener and Sussman are quoted in this issue.

Beth is Beth Black, founder of the Cherokee Creek School for Boys in South Carolina.

## Are Grandmothers and Grandfathers Different?

Marianne Legato, *Why Men Die First* (New York: Palgrave Macmillan, 2008).

Shirley Aresvik lives in Spokane, Washington. She is working on a number of volumes of poetry regarding her own and her family's life.

## The Sacred Stories of the Grandparents

Saint John is quoted from Swami Abhayanada's *History of Mysticism* (London: Watkins, 2002).

## Stress and the Amazing Grandparent Brain

F. Grodstein, "How Early Can Cognitive Decline Be Detected?" *British Medical Journal* (January 5, 2011): 7652: 344.

B. Carey, "Too Much Stress May Give Genes Gray Hair," *New York Times*, November 4, 2004.

Sara W. Lazar et al., "Functional Brain Mapping of the Relaxation Response and Meditation," *NeuroReport* 11, no. 7 (May 15, 2000): 1581–85. This study's abstract reads: "Meditation is a conscious mental process that induces a set of integrated physiologic changes termed the relaxation response. Functional magnetic resonance imaging (fMRI) was used to identify and characterize the brain regions that are active during a simple form of meditation. Significant signal increases were observed in the group-averaged data in the dorsolateral prefrontal and parietal cortices, hippocampus/parahippocampus, temporal lobe, pregenual anterior cingulate cortex, striatum, and pre- and post-central gyri during meditation. Global fMRI signal decreases were also noted, although these were probably secondary to cardiorespiratory changes that often accompany meditation. The results indicate that the practice of meditation activates neural structures involved in attention and control of the autonomic nervous system."

Meditation (or prayer) is universally powerful as a stress reducer, even if one does not have a formal belief in God, because of the concentration effects on various parts of the brain.

A. Newberg, *Why God Won't Go Away* (New York: Ballantine Books, 2004).

Skoryna's research at Easter Island is reported in D. Stipp, "A New Path to Longevity," *Scientific American* 306(1) (January 2012): 32–39.

Larkin's story appears in Larkin Warren, "When Is Life Too Long?" *AARP Magazine* (August–September 2012): 58–60 and at aarp.org.

**You Are in the Driver's Seat**
Mehmet Oz is quoted from "More Sex, Less Stress" in *AARP Magazine* (September/October, 2011).

### CHAPTER 7: A NEW LIFETIME OF SECOND CHANCES

The Meyer and Whately words were sent to me by my friend and colleague Kathy Stevens.

Anna Quindlen, commencement speech, Villanova University, June 23, 2000.

**Completion Spirituality**
M. Gazzaniga, "The Split Brain Revisited," *Scientific American* (July 1998): 51–55.

Fran Spielhagen has been my friend and a friend to the Gurian Institute for six years. She teaches at Mount Saint Mary College in Newburgh, New York. We have spoken together a number of times on topics regarding teaching, learning, and aging.

Amichai is one of the world's finest poets, but he is little known in the United States. I hope you will go to *Selected Poetry*, translated by Chana Bloch and Stephen Mitchell (Los Angeles: University of California Press, 1994) and *Open Closed Open*, translated by Chana Bloch (New York: Mariner Books, 2006). The latter is very much about aging. It can serve as a meditation companion and as a friend in the journey.

## CHAPTER 8: THE MIRACLE OF DYING AND DEATH

See Robert Bly et al., *The Rag and Bone Shop of the Heart.*

Theodore Roethke, *Collected Poems* (New York: Anchor, 1974).

Socrates quoted from Plato's *Apology.*

"October Fullness" is translated by Mark Eisner in *The Essential Neruda: Selected Poems*, ed. and trans. Mark Eisner (San Francisco: City Lights, 2004).

### There Is No Right Way to Die, but There Is a Better Way

Elisabeth Kübler-Ross, *Death: The Final Stage of Growth* (New York: Scribner, 1997).

### Protecting the Miracle of Your Death

Dr. Halpern and I have been friends for almost fifteen years. I performed the wedding ceremony for his eldest daughter, and he and his wife, Carmen, and my wife and I have all been friends for years. My dialogues with Lloyd have evolved around the topic of dying and death as a way of looking carefully at all the generations we must each serve as we live and die.

For Rilke lines, see *Duino Elegies.*

Muriel Spark appears in *Cries of the Spirit.*

Yehuda Amichai, *Open Closed Open.*

Rev. Houff: private conversations.

Curtis Johnson shared his story and wisdom in his article, "Put Real Dignity in Choice to Die," in the *Spokesman-Review*, June 10, 2012.

## Confronting Our Fear of Abandonment

The statistics appear in Frank Jordans, "WHO: Dementia Cases Worldwide Will Triple by 2050," Associated Press, April 11, 2012.

A. Bennett, *The Cost of Hope* (New York: Random House, 2012).

Amanda Bennett, "The Cost of Hope," *Newsweek*, June 4 and 11, 2012.

Thank you to Karen Boyd for her story.

See also Joe Klein's moving "The Long Goodbye," *Time*, June 11, 2012.

### EPILOGUE

Meryl Streep and Tommy Lee Jones are quoted from "We Ask Meryl Streep and

Tommy Lee Jones, 'Can Passion Last?'," *AARP Magazine* (August–September 2012): 43.

Wendell Berry appears in *Risking Everything.*

Robert Hass is quoted from his introduction to *Best American Poetry 2001* (New York: Scribner, 2001).

Goethe's "The Holy Longing" appears in *Risking Everything,* translated by Robert Bly.

# BIBLIOGRAPHY

Amen, Daniel. *Use Your Brain to Change Your Age.* New York: Bantam, 2011.

———. *Sex on the Brain.* New York: Bantam, 2005.

Amichai, Yehuda. *Open Closed Open.* Trans. Chana Bloch. New York: Mariner Books, 2006.

———. *Selected Poetry.* Trans. Chana Bloch and Stephen Mitchell. Los Angeles: University of California Press, 1994.

Arnot, Robert. *The Biology of Success.* Boston: Little, Brown & Company, 2001.

Arrien, Angeles. *The Second Half of Life.* Boulder, CO: Sounds True, 2007.

Barks, Coleman, and John Moyne. *The Essential Rumi.* New York: HarperOne, 2004.

Baron-Cohen, Simon. *The Essential Difference.* New York: Basic Books, 2003.

Barrows, Anita, and Joanna Marie Macy. *Rilke's Book of Hours.* New York: Riverhead Books, 2005.

Bear, Mark, Barry Connors, and Michael Paradiso. *Neuroscience.* Baltimore: Williams and Wilkins, 1996.

Bennett, Amanda. *The Cost of Hope.* New York: Random House, 2012.

Blum, Deborah. *Sex on the Brain.* New York: Penguin Books, 1998.

Boston Women's Health Collective. *Our Bodies, Ourselves.* New York: Touchstone, 2005.

Brizendine, Louann. *The Female Brain.* New York: Three Rivers Press, 2007.

Bulettner, Daniel. *The Blue Zones.* Washington, D.C.: National Geographic, 2010.

Buss, David. *Dangerous Passions.* New York: Free Press, 2011.

———. *The Evolution of Desire.* New York: Basic Books, 2003.

Carter, Rita. *Mapping the Mind.* Los Angeles: University of California Press, 1998.

Deak, JoAnn. *Girls Will Be Girls.* New York: Hyperion, 2003.

Diamond, Jared. *Guns, Germs, and Steel.* New York: W. W. Norton, 1997.

———. *The Third Chimpanzee.* New York: HarperPerennial, 1992.

Diamond, Jed. *Mr. Mean.* New York: Vox Novus, 2010.

———. *Surviving Male Menopause.* New York: Sourcebooks, 2000.

Dychtwald, Ken. *Age Power.* New York:

Tarcher/Putnam, 2000.

Eisner, Mark, ed. and trans. *The Essential Neruda: Selected Poems.* San Francisco: City Lights, 2004.

Faludi, S. *Stiffed: The Betrayal of the American Man.* New York: Harper Perennial, 2000.

Farrell, W. *The Myth of Male Power.* New York: Berkley Books, 2001.

Fisher, Helen. *Anatomy of Love.* New York: Ballantine Books, 2000.

Flinders, Carol. *The Values of Belonging.* San Francisco: HarperSanFrancisco, 2002.

Friedan, B. *The Second Stage.* Cambridge, MA: Harvard University Press, 1981/1998.

Gilmore, David. *Manhood in the Making.* New Haven, CT: Yale University Press, 1990.

Golden, T. R. *Swallowed by a Snake.* Gaithersburg, MD: G H Publishing, LLC, 2000.

Goleman, Daniel. *Emotional Intelligence.* New York: Bantam Books, 1995.

Gurian, J. P., and J. Gurian. *The Dependency Tendency.* New York: Rowman and Littlefield, 1983.

Gurian, Michael. *The Invisible Presence.* Boston: Shambhala, 2010.

———. *Leadership and the Sexes.* San Francisco: Jossey-Bass/John Wiley, 2008.

———. *What Could He Be Thinking?* New York: St. Martin's Press, 2004.

Harris, Judith R. *The Nurture Assumption.*

New York: Free Press, 1998.

Jessel, David, and Anne Moir. *Brain Sex.* New York: Dell, 1989.

Johnson, Stephen. *The Sacred Path.* Los Angeles: Sacred Path Press, 2012.

Johnson, Steven. *Mind Wide Open.* New York: Scribner, 2004.

Kandel, Eric, James Schwartz, and Thomas Jessell. *Essentials of Neural Science and Behavior.* Norwalk, CT: Appleton & Lange, 1995.

Kinnell, Galway. *A New Selected Poems.* New York: Mariner Books, 2001.

Kübler-Ross, Elisabeth. *Death: The Final Stage of Growth.* New York: Scribner, 1997.

———. *On Death and Dying.* New York: Scribner, 1997.

Ladinsky, Daniel. *Love Poems from God.* New York: Penguin Compass, 2002.

Legato, Marianne. *Why Men Die First.* New York: Macmillan, 2008.

Moir, Anne, and David Jessel. *Brain Sex.* New York: Laurel, 1990.

Moir, Anne, and Bill Moir. *Why Men Don't Iron.* New York: Citadel, 1999.

Newberg, Andrew, et al. *Why God Won't Go Away.* New York: Ballantine Books, 2002.

Northrup, Christiane. *The Wisdom of Menopause.* Rev. ed. New York: Bantam, 2012.

Oliver, Mary. *New and Selected Poems.* Vols.

1 and 2. Boston: Beacon Press, 2005, 2007.

Payne, Ruby. *A Framework for Understanding Poverty.* Highlands, TX: AhaProcess, Inc., 2000.

Ratey, John, and Eric Hagerman. *Spark: The Revolutionary New Science of Exercise and the Brain.* New York: Little, Brown, 2008.

Real, Terrence. *I Don't Want to Talk About It.* New York: Fireside, 1997.

Rhoads, Steven E. *Taking Sex Differences Seriously.* San Francisco: Encounter Books, 2004.

Robbins, John. *Healthy at 100.* New York: Ballantine Books, 2006.

Roizen, Michael, and Mehmet Oz. *You.* New York: Free Press, 2007.

Roizen, Michael, and Mary Jo Putney. *RealAge.* New York: William Morrow, 1999.

Sewell, Marilyn. *Cries of the Spirit.* Boston: Beacon Press, 2000.

Siegel, Daniel J. *The Developing Mind.* New York: Guilford Press, 1999.

Snyderman, Nancy. *Medical Myths That Can Kill You.* New York: Three Rivers Press, 2009.

Swami, Abhayanada. *A History of Mysticism.* San Francisco: Watkins Publishing, 2002.

Sykes, Bryan. *Adam's Curse.* New York: W. W. Norton & Company, 2003.

Tannen, Deborah. *You Just Don't Understand:*

*Women and Men in Conversation.* New York: William Morrow, 1991.

Taylor, Shelley E. *The Tending Instinct.* New York: Times Books, 2002.

Thompson, Michael. *Homesick and Happy.* New York: Ballantine Books, 2012.

Weil, Andrew. *Healthy Aging.* New York: Anchor Books, 2007.

Woody, Jane DiVita. *How Can We Talk About That?* San Francisco: Jossey-Bass, 2002.

# ABOUT THE AUTHOR

**Michael Gurian** is a social philosopher, certified mental health counselor in private practice, and the *New York Times* bestselling author of twenty-six books published in twenty-one languages. The Gurian Institute, which he cofounded in 1996, conducts research internationally, launches pilot programs, and trains professionals. Michael has been called "the people's philosopher" for his ability to bring together people's ordinary lives and scientific ideas.

Gurian provides between twenty and thirty keynote speeches a year at conferences and provides consulting to community agencies, schools, corporations, physicians, hospitals, and faith communities. He has provided training at NASA, Google, Cisco Systems, Boeing, Frito-Lay/Pepsico, World Presidents Organization, and many other corporations, as well as the U.S. Departments of Treasury and Corrections and many other government agencies.

As an educator, Michael previously taught at Gonzaga University, Eastern Washington University, and Ankara University. His more recent academic speaking engagements include Harvard University, Johns Hopkins University, Stanford University, Morehouse College, the University of Colorado, the University of Missouri–Kansas City, and UCLA. His multicultural philosophy reflects the diverse cultures (European, Asian, Middle Eastern, and American) in which he has lived, worked, and studied.

Gurian's work has been featured multiple times in nearly all the major media, including *The New York Times*, *The Washington Post*, *USA Today*, *Newsweek*, *Time*, *Psychology Today*, *AARP Magazine*, *People*, *Reader's Digest*, *The Wall Street Journal*, *Forbes Magazine*, *Parenting*, *Good Housekeeping*, *Redbook*, and many others. Gurian has also made multiple appearances on the *Today* show, *Good Morning America*, CNN, PBS, National Public Radio, and many others.

Gurian lives in Spokane, Washington, with his wife, Gail, a family therapist in private practice, and their three pets. The couple has two grown daughters, Gabrielle and Davita.

# ABOUT THE
# GURIAN INSTITUTE

The Gurian Institute, founded in 1996, provides professional development, training services, and pilot programs. All of the institute's work is science based, research driven, and practice oriented. The institute has gender trainers throughout the world. The institute also provides products such as DVDs, books, workbooks, newsletters, and a user-friendly Web site at www.gurianinstitute.com.

The Gurian Institute Corporate Division provides training and consulting in gender diversity for businesses, corporations, and government agencies. This work has inspired the book *Leadership and the Sexes*, which looks at both women and men in our workforce from a gender science perspective. For more about this work, see www.gender leadership.com.

If you are interested in expanding and teaching new paradigms for the wonder of aging, visit www.michaelgurian.com.

The employees of Thorndike Press hope you have enjoyed this Large Print book. All our Thorndike, Wheeler, and Kennebec Large Print titles are designed for easy reading, and all our books are made to last. Other Thorndike Press Large Print books are available at your library, through selected bookstores, or directly from us.

For information about titles, please call:
    (800) 223-1244

or visit our Web site at:
    http://gale.cengage.com/thorndike

To share your comments, please write:
    Publisher
    Thorndike Press
    10 Water St., Suite 310
    Waterville, ME 04901